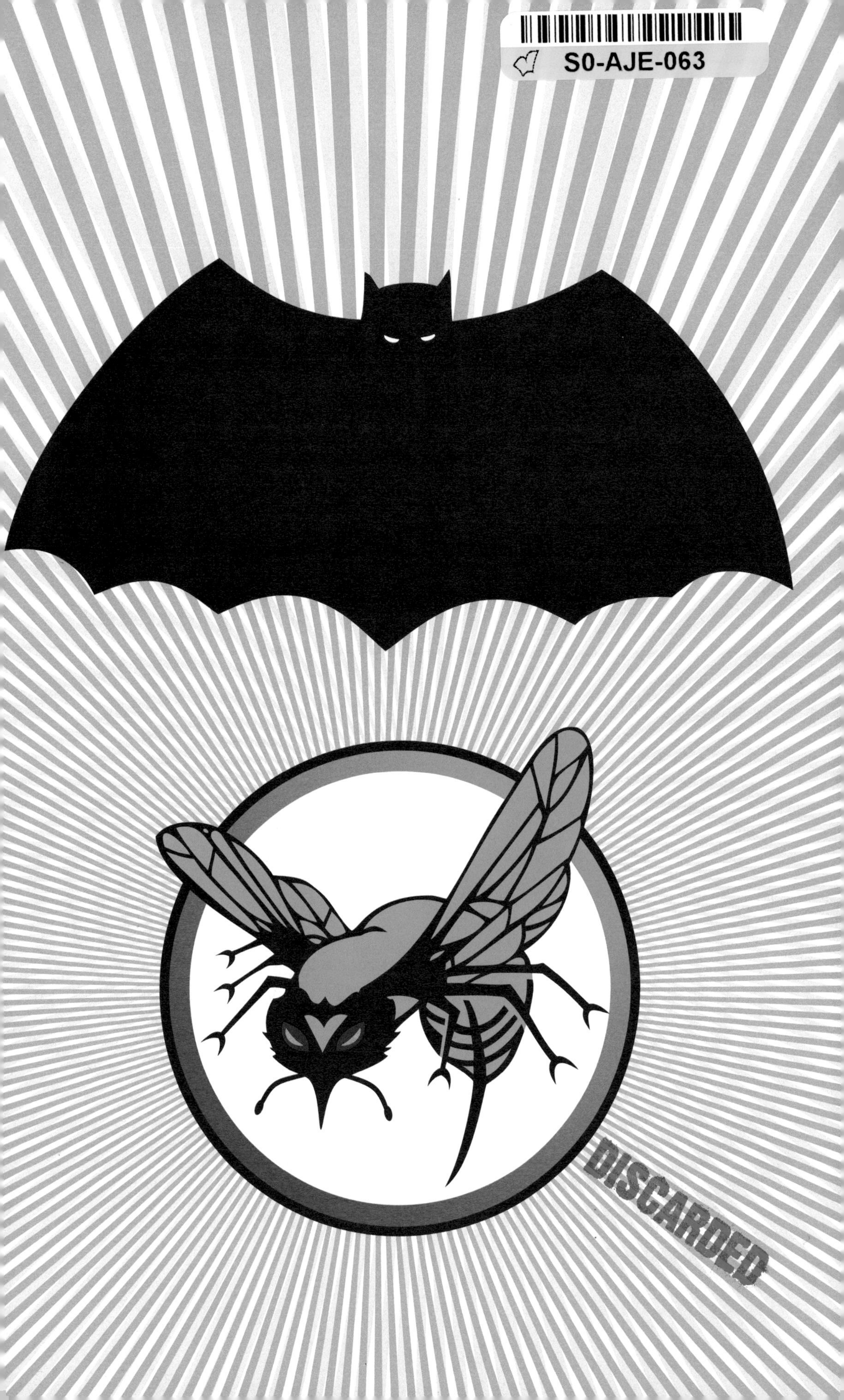

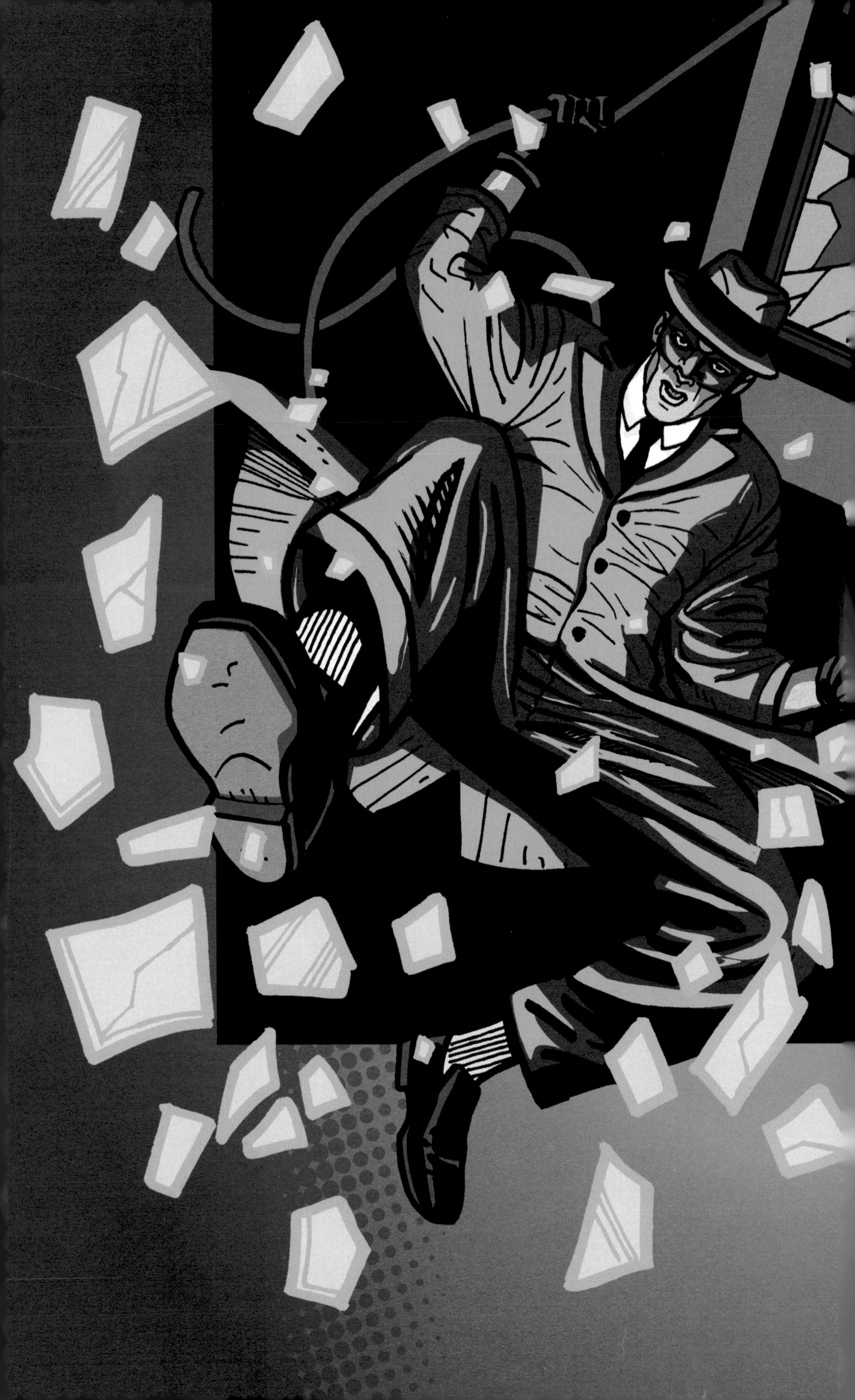

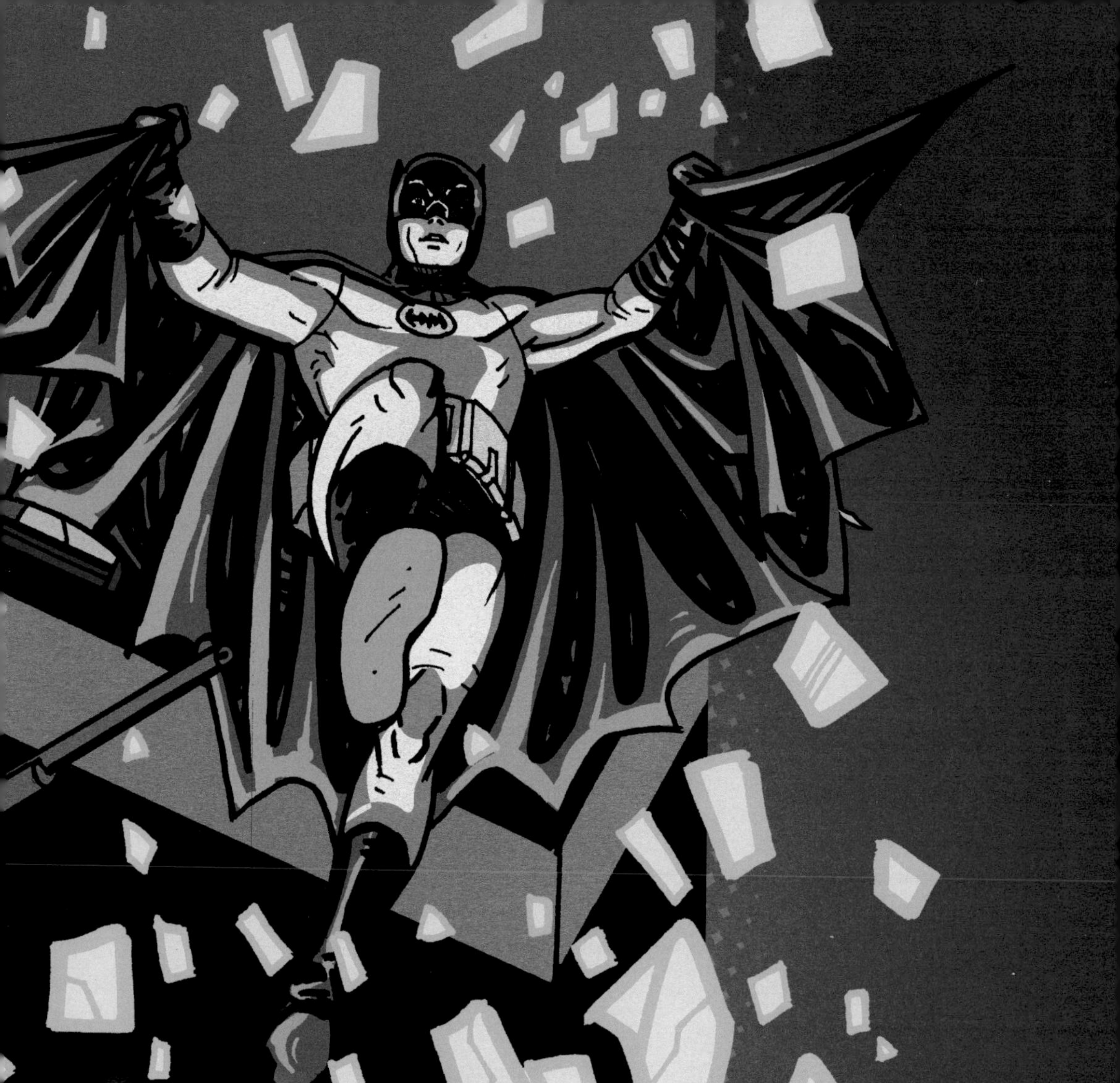

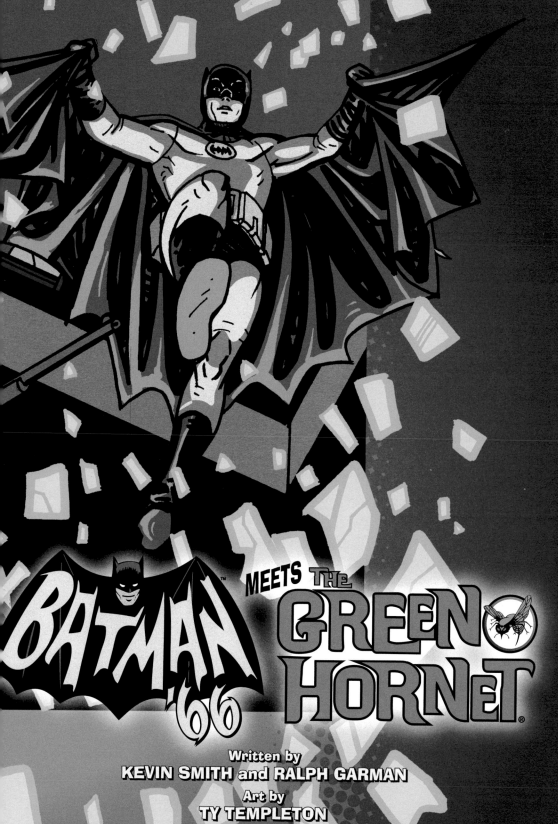

BATMAN™ '66 MEETS THE GREEN HORNET®

Written by
KEVIN SMITH and RALPH GARMAN

Art by
TY TEMPLETON
with **JON BOGDANOVE VICENTE CIFUENTES ROBERTO FLORES ANDRES CRUZ CARLOS MUÑOZ TED KEYS**

Colors by **TONY AVIÑA** Letters by **WES ABBOTT**

Cover Art & Original Series Covers by **ALEX ROSS**

Special Thanks to **DAVID GRACE** at Green Hornet Inc.

BATMAN created by **BOB KANE**

BATMAN '66 MEETS THE GREEN HORNET
Published by DC Comics. Copyright © 2015 DC Comics and The Green Hornet, Inc.
All Rights Reserved. Originally published in single magazine form as BATMAN '66 MEETS
THE GREEN HORNET 1-6 and online as BATMAN '66 MEETS THE GREEN HORNET Digital
Chapters 1-12. Copyright © 2014. All Rights Reserved. BATMAN '66, DC Comics and logo
are trademarks of DC Comics. The Green Hornet, Black Beauty, Kato, and the hornet logos
are trademarks of The Green Hornet, Inc. All Rights Reserved. Dynamite, Dynamite
Entertainment, and its logo are ® & © 2015 Dynamite. All Rights Reserved. The stories,
characters and incidents featured in this publication are entirely fictional. DC Comics does
not read or accept unsolicited submissions of ideas, stories or artwork.

DC Comics, 4000 Warner Blvd., Burbank, CA 91522. A Warner Bros. Entertainment Company.
Printed by RR Donnelley, Salem, VA, USA. 10/23/15. First Printing. ISBN: 978-1-4012-5799-6

Library of Congress Cataloging-in-Publication Data

Smith, Kevin, 1970-
  Batman '66 Meets the Green Hornet / Kevin Smith, Ralph Garman ; illustrated by Ty
Templeton.
    pages cm
  ISBN 978-1-4012-5799-6
  1. Graphic novels. I. Garman, Ralph. II. Templeton, Ty, illustrator. III. Title.

PN6728.B36S63 2015
741.5'973— dc23

TABLE OF CONTENTS

BATMAN™ '66 MEETS THE GREEN HORNET®

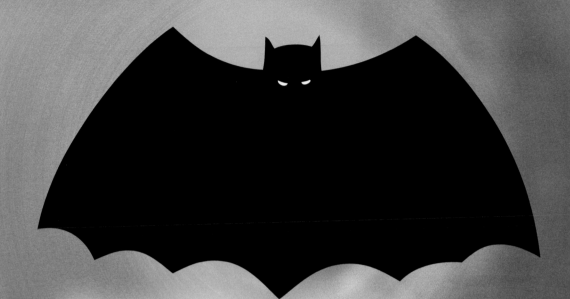

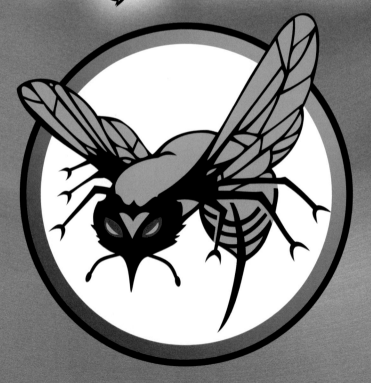

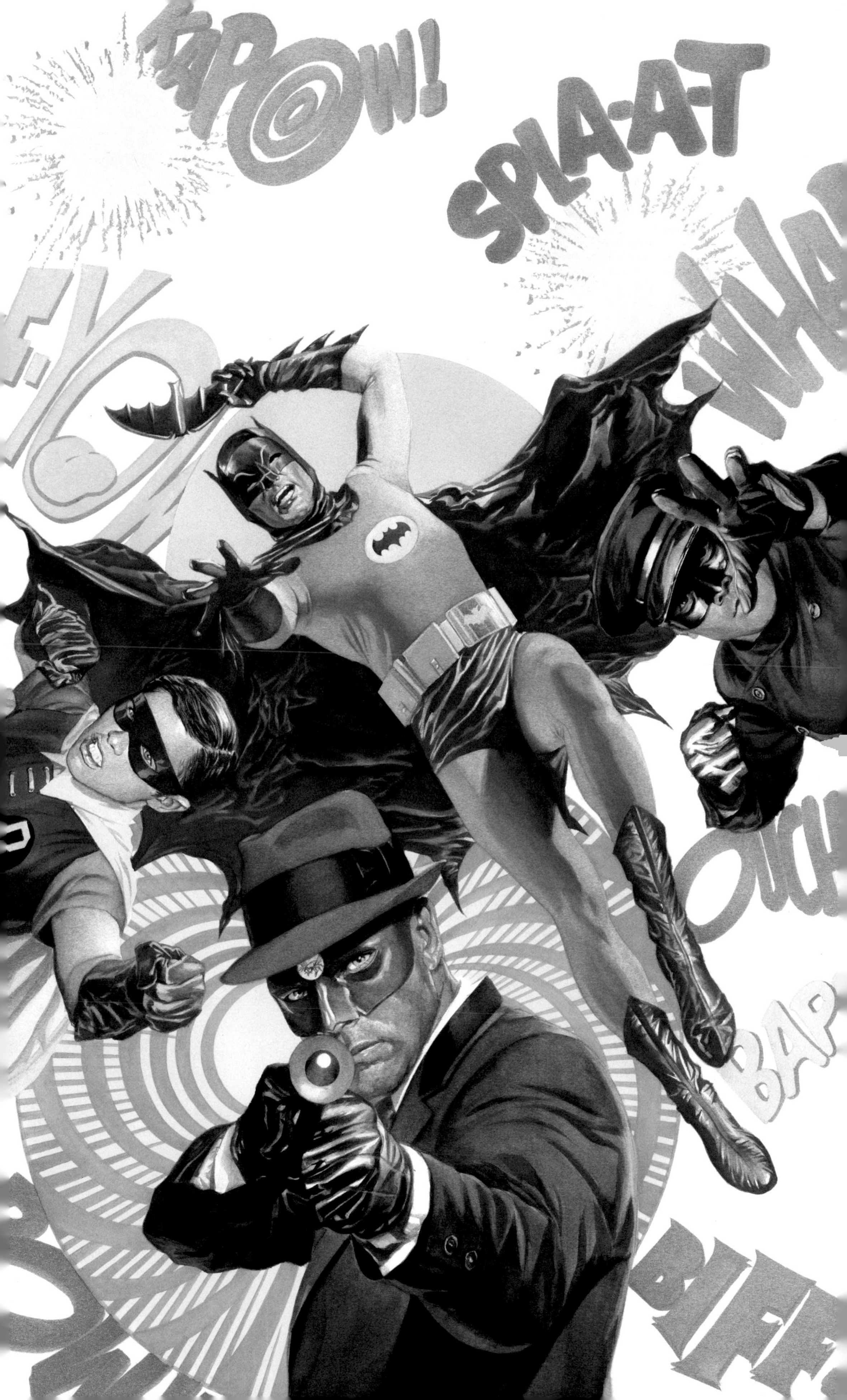
KAPOW!
SPLA-A-T

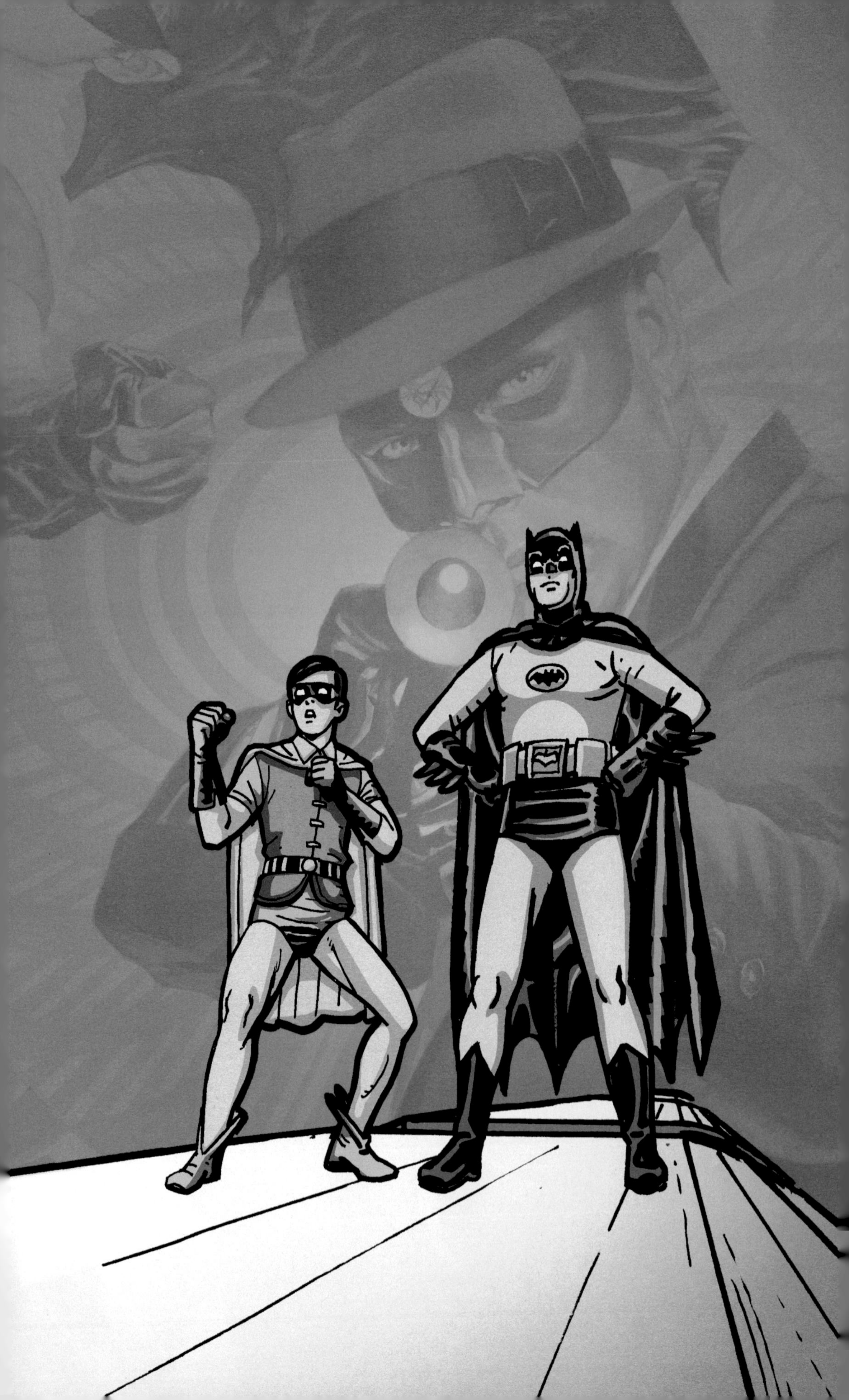

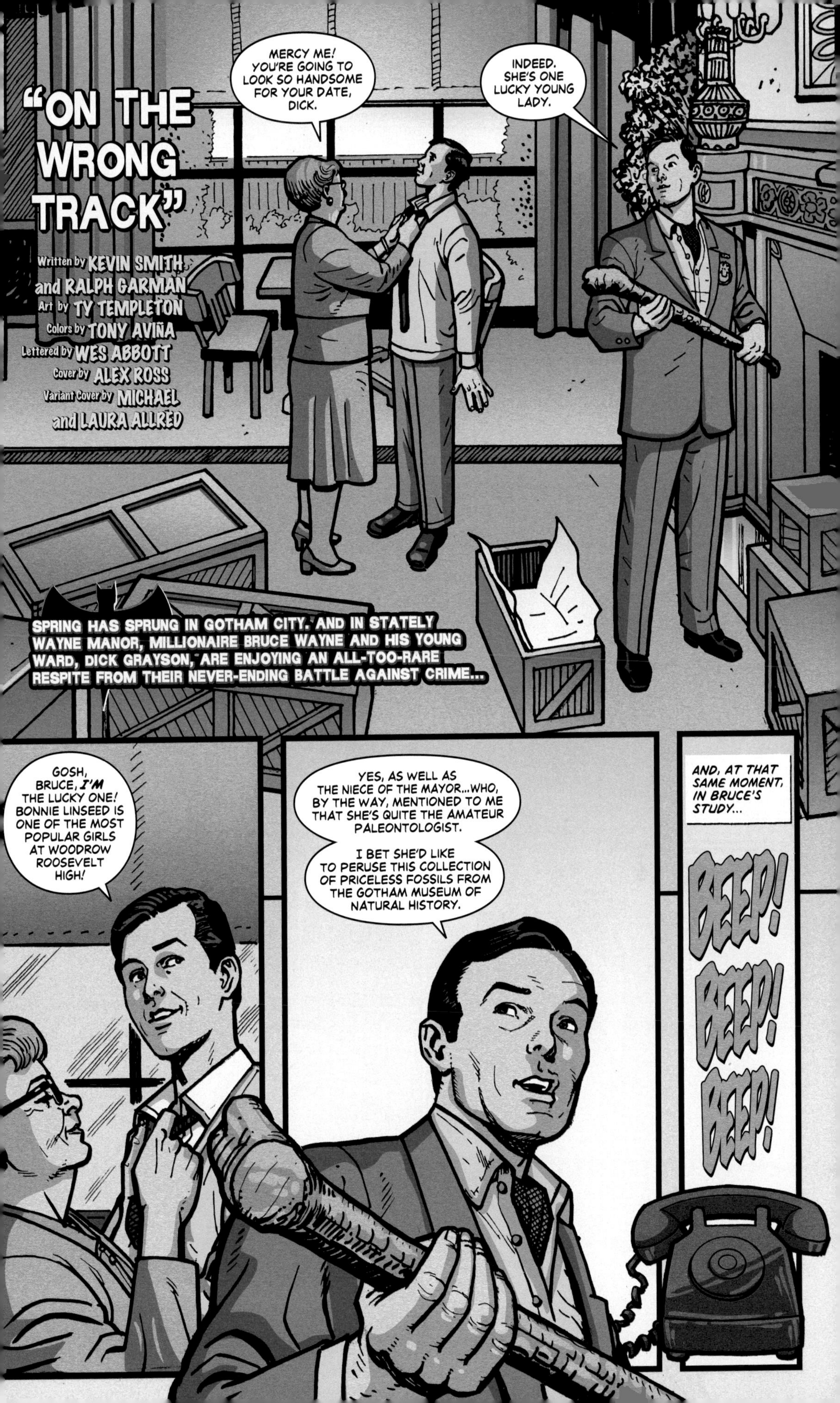
"ON THE WRONG TRACK"
Written by KEVIN SMITH and RALPH GARMAN
Art by TY TEMPLETON
Colors by TONY AVIÑA
Lettered by WES ABBOTT
Cover by ALEX ROSS
Variant Cover by MICHAEL and LAURA ALLRED
MERCY ME! YOU'RE GOING TO LOOK SO HANDSOME FOR YOUR DATE, DICK.
INDEED. SHE'S ONE LUCKY YOUNG LADY.
SPRING HAS SPRUNG IN GOTHAM CITY. AND IN STATELY WAYNE MANOR, MILLIONAIRE BRUCE WAYNE AND HIS YOUNG WARD, DICK GRAYSON, ARE ENJOYING AN ALL-TOO-RARE RESPITE FROM THEIR NEVER-ENDING BATTLE AGAINST CRIME...
GOSH, BRUCE, I'M THE LUCKY ONE! BONNIE LINSEED IS ONE OF THE MOST POPULAR GIRLS AT WOODROW ROOSEVELT HIGH!
YES, AS WELL AS THE NIECE OF THE MAYOR...WHO, BY THE WAY, MENTIONED TO ME THAT SHE'S QUITE THE AMATEUR PALEONTOLOGIST.
I BET SHE'D LIKE TO PERUSE THIS COLLECTION OF PRICELESS FOSSILS FROM THE GOTHAM MUSEUM OF NATURAL HISTORY.
AND, AT THAT SAME MOMENT, IN BRUCE'S STUDY...
BEEP! BEEP! BEEP!

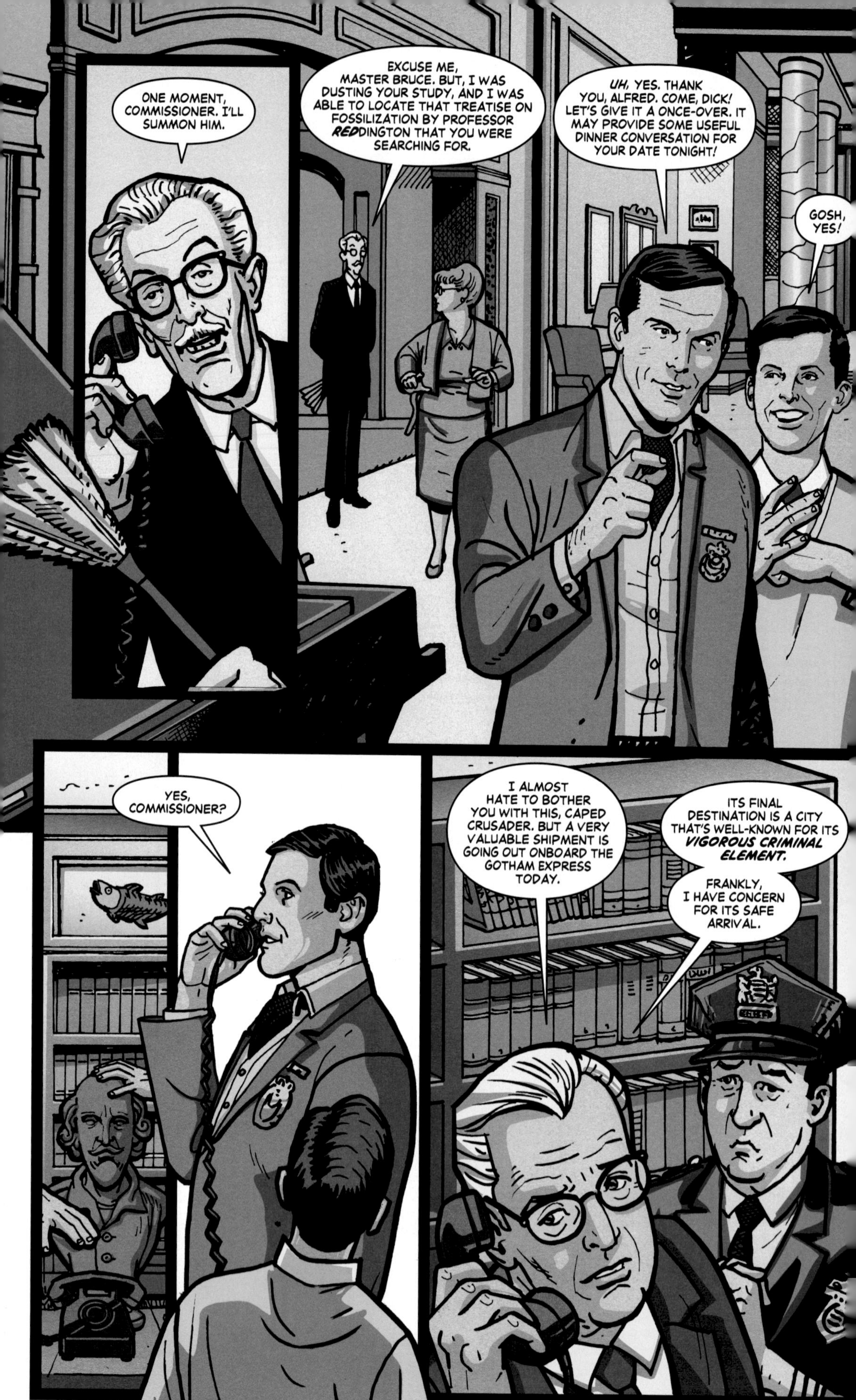
ONE MOMENT, COMMISSIONER. I'LL SUMMON HIM.
EXCUSE ME, MASTER BRUCE. BUT, I WAS DUSTING YOUR STUDY, AND I WAS ABLE TO LOCATE THAT TREATISE ON FOSSILIZATION BY PROFESSOR REDDINGTON THAT YOU WERE SEARCHING FOR.
UH, YES. THANK YOU, ALFRED. COME, DICK! LET'S GIVE IT A ONCE-OVER. IT MAY PROVIDE SOME USEFUL DINNER CONVERSATION FOR YOUR DATE TONIGHT!
GOSH, YES!
YES, COMMISSIONER?
I ALMOST HATE TO BOTHER YOU WITH THIS, CAPED CRUSADER. BUT A VERY VALUABLE SHIPMENT IS GOING OUT ONBOARD THE GOTHAM EXPRESS TODAY.
ITS FINAL DESTINATION IS A CITY THAT'S WELL-KNOWN FOR ITS VIGOROUS CRIMINAL ELEMENT.
FRANKLY, I HAVE CONCERN FOR ITS SAFE ARRIVAL.

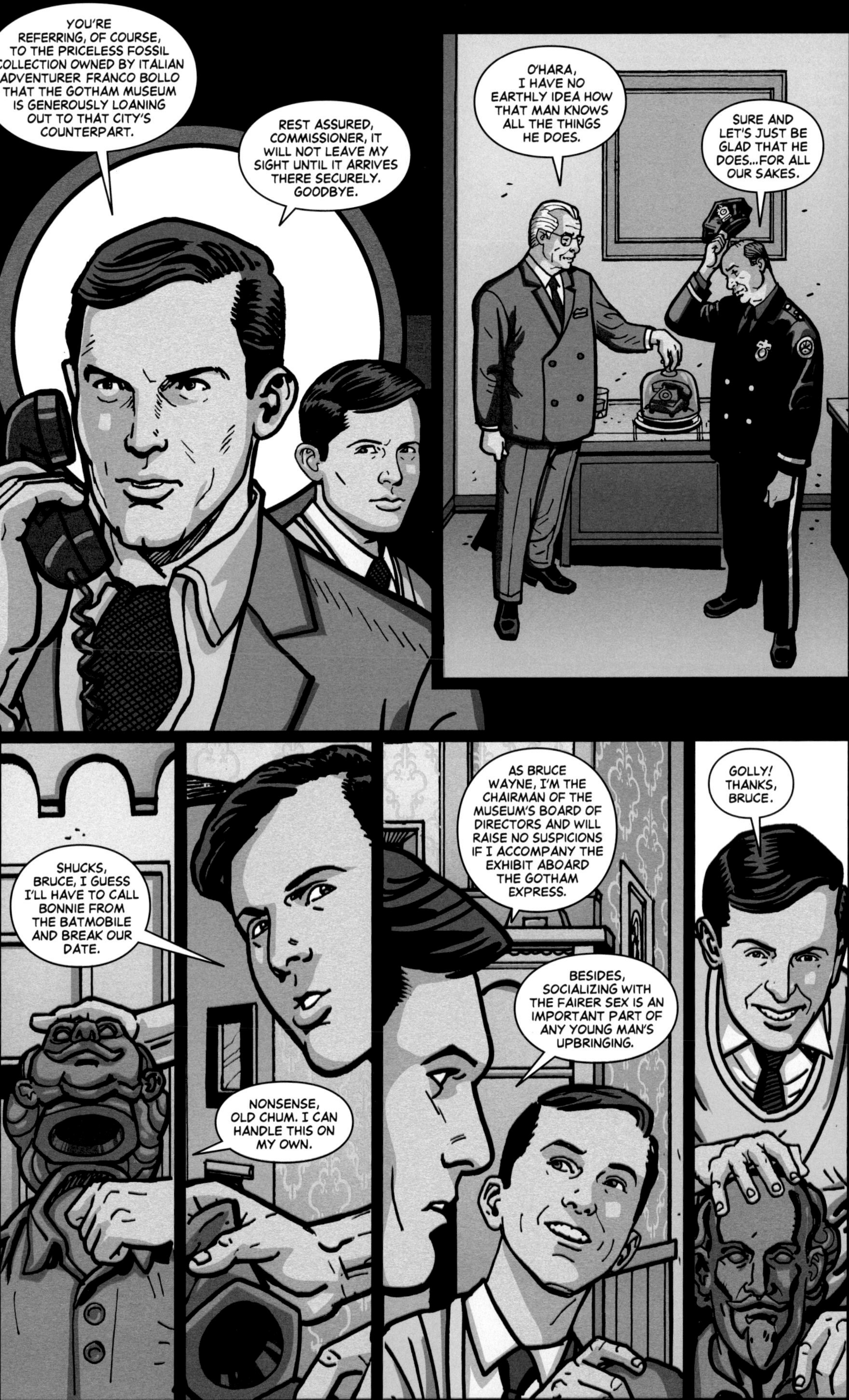
YOU'RE REFERRING, OF COURSE, TO THE PRICELESS FOSSIL COLLECTION OWNED BY ITALIAN ADVENTURER FRANCO BOLLO THAT THE GOTHAM MUSEUM IS GENEROUSLY LOANING OUT TO THAT CITY'S COUNTERPART.
REST ASSURED, COMMISSIONER, IT WILL NOT LEAVE MY SIGHT UNTIL IT ARRIVES THERE SECURELY. GOODBYE.
O'HARA, I HAVE NO EARTHLY IDEA HOW THAT MAN KNOWS ALL THE THINGS HE DOES.
SURE AND LET'S JUST BE GLAD THAT HE DOES...FOR ALL OUR SAKES.
SHUCKS, BRUCE, I GUESS I'LL HAVE TO CALL BONNIE FROM THE BATMOBILE AND BREAK OUR DATE.
NONSENSE, OLD CHUM. I CAN HANDLE THIS ON MY OWN.
AS BRUCE WAYNE, I'M THE CHAIRMAN OF THE MUSEUM'S BOARD OF DIRECTORS AND WILL RAISE NO SUSPICIONS IF I ACCOMPANY THE EXHIBIT ABOARD THE GOTHAM EXPRESS.
BESIDES, SOCIALIZING WITH THE FAIRER SEX IS AN IMPORTANT PART OF ANY YOUNG MAN'S UPBRINGING.
GOLLY! THANKS, BRUCE.

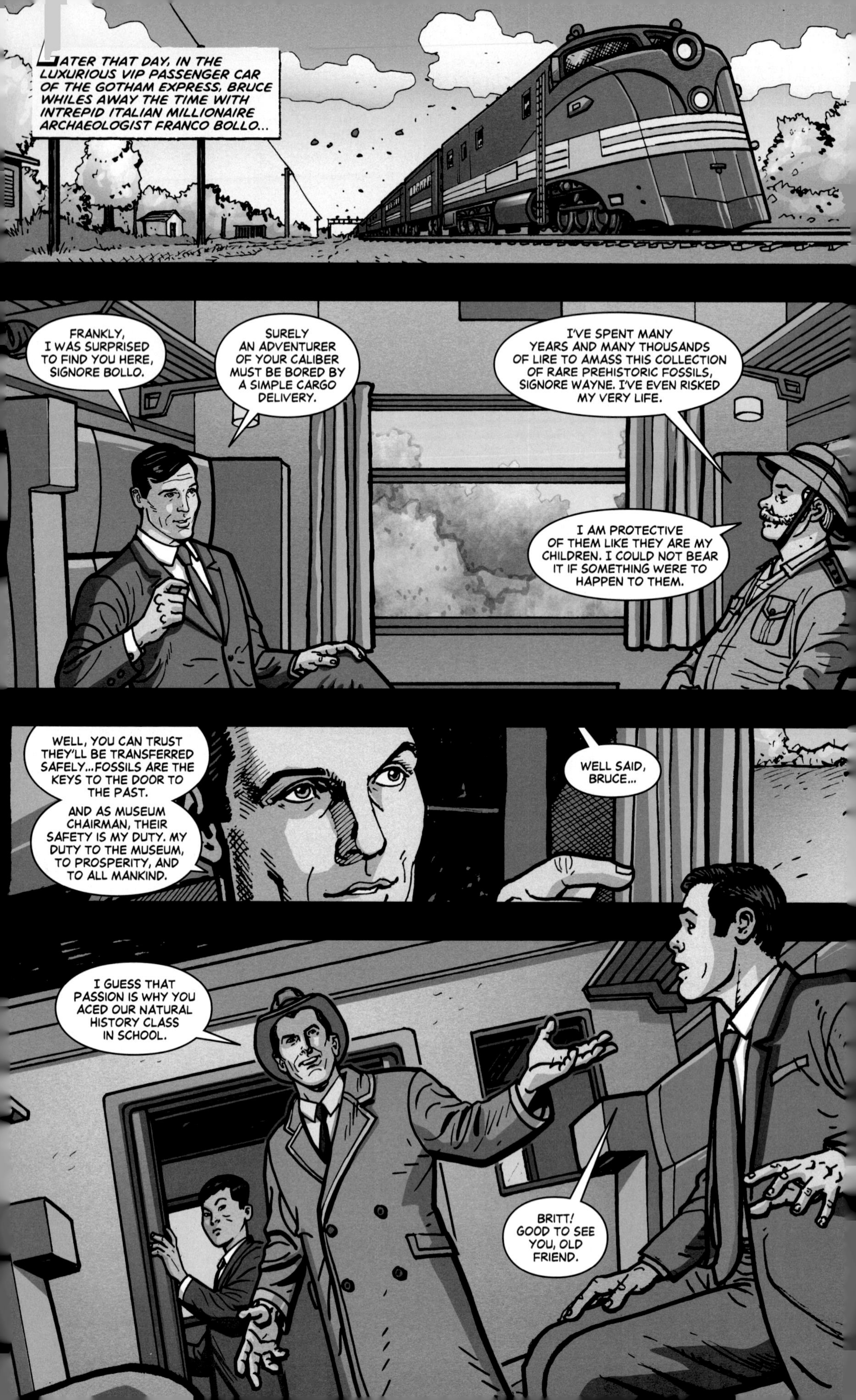
LATER THAT DAY, IN THE LUXURIOUS VIP PASSENGER CAR OF THE GOTHAM EXPRESS, BRUCE WHILES AWAY THE TIME WITH INTREPID ITALIAN MILLIONAIRE ARCHAEOLOGIST FRANCO BOLLO...
FRANKLY, I WAS SURPRISED TO FIND YOU HERE, SIGNORE BOLLO.
SURELY AN ADVENTURER OF YOUR CALIBER MUST BE BORED BY A SIMPLE CARGO DELIVERY.
I'VE SPENT MANY YEARS AND MANY THOUSANDS OF LIRE TO AMASS THIS COLLECTION OF RARE PREHISTORIC FOSSILS, SIGNORE WAYNE. I'VE EVEN RISKED MY VERY LIFE.
I AM PROTECTIVE OF THEM LIKE THEY ARE MY CHILDREN. I COULD NOT BEAR IT IF SOMETHING WERE TO HAPPEN TO THEM.
WELL, YOU CAN TRUST THEY'LL BE TRANSFERRED SAFELY...FOSSILS ARE THE KEYS TO THE DOOR TO THE PAST.
AND AS MUSEUM CHAIRMAN, THEIR SAFETY IS MY DUTY. MY DUTY TO THE MUSEUM, TO PROSPERITY, AND TO ALL MANKIND.
WELL SAID, BRUCE...
I GUESS THAT PASSION IS WHY YOU ACED OUR NATURAL HISTORY CLASS IN SCHOOL.
BRITT! GOOD TO SEE YOU, OLD FRIEND.

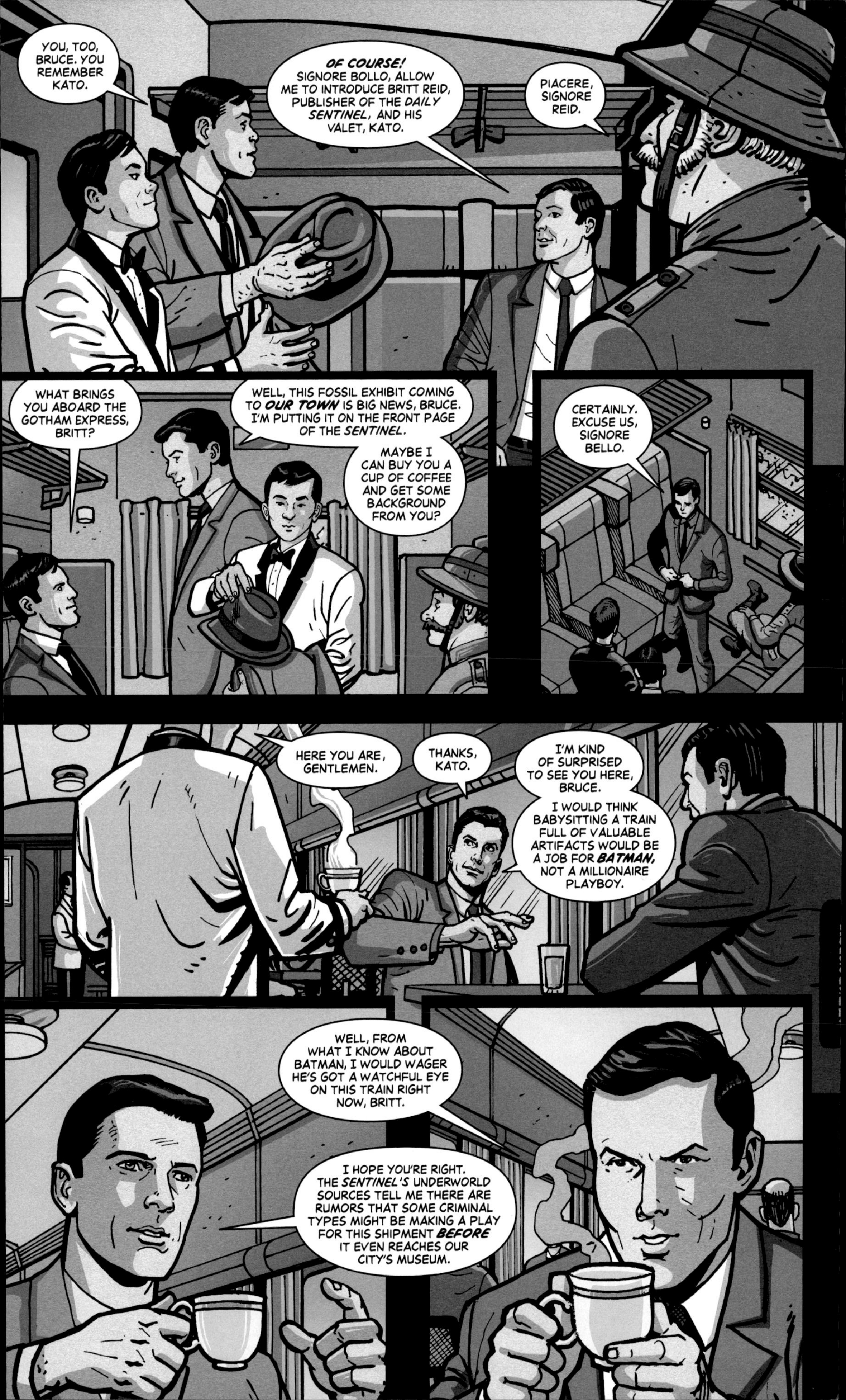

YOU, TOO, BRUCE. YOU REMEMBER KATO.
OF COURSE! SIGNORE BOLLO, ALLOW ME TO INTRODUCE BRITT REID, PUBLISHER OF THE DAILY SENTINEL, AND HIS VALET, KATO.
PIACERE, SIGNORE REID.
WHAT BRINGS YOU ABOARD THE GOTHAM EXPRESS, BRITT?
WELL, THIS FOSSIL EXHIBIT COMING TO OUR TOWN IS BIG NEWS, BRUCE. I'M PUTTING IT ON THE FRONT PAGE OF THE SENTINEL.
MAYBE I CAN BUY YOU A CUP OF COFFEE AND GET SOME BACKGROUND FROM YOU?
CERTAINLY. EXCUSE US, SIGNORE BELLO.
HERE YOU ARE, GENTLEMEN.
THANKS, KATO.
I'M KIND OF SURPRISED TO SEE YOU HERE, BRUCE.
I WOULD THINK BABYSITTING A TRAIN FULL OF VALUABLE ARTIFACTS WOULD BE A JOB FOR BATMAN, NOT A MILLIONAIRE PLAYBOY.
WELL, FROM WHAT I KNOW ABOUT BATMAN, I WOULD WAGER HE'S GOT A WATCHFUL EYE ON THIS TRAIN RIGHT NOW, BRITT.
I HOPE YOU'RE RIGHT. THE SENTINEL'S UNDERWORLD SOURCES TELL ME THERE ARE RUMORS THAT SOME CRIMINAL TYPES MIGHT BE MAKING A PLAY FOR THIS SHIPMENT BEFORE IT EVEN REACHES OUR CITY'S MUSEUM.

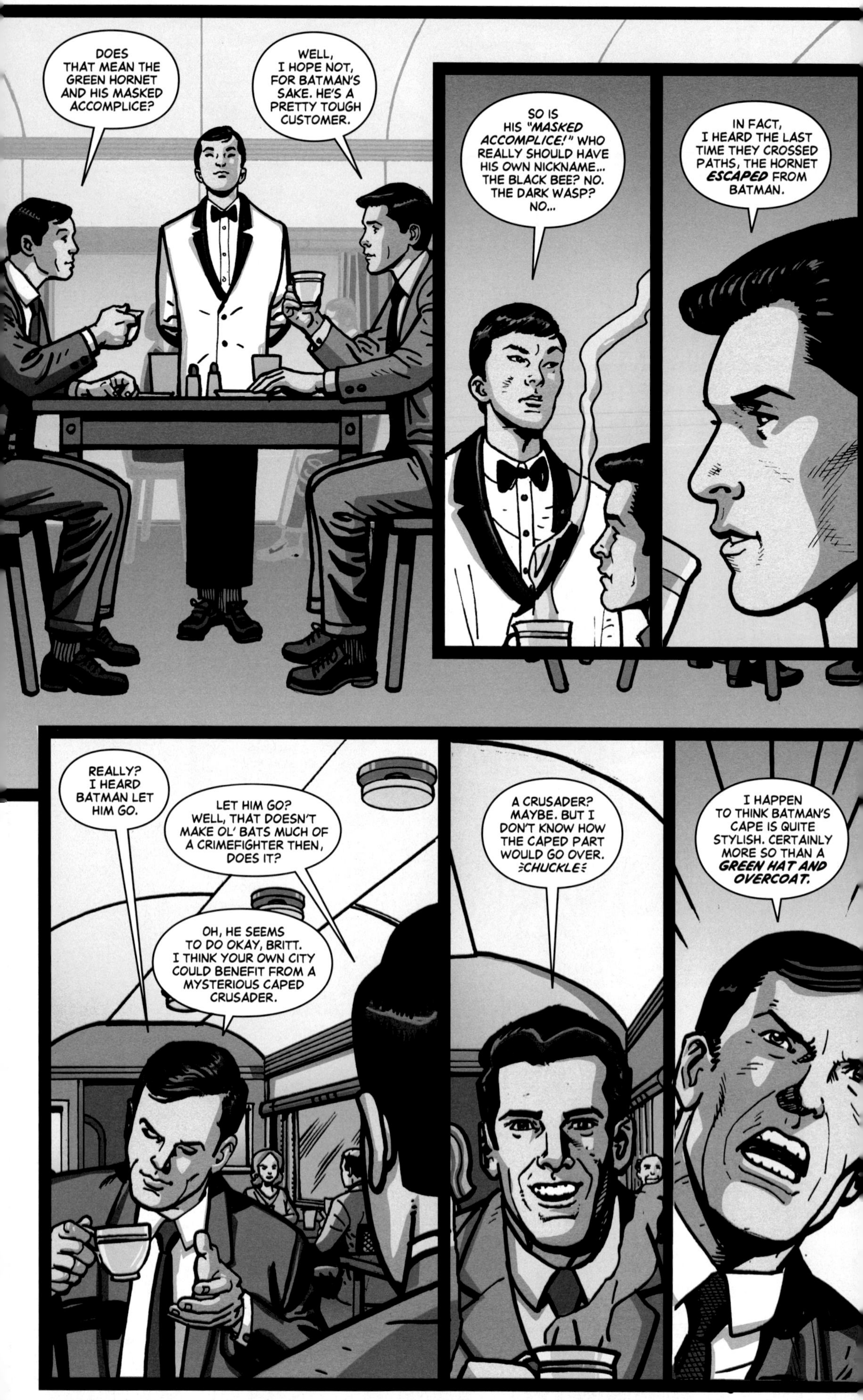
DOES THAT MEAN THE GREEN HORNET AND HIS MASKED ACCOMPLICE?
WELL, I HOPE NOT, FOR BATMAN'S SAKE. HE'S A PRETTY TOUGH CUSTOMER.
SO IS HIS "MASKED ACCOMPLICE!" WHO REALLY SHOULD HAVE HIS OWN NICKNAME... THE BLACK BEE? NO. THE DARK WASP? NO...
IN FACT, I HEARD THE LAST TIME THEY CROSSED PATHS, THE HORNET ESCAPED FROM BATMAN.
REALLY? I HEARD BATMAN LET HIM GO.
LET HIM GO? WELL, THAT DOESN'T MAKE OL' BATS MUCH OF A CRIMEFIGHTER THEN, DOES IT?
OH, HE SEEMS TO DO OKAY, BRITT. I THINK YOUR OWN CITY COULD BENEFIT FROM A MYSTERIOUS CAPED CRUSADER.
A CRUSADER? MAYBE. BUT I DON'T KNOW HOW THE CAPED PART WOULD GO OVER. ≈CHUCKLE≈
I HAPPEN TO THINK BATMAN'S CAPE IS QUITE STYLISH. CERTAINLY MORE SO THAN A GREEN HAT AND OVERCOAT.

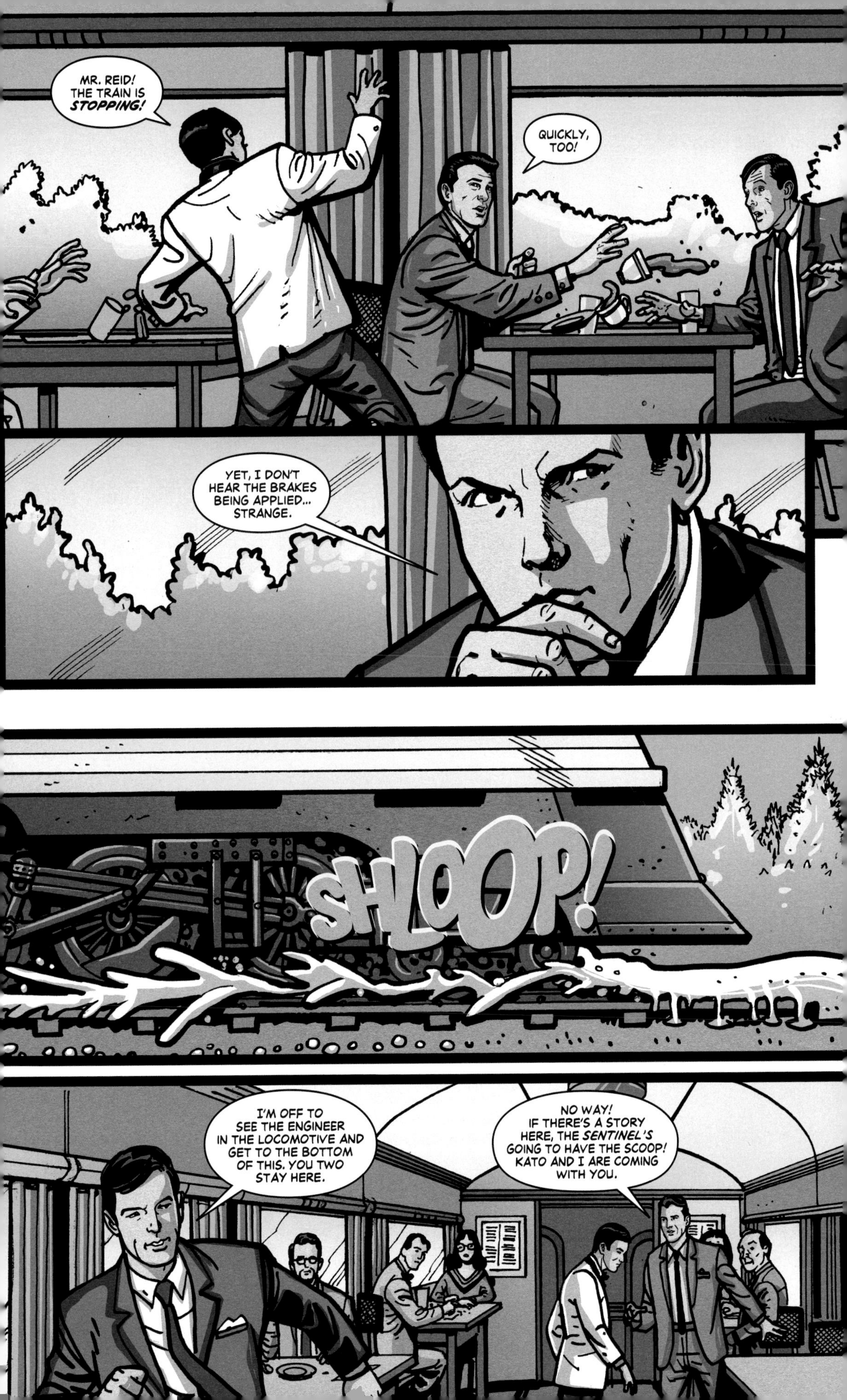
MR. REID! THE TRAIN IS *STOPPING!*
QUICKLY, TOO!
YET, I DON'T HEAR THE BRAKES BEING APPLIED... STRANGE.
SHLOOP!
I'M OFF TO SEE THE ENGINEER IN THE LOCOMOTIVE AND GET TO THE BOTTOM OF THIS. YOU TWO STAY HERE.
NO WAY! IF THERE'S A STORY HERE, THE *SENTINEL'S* GOING TO HAVE THE SCOOP! KATO AND I ARE COMING WITH YOU.

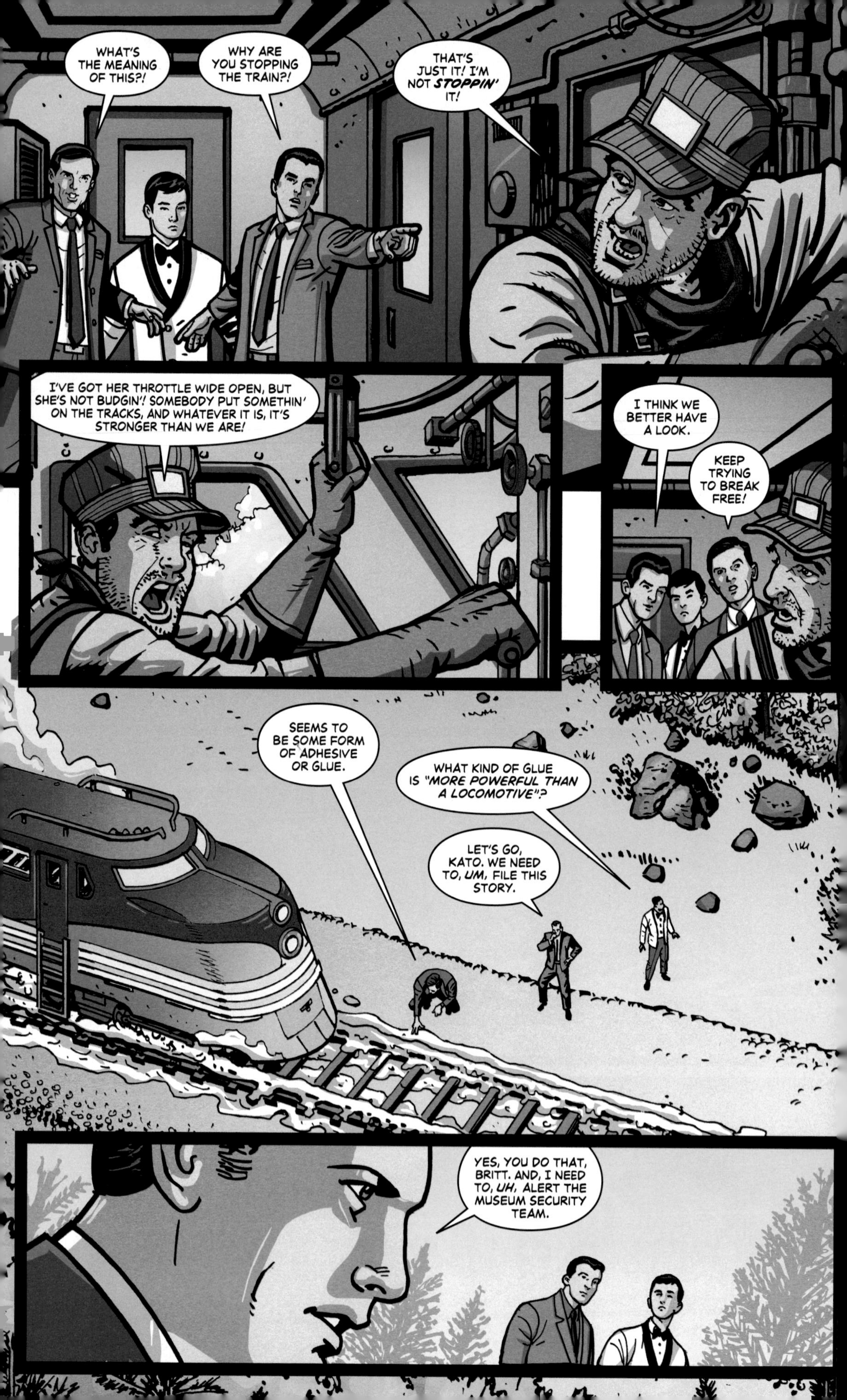
WHAT'S THE MEANING OF THIS?!
WHY ARE YOU STOPPING THE TRAIN?!
THAT'S JUST IT! I'M NOT *STOPPIN'* IT!
I'VE GOT HER THROTTLE WIDE OPEN, BUT SHE'S NOT BUDGIN'! SOMEBODY PUT SOMETHIN' ON THE TRACKS, AND WHATEVER IT IS, IT'S STRONGER THAN WE ARE!
I THINK WE BETTER HAVE A LOOK.
KEEP TRYING TO BREAK FREE!
SEEMS TO BE SOME FORM OF ADHESIVE OR GLUE.
WHAT KIND OF GLUE IS *"MORE POWERFUL THAN A LOCOMOTIVE"*?
LET'S GO, KATO. WE NEED TO, *UM,* FILE THIS STORY.
YES, YOU DO THAT, BRITT. AND, I NEED TO, *UH,* ALERT THE MUSEUM SECURITY TEAM.

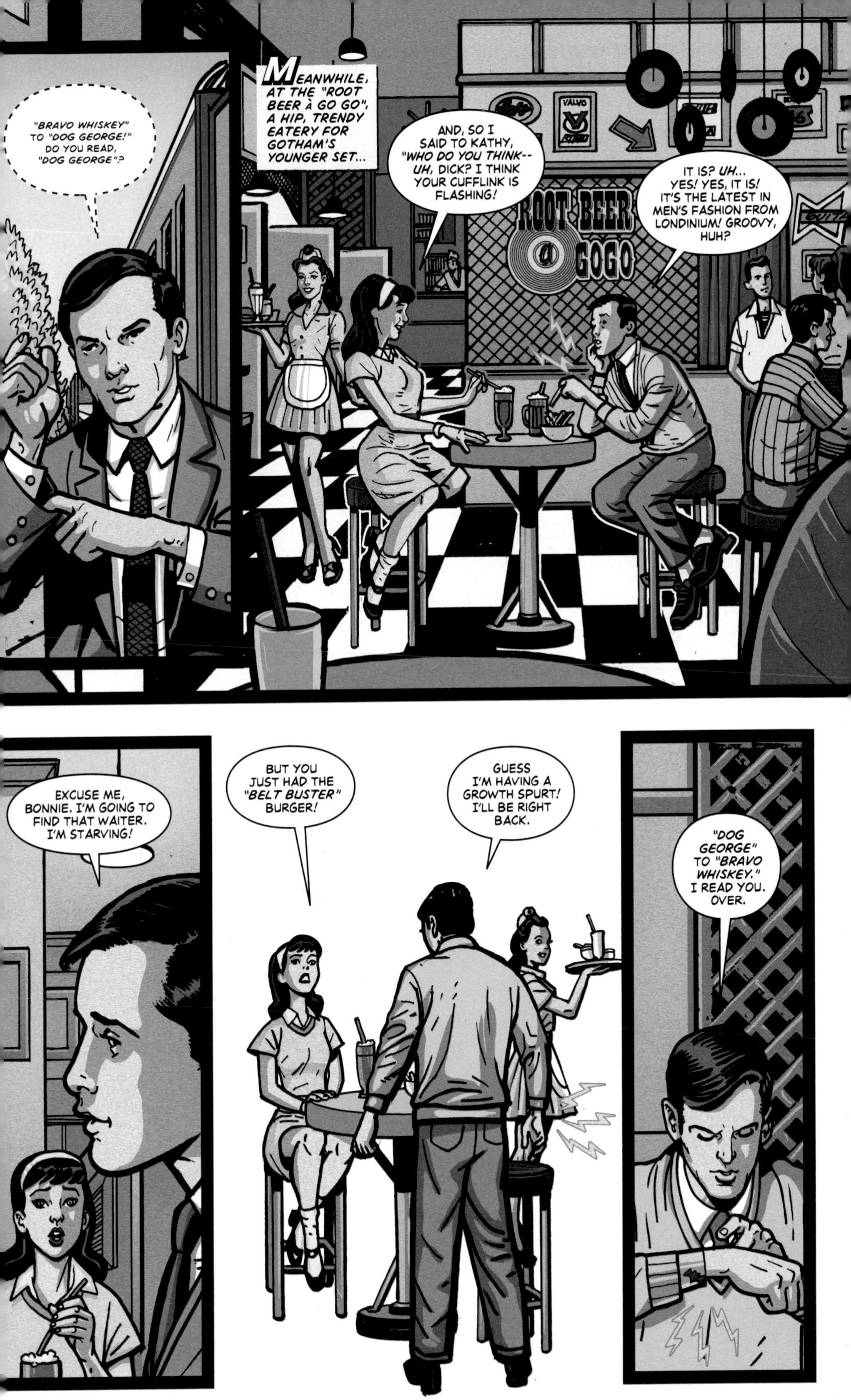
"BRAVO WHISKEY" TO "DOG GEORGE!" DO YOU READ, "DOG GEORGE"?
MEANWHILE, AT THE "ROOT BEER À GO GO", A HIP, TRENDY EATERY FOR GOTHAM'S YOUNGER SET...
AND, SO I SAID TO KATHY, "WHO DO YOU THINK-- UH, DICK? I THINK YOUR CUFFLINK IS FLASHING!
IT IS? UH... YES! YES, IT IS! IT'S THE LATEST IN MEN'S FASHION FROM LONDINIUM! GROOVY, HUH?
ROOT BEER @ GOGO
VALVO
EXCUSE ME, BONNIE. I'M GOING TO FIND THAT WAITER. I'M STARVING!
BUT YOU JUST HAD THE "BELT BUSTER" BURGER!
GUESS I'M HAVING A GROWTH SPURT! I'LL BE RIGHT BACK.
"DOG GEORGE" TO "BRAVO WHISKEY." I READ YOU. OVER.

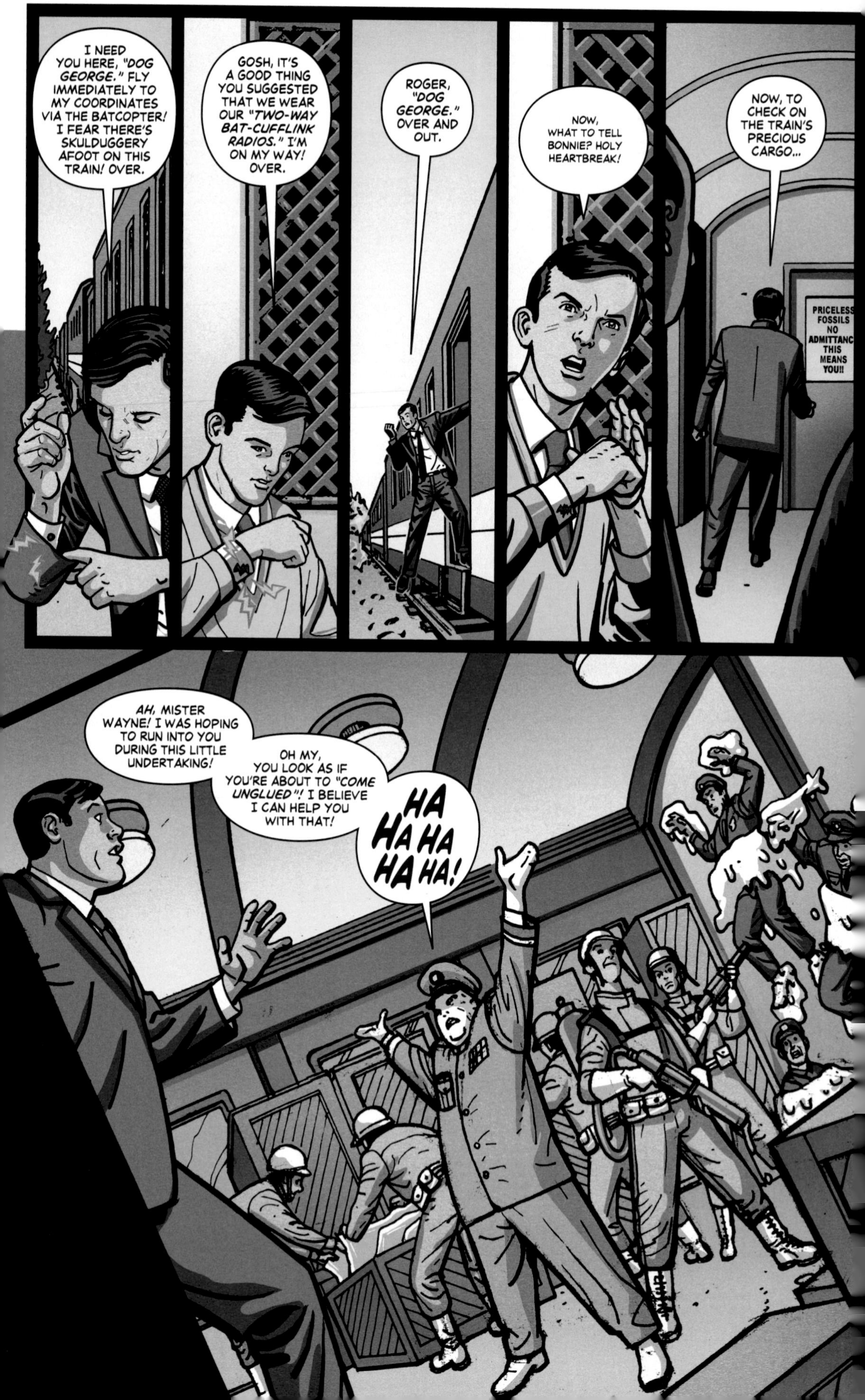

I NEED YOU HERE, "DOG GEORGE." FLY IMMEDIATELY TO MY COORDINATES VIA THE BATCOPTER! I FEAR THERE'S SKULDUGGERY AFOOT ON THIS TRAIN! OVER.
GOSH, IT'S A GOOD THING YOU SUGGESTED THAT WE WEAR OUR "TWO-WAY BAT-CUFFLINK RADIOS." I'M ON MY WAY! OVER.
ROGER, "DOG GEORGE." OVER AND OUT.
NOW, WHAT TO TELL BONNIE? HOLY HEARTBREAK!
NOW, TO CHECK ON THE TRAIN'S PRECIOUS CARGO...
PRICELESS FOSSILS NO ADMITTANC THIS MEANS YOU!!
AH, MISTER WAYNE! I WAS HOPING TO RUN INTO YOU DURING THIS LITTLE UNDERTAKING!
OH MY, YOU LOOK AS IF YOU'RE ABOUT TO "COME UNGLUED"! I BELIEVE I CAN HELP YOU WITH THAT!
HA HA HA HA HA!

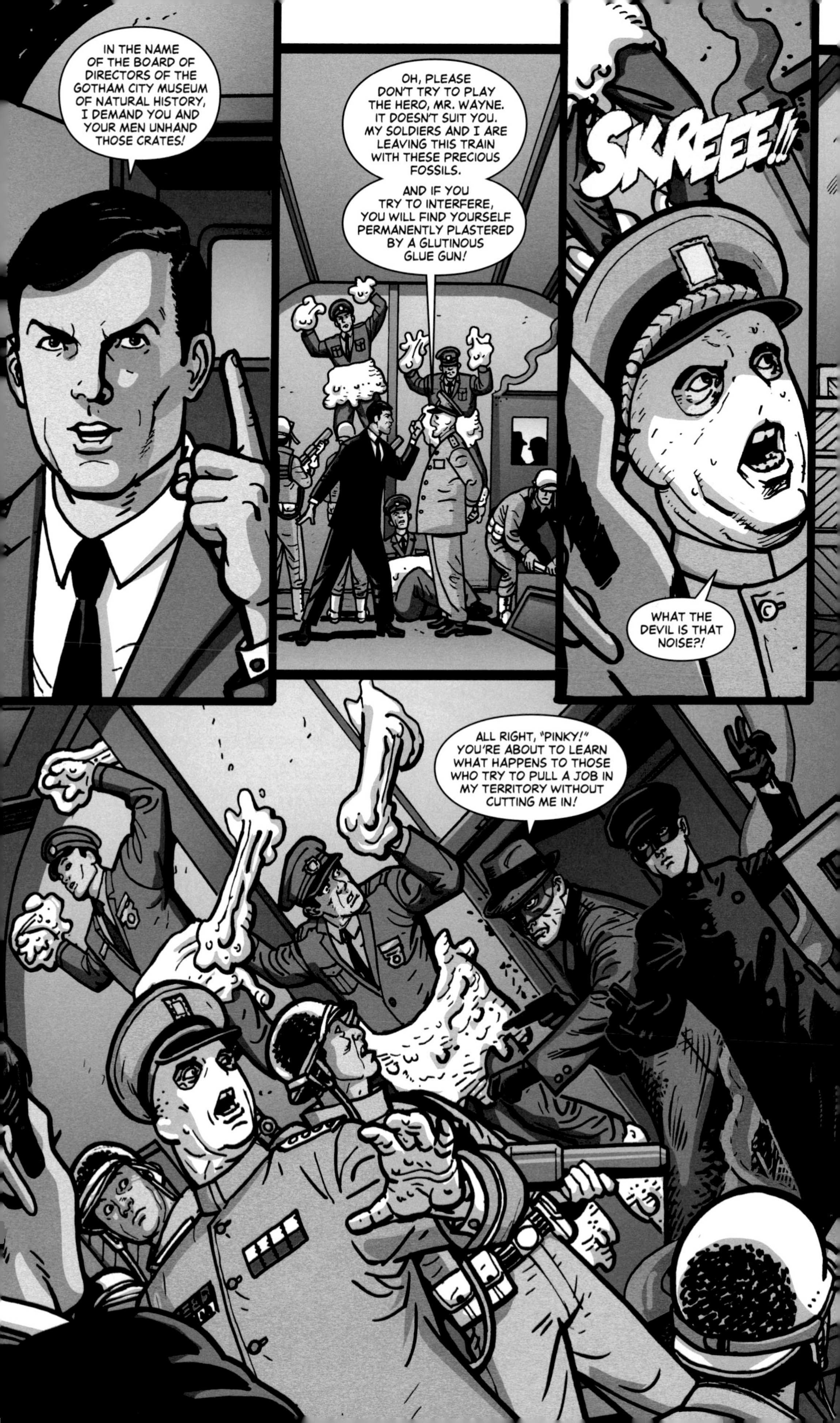
IN THE NAME OF THE BOARD OF DIRECTORS OF THE GOTHAM CITY MUSEUM OF NATURAL HISTORY, I DEMAND YOU AND YOUR MEN UNHAND THOSE CRATES!
OH, PLEASE DON'T TRY TO PLAY THE HERO, MR. WAYNE. IT DOESN'T SUIT YOU. MY SOLDIERS AND I ARE LEAVING THIS TRAIN WITH THESE PRECIOUS FOSSILS.
AND IF YOU TRY TO INTERFERE, YOU WILL FIND YOURSELF PERMANENTLY PLASTERED BY A GLUTINOUS GLUE GUN!
SKREEE!!
WHAT THE DEVIL IS THAT NOISE?!
ALL RIGHT, "PINKY!" YOU'RE ABOUT TO LEARN WHAT HAPPENS TO THOSE WHO TRY TO PULL A JOB IN MY TERRITORY WITHOUT CUTTING ME IN!

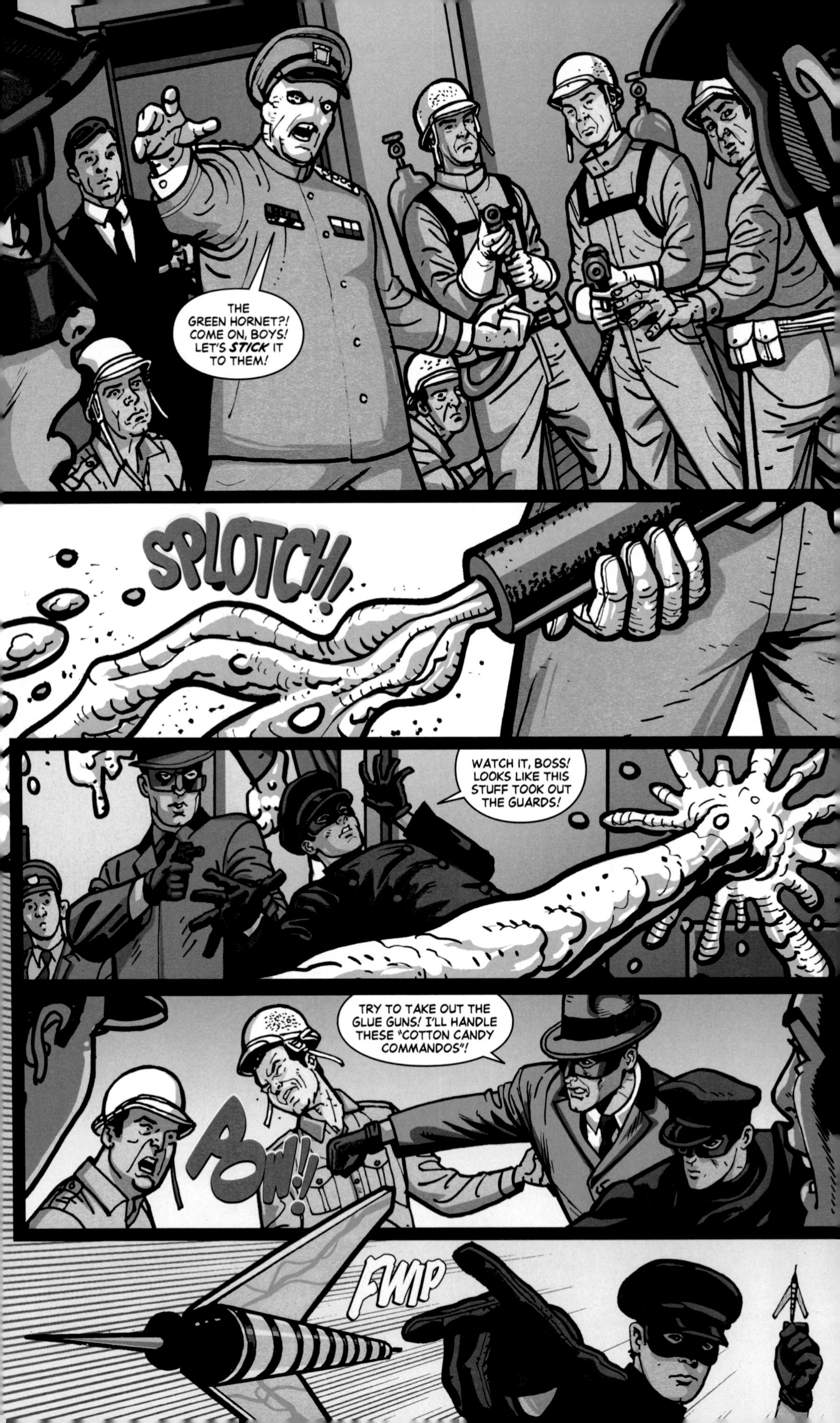
THE GREEN HORNET?! COME ON, BOYS! LET'S STICK IT TO THEM!
SPLOTCH!
WATCH IT, BOSS! LOOKS LIKE THIS STUFF TOOK OUT THE GUARDS!
TRY TO TAKE OUT THE GLUE GUNS! I'LL HANDLE THESE "COTTON CANDY COMMANDOS"!
POW!!
FWIP

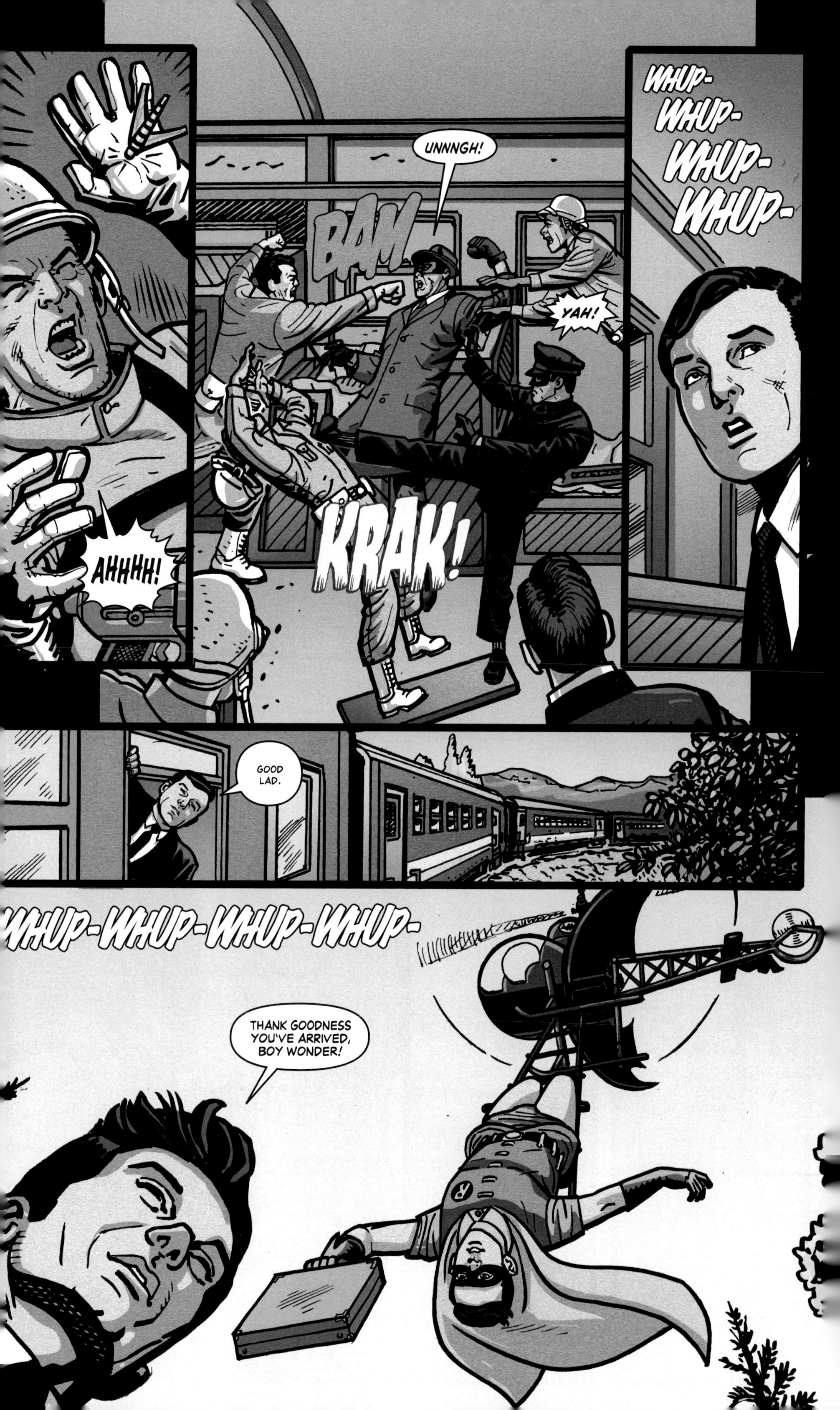

UNNNGH!
BAM
YAH!
AHHHH!
KRAK!
WHUP-
WHUP-
WHUP-
WHUP-
GOOD LAD.
WHUP-WHUP-WHUP-WHUP-
THANK GOODNESS YOU'VE ARRIVED, BOY WONDER!

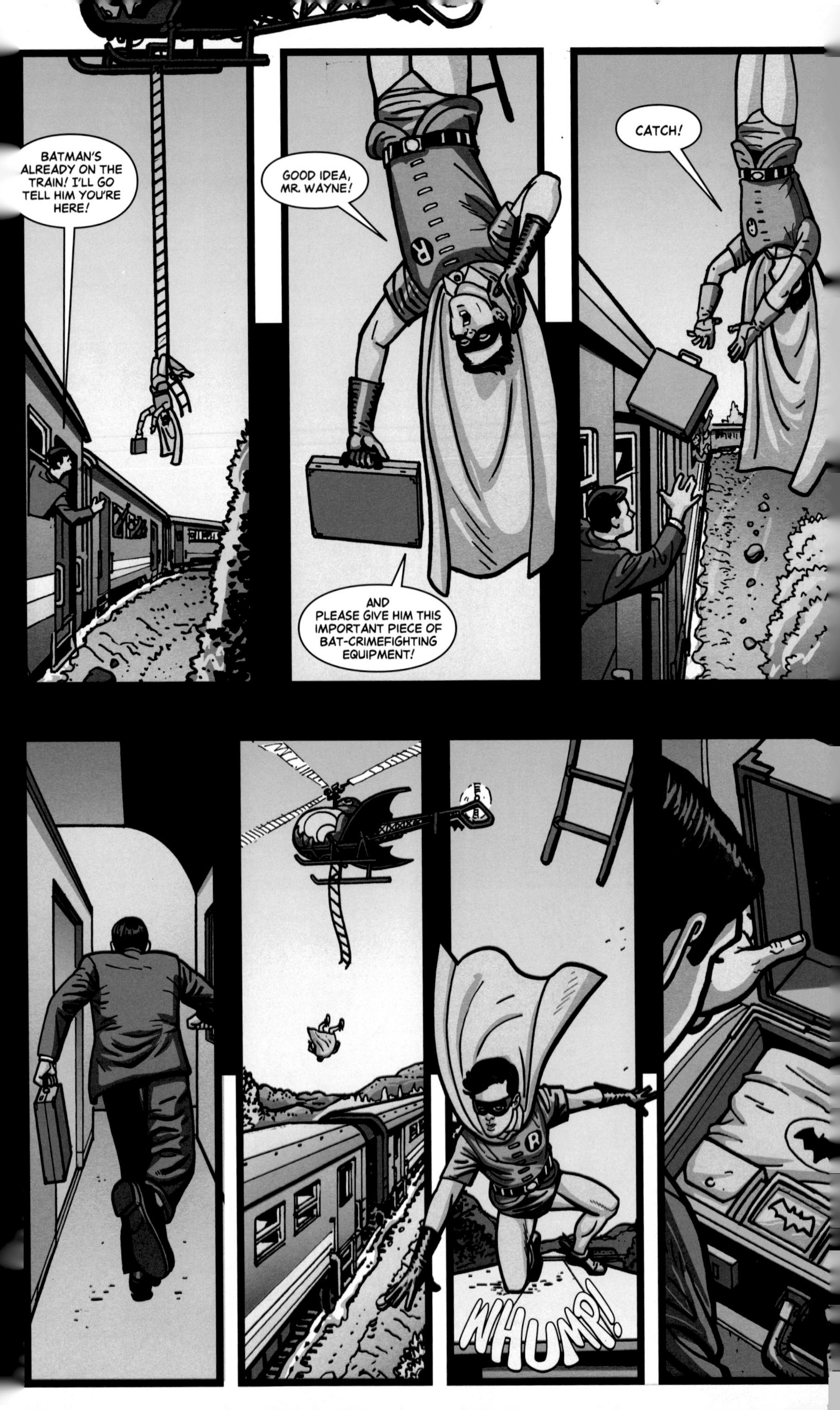
BATMAN'S ALREADY ON THE TRAIN! I'LL GO TELL HIM YOU'RE HERE!
GOOD IDEA, MR. WAYNE!
AND PLEASE GIVE HIM THIS IMPORTANT PIECE OF BAT-CRIMEFIGHTING EQUIPMENT!
CATCH!
WHUMP!

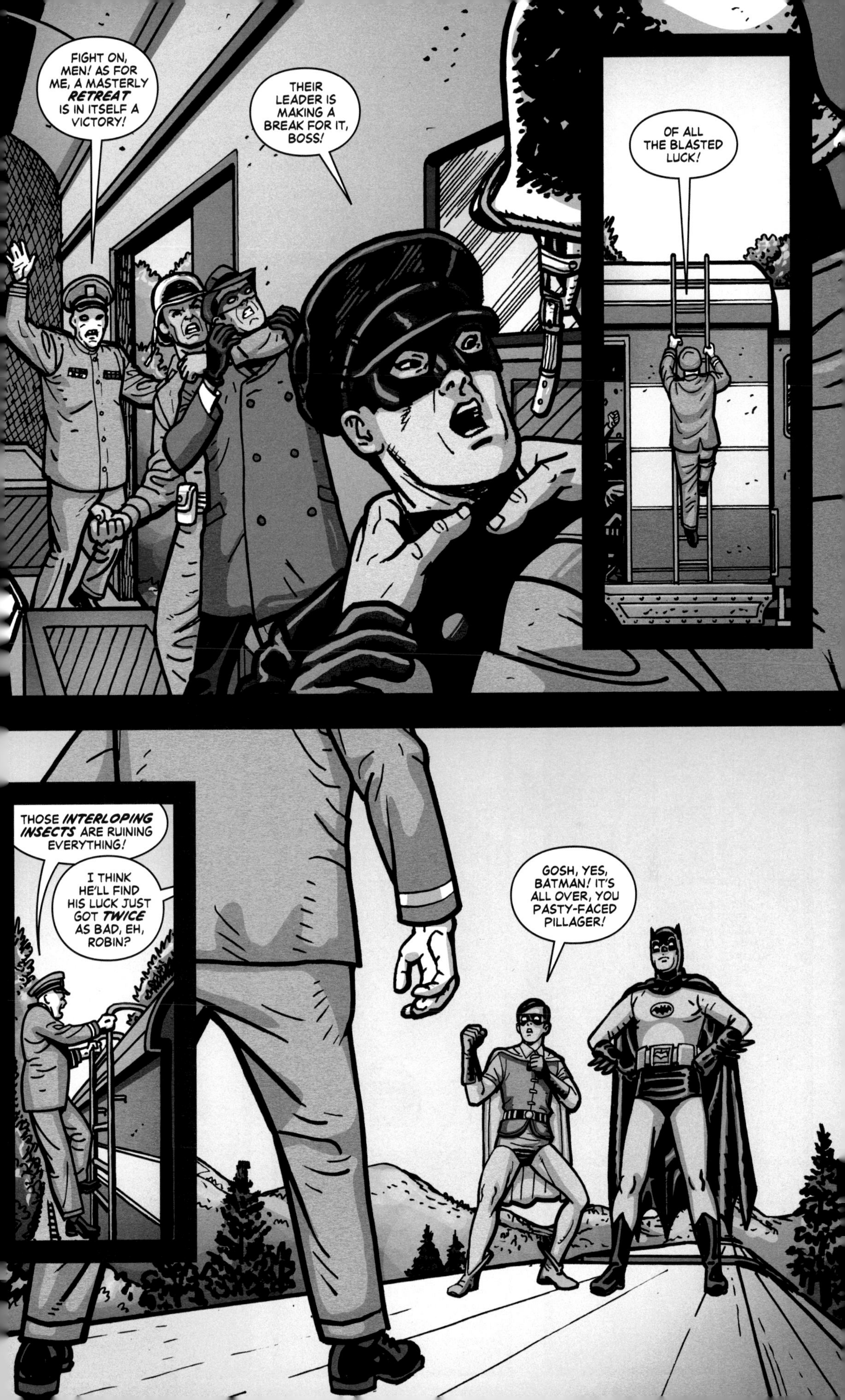
FIGHT ON, MEN! AS FOR ME, A MASTERLY RETREAT IS IN ITSELF A VICTORY!
THEIR LEADER IS MAKING A BREAK FOR IT, BOSS!
OF ALL THE BLASTED LUCK!
THOSE INTERLOPING INSECTS ARE RUINING EVERYTHING!
I THINK HE'LL FIND HIS LUCK JUST GOT TWICE AS BAD, EH, ROBIN?
GOSH, YES, BATMAN! IT'S ALL OVER, YOU PASTY-FACED PILLAGER!

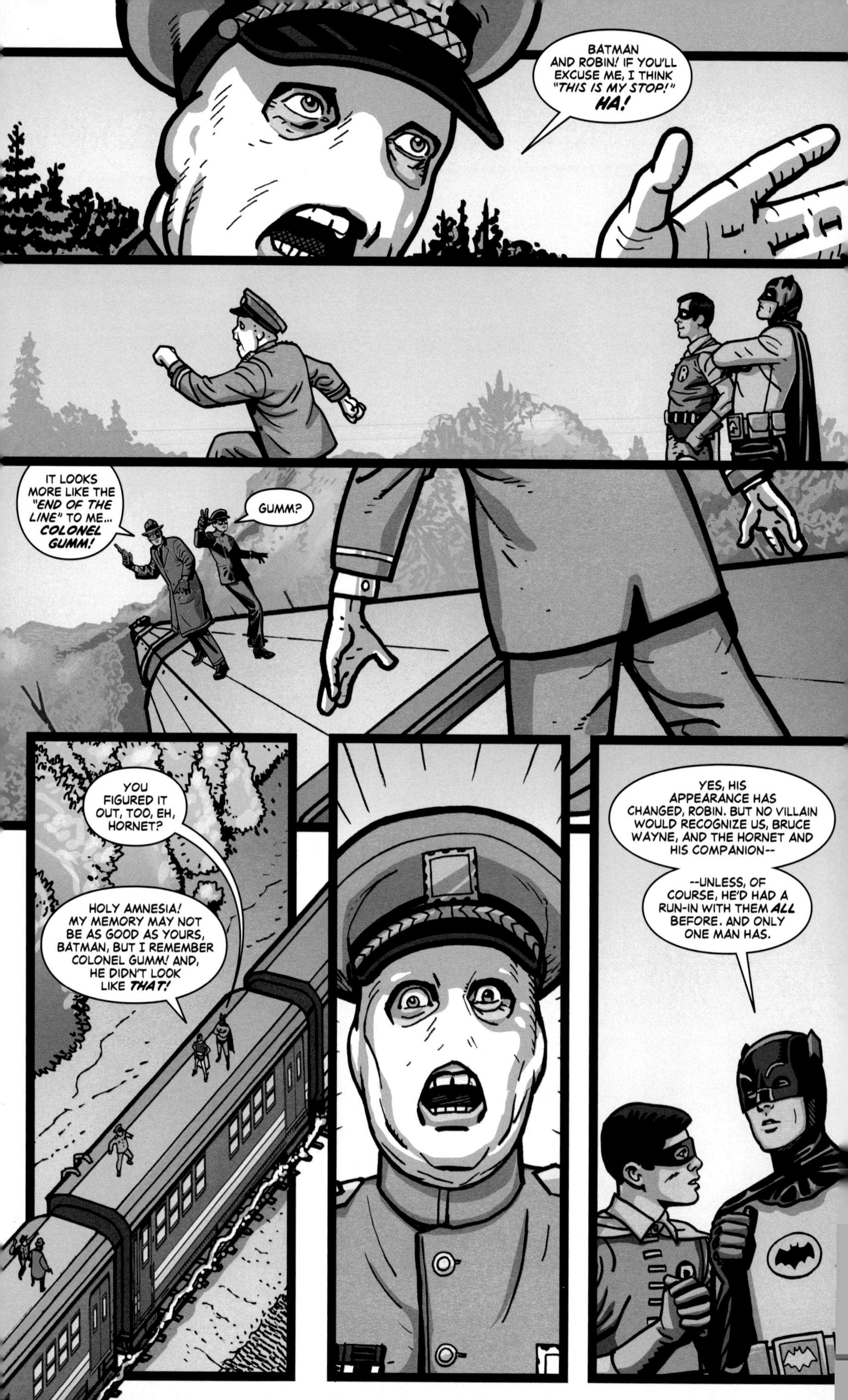
BATMAN AND ROBIN! IF YOU'LL EXCUSE ME, I THINK "THIS IS MY STOP!" HA!
IT LOOKS MORE LIKE THE "END OF THE LINE" TO ME... COLONEL GUMM!
GUMM?
YOU FIGURED IT OUT, TOO, EH, HORNET?
HOLY AMNESIA! MY MEMORY MAY NOT BE AS GOOD AS YOURS, BATMAN, BUT I REMEMBER COLONEL GUMM! AND, HE DIDN'T LOOK LIKE THAT!
YES, HIS APPEARANCE HAS CHANGED, ROBIN. BUT NO VILLAIN WOULD RECOGNIZE US, BRUCE WAYNE, AND THE HORNET AND HIS COMPANION--
--UNLESS, OF COURSE, HE'D HAD A RUN-IN WITH THEM ALL BEFORE. AND ONLY ONE MAN HAS.

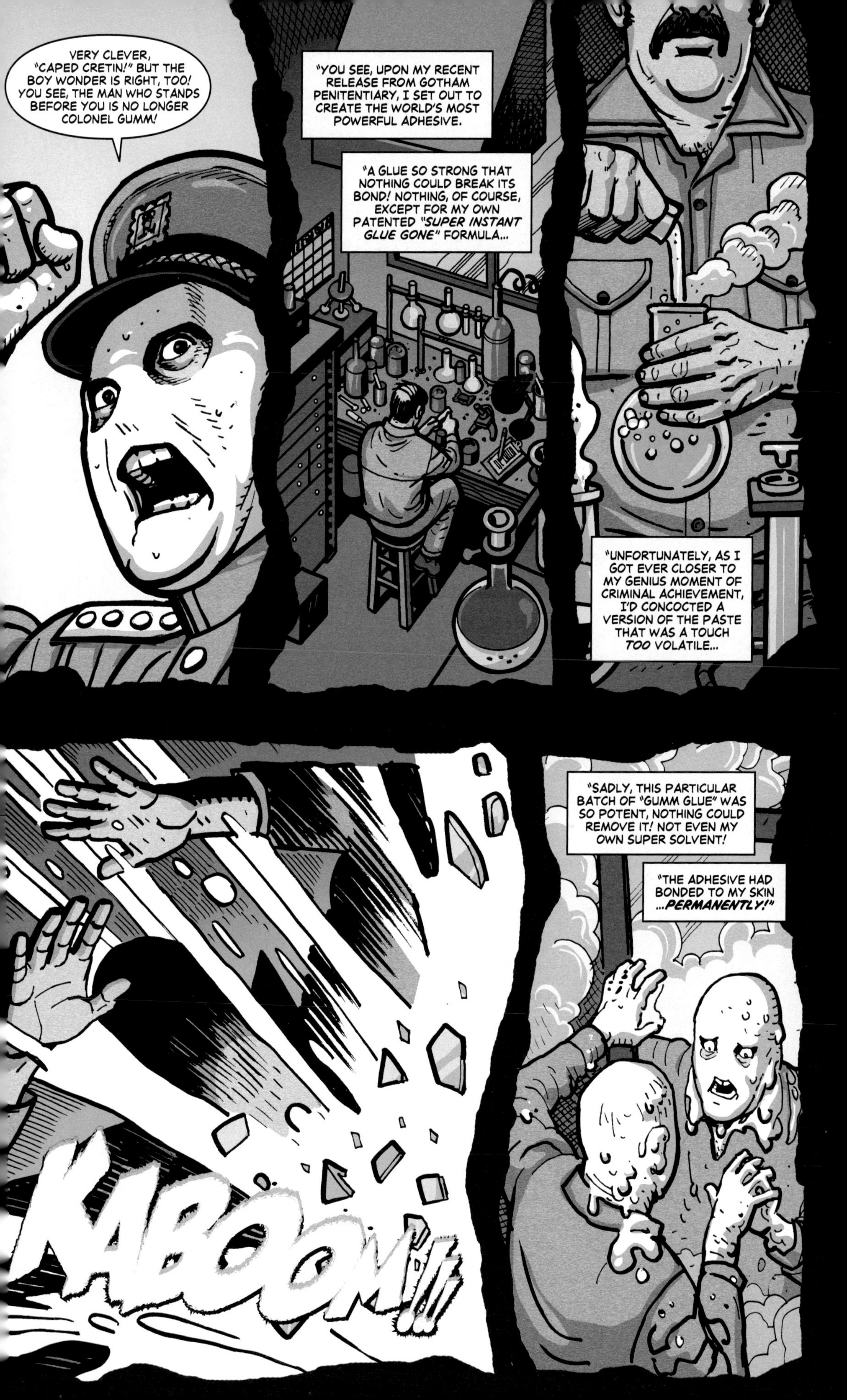
VERY CLEVER, "CAPED CRETIN!" BUT THE BOY WONDER IS RIGHT, TOO! YOU SEE, THE MAN WHO STANDS BEFORE YOU IS NO LONGER COLONEL GUMM!
"YOU SEE, UPON MY RECENT RELEASE FROM GOTHAM PENITENTIARY, I SET OUT TO CREATE THE WORLD'S MOST POWERFUL ADHESIVE.
"A GLUE SO STRONG THAT NOTHING COULD BREAK ITS BOND! NOTHING, OF COURSE, EXCEPT FOR MY OWN PATENTED "SUPER INSTANT GLUE GONE" FORMULA...
"UNFORTUNATELY, AS I GOT EVER CLOSER TO MY GENIUS MOMENT OF CRIMINAL ACHIEVEMENT, I'D CONCOCTED A VERSION OF THE PASTE THAT WAS A TOUCH TOO VOLATILE...
KABOOM!!!
"SADLY, THIS PARTICULAR BATCH OF "GUMM GLUE" WAS SO POTENT, NOTHING COULD REMOVE IT! NOT EVEN MY OWN SUPER SOLVENT!
"THE ADHESIVE HAD BONDED TO MY SKIN ...PERMANENTLY!"

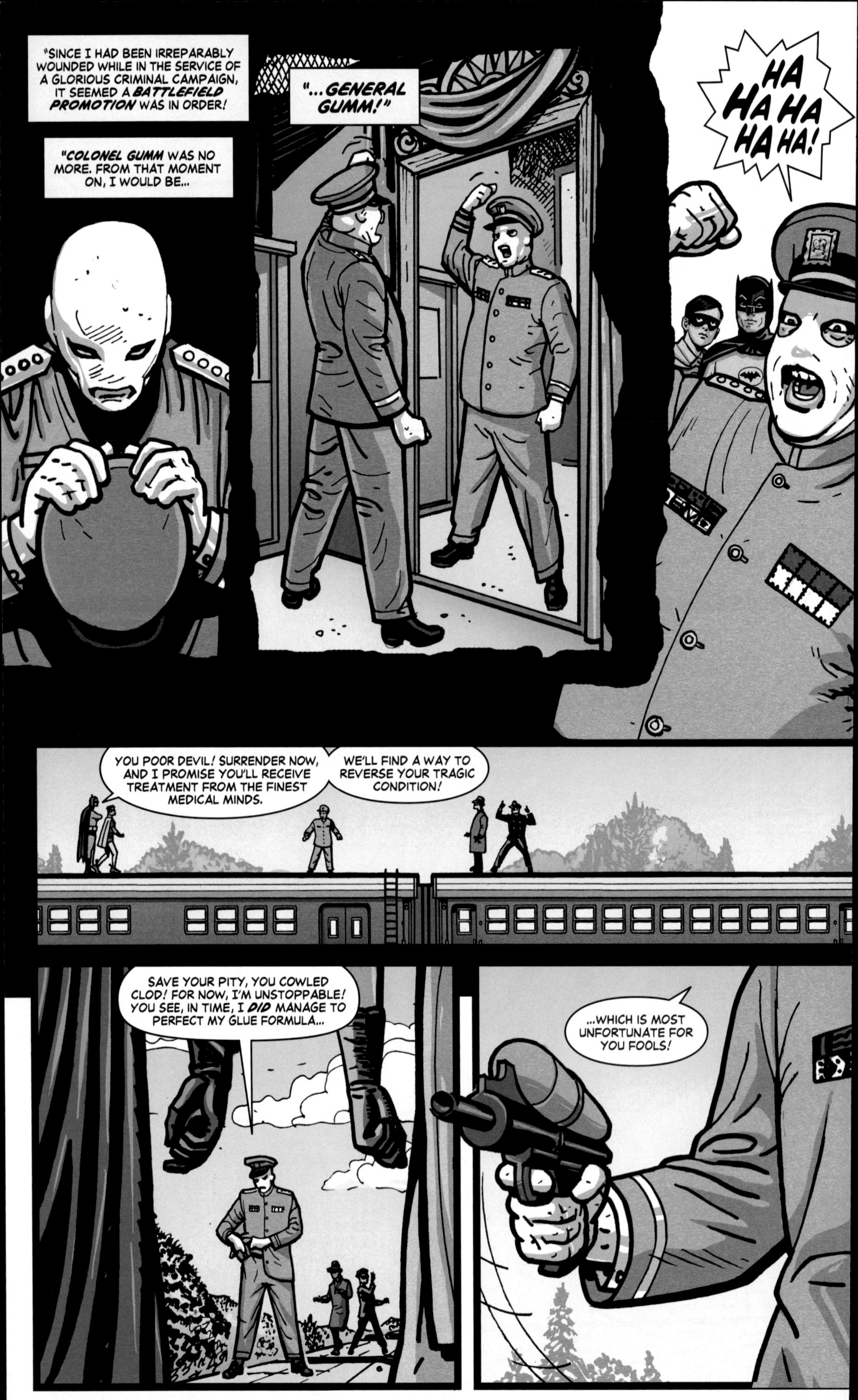

"SINCE I HAD BEEN IRREPARABLY WOUNDED WHILE IN THE SERVICE OF A GLORIOUS CRIMINAL CAMPAIGN, IT SEEMED A BATTLEFIELD PROMOTION WAS IN ORDER!
"COLONEL GUMM WAS NO MORE. FROM THAT MOMENT ON, I WOULD BE...
"...GENERAL GUMM!"
HA HA HA HA HA HA!
YOU POOR DEVIL! SURRENDER NOW, AND I PROMISE YOU'LL RECEIVE TREATMENT FROM THE FINEST MEDICAL MINDS.
WE'LL FIND A WAY TO REVERSE YOUR TRAGIC CONDITION!
SAVE YOUR PITY, YOU COWLED CLOD! FOR NOW, I'M UNSTOPPABLE! YOU SEE, IN TIME, I DID MANAGE TO PERFECT MY GLUE FORMULA...
...WHICH IS MOST UNFORTUNATE FOR YOU FOOLS!

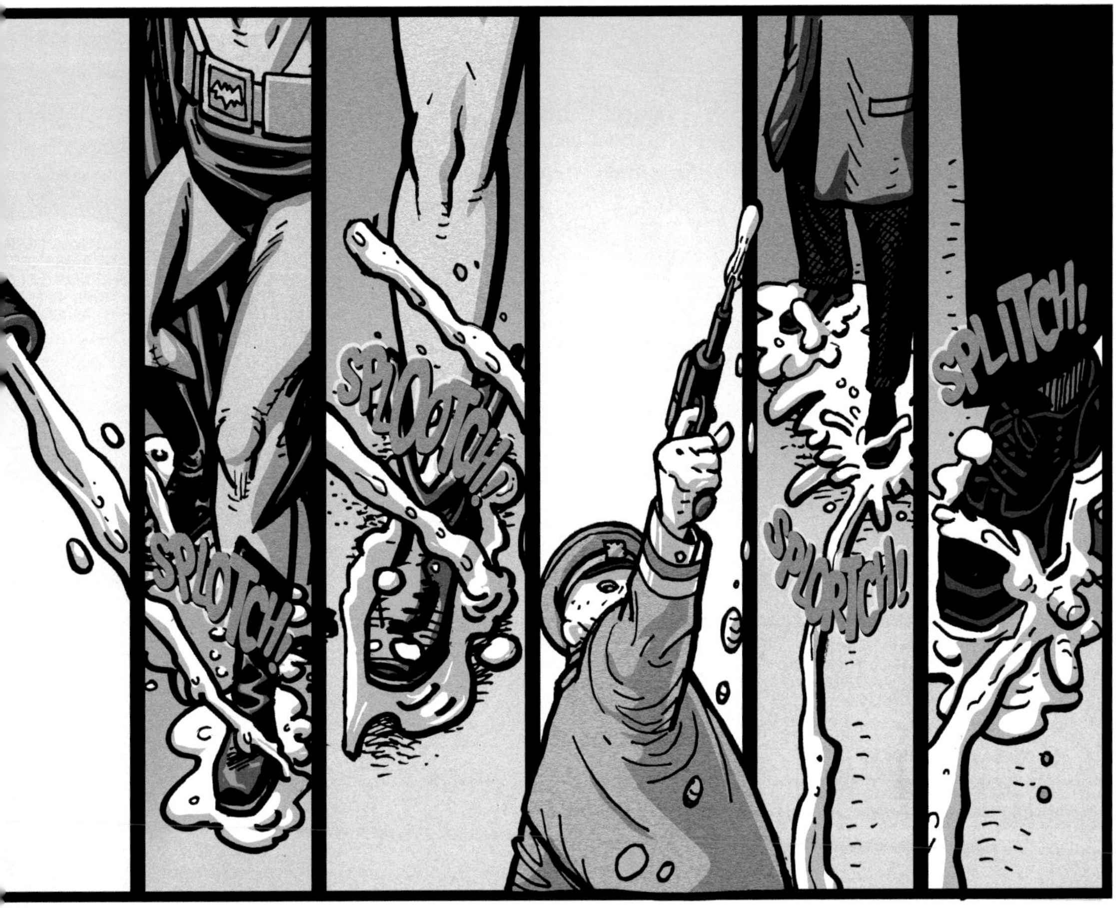
SPLOTCH!
SPLOOTCH!
SPLORTCH!
SPLITCH!

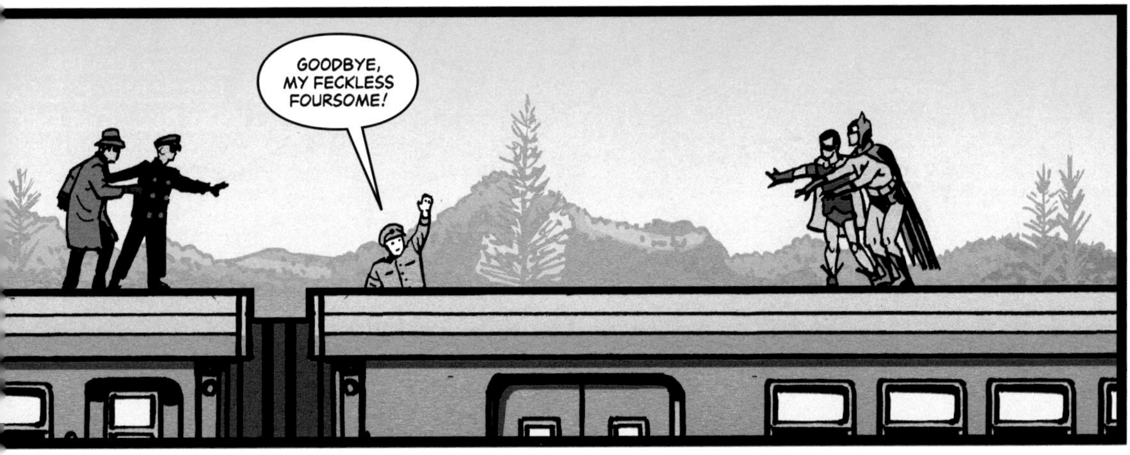
GOODBYE, MY FECKLESS FOURSOME!

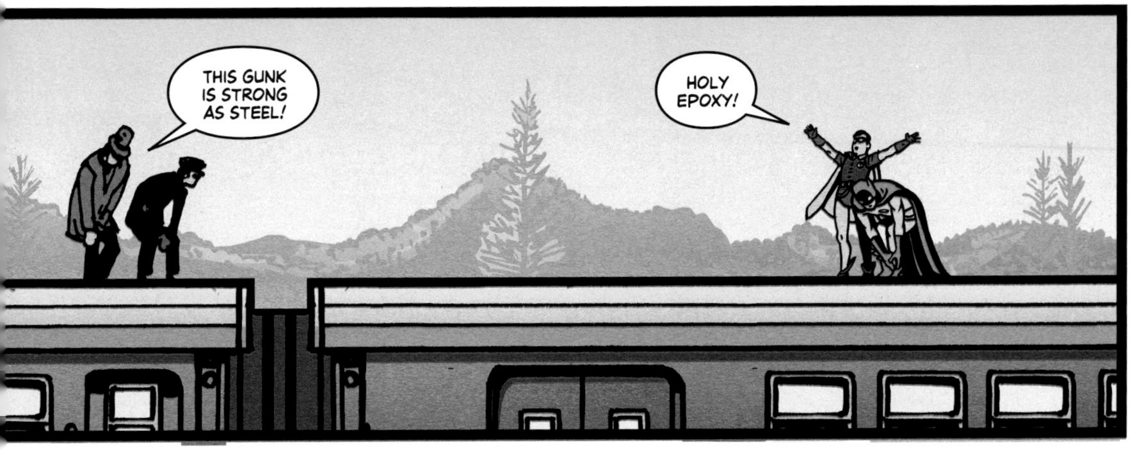
THIS GUNK IS STRONG AS STEEL!
HOLY EPOXY!

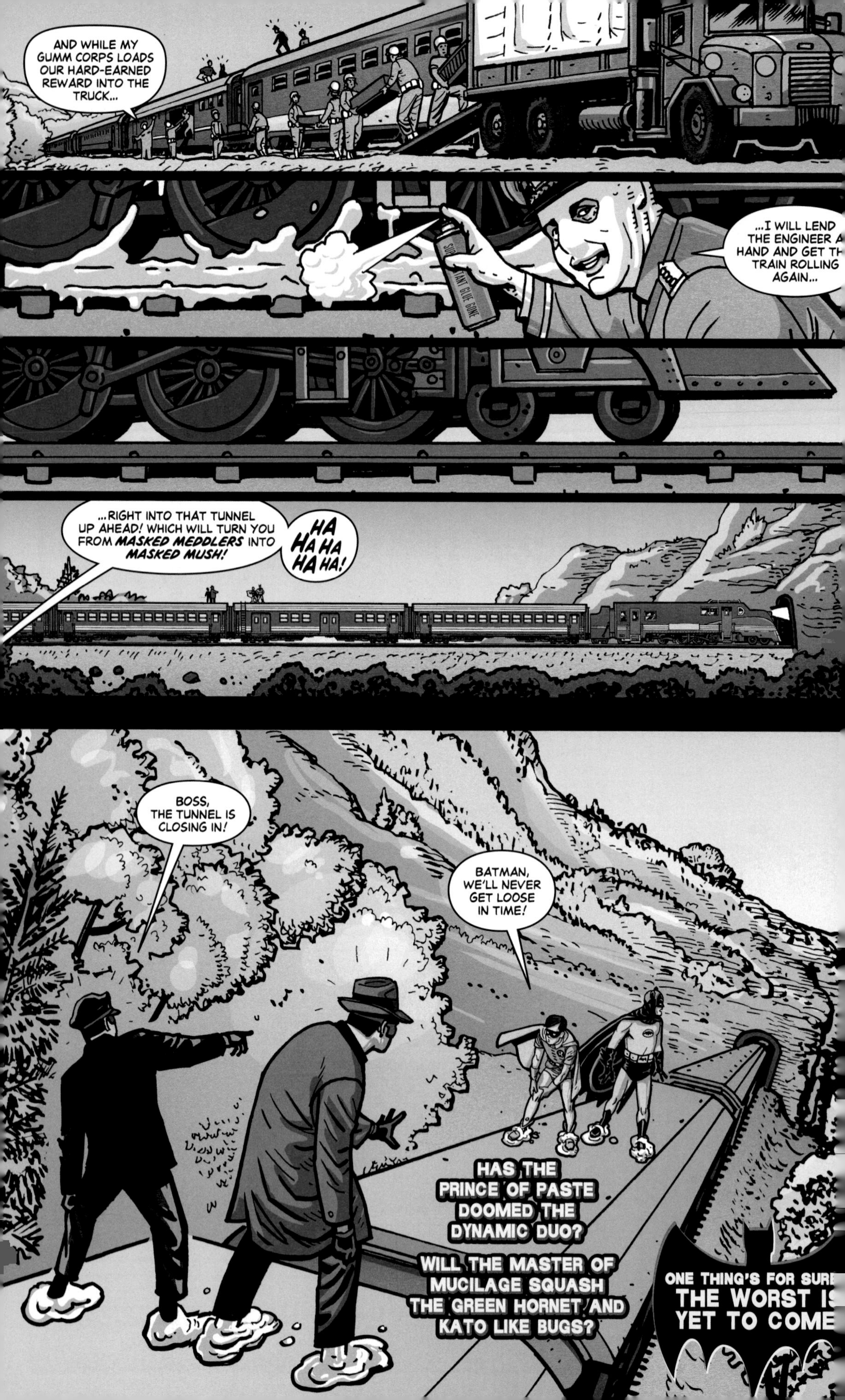
AND WHILE MY GUMM CORPS LOADS OUR HARD-EARNED REWARD INTO THE TRUCK...
...I WILL LEND THE ENGINEER A HAND AND GET TH TRAIN ROLLING AGAIN...
...RIGHT INTO THAT TUNNEL UP AHEAD! WHICH WILL TURN YOU FROM *MASKED MEDDLERS* INTO *MASKED MUSH!*
HA HA HA HA HA!
BOSS, THE TUNNEL IS CLOSING IN!
BATMAN, WE'LL NEVER GET LOOSE IN TIME!
HAS THE PRINCE OF PASTE DOOMED THE DYNAMIC DUO?
WILL THE MASTER OF MUCILAGE SQUASH THE GREEN HORNET AND KATO LIKE BUGS?
ONE THING'S FOR SURE THE WORST IS YET TO COME

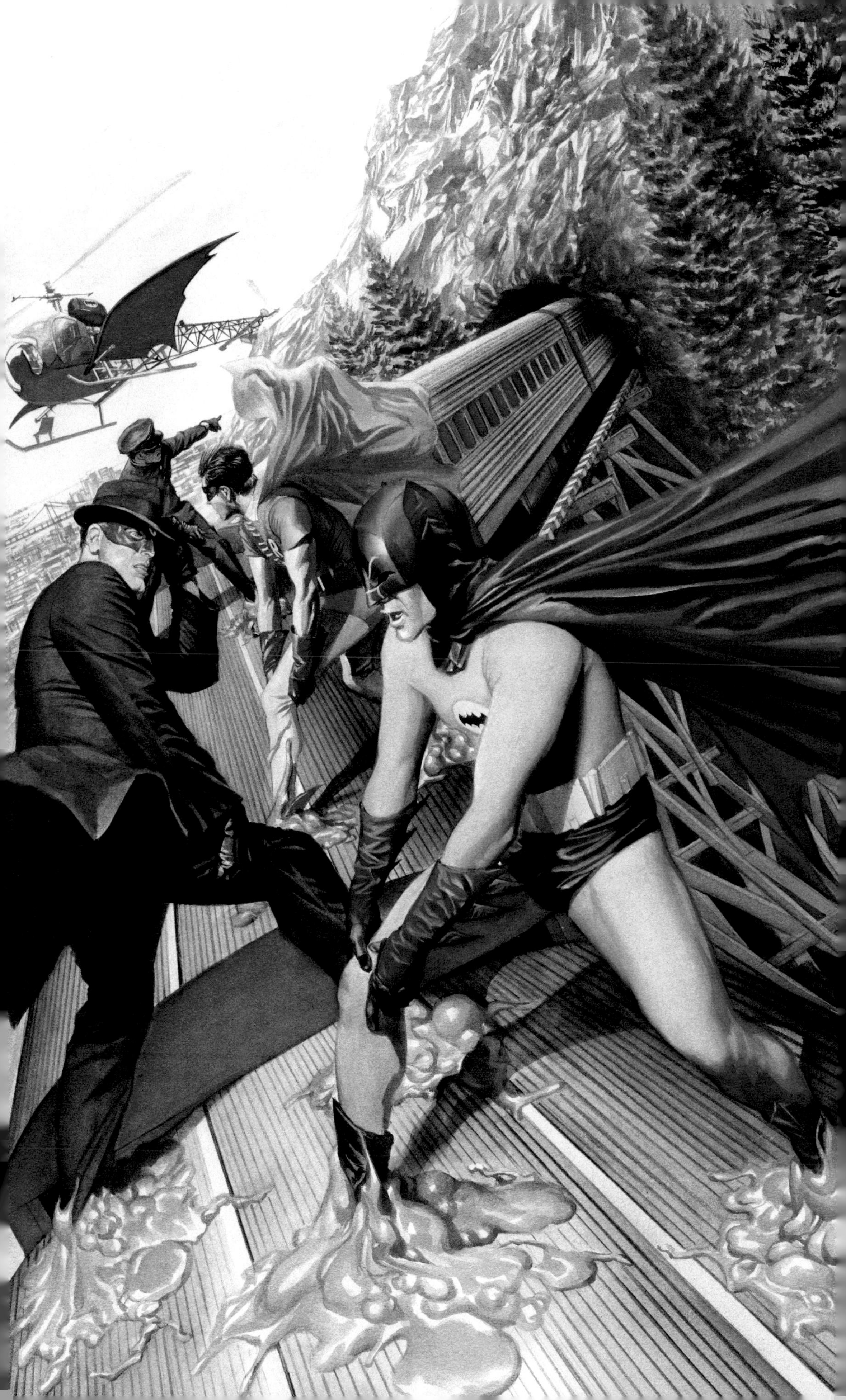

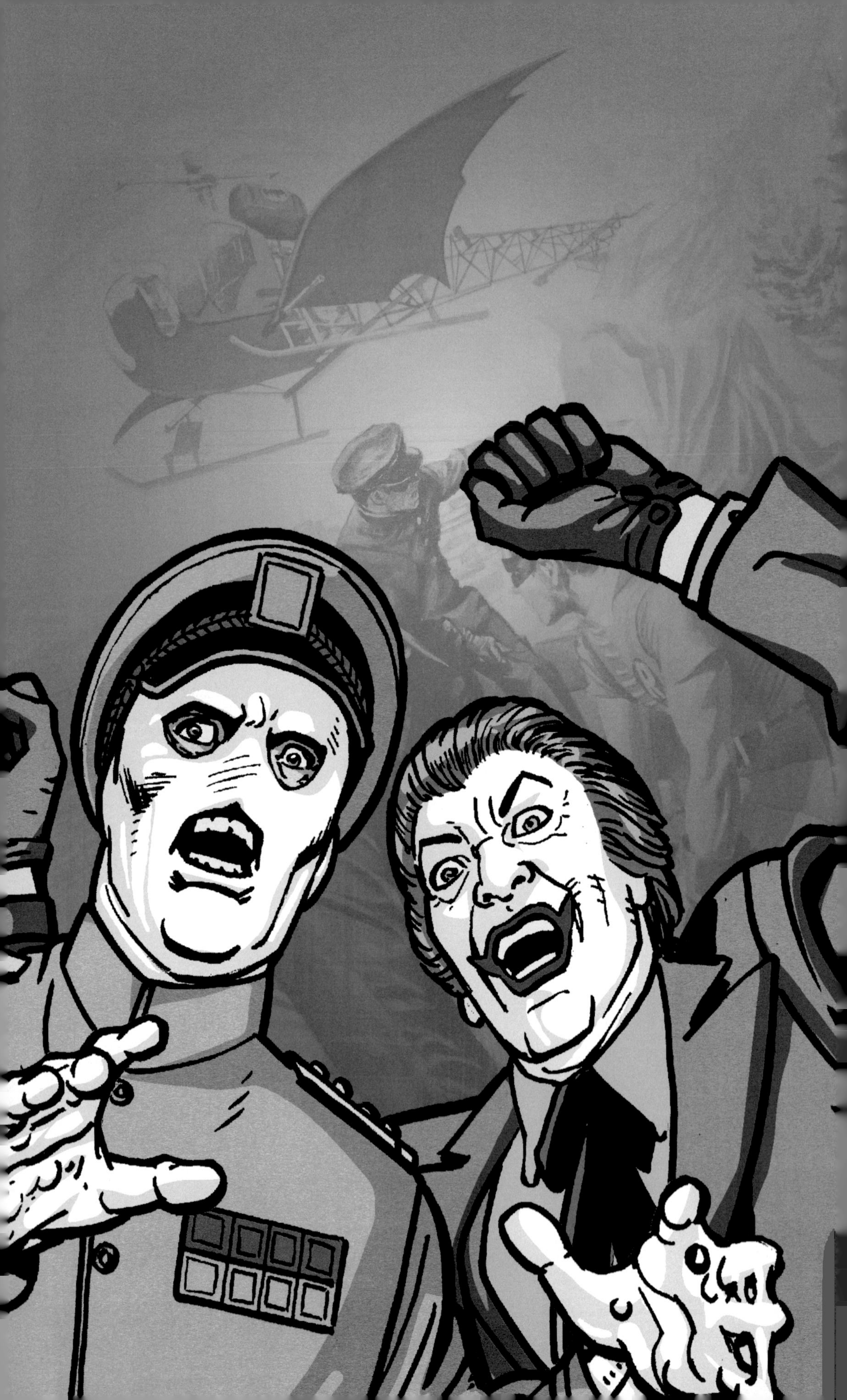

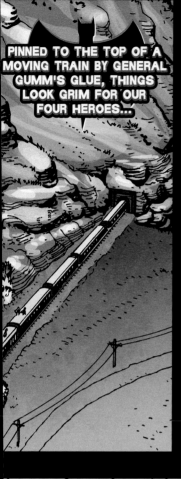

PINNED TO THE TOP OF A MOVING TRAIN BY GENERAL GUMM'S GLUE, THINGS LOOK GRIM FOR OUR FOUR HEROES...

IT'S NO USE, BOSS!

THERE'S NO WAY TO GET *UNSTUCK!*

≡GULP!≡ HOLY ANNIHILATION, BATMAN!

WE'RE GOING TO GET SPLATTERED AGAINST THAT MOUNTAIN!

DON'T LOSE HOPE, OLD CHUM!

I THINK I'VE FIGURED OUT A WAY TO PULL US FREE FROM THIS HEINOUS ADHESIVE!

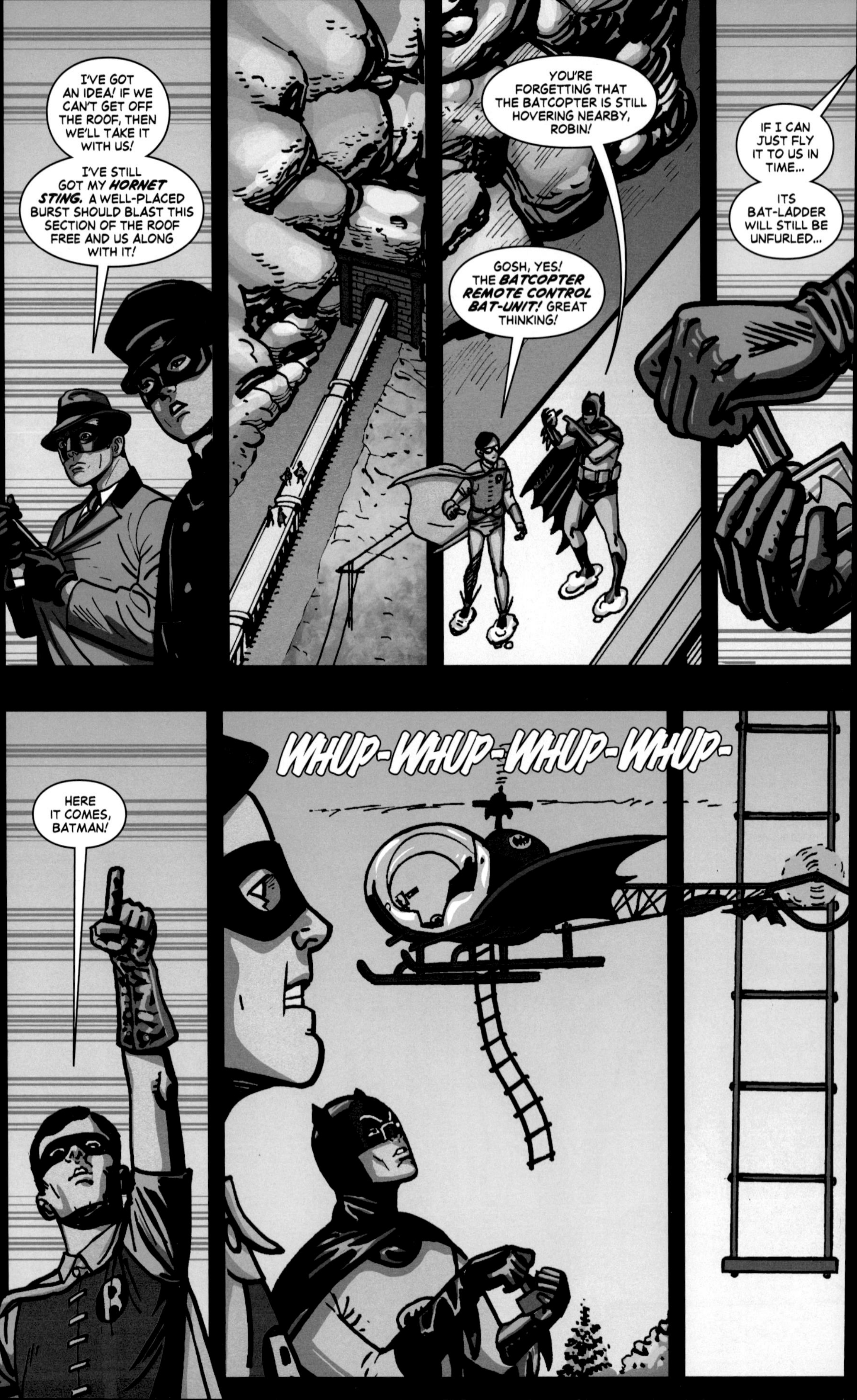
I'VE GOT AN IDEA! IF WE CAN'T GET OFF THE ROOF, THEN WE'LL TAKE IT WITH US!
I'VE STILL GOT MY HORNET STING. A WELL-PLACED BURST SHOULD BLAST THIS SECTION OF THE ROOF FREE AND US ALONG WITH IT!
YOU'RE FORGETTING THAT THE BATCOPTER IS STILL HOVERING NEARBY, ROBIN!
GOSH, YES! THE BATCOPTER REMOTE CONTROL BAT-UNIT! GREAT THINKING!
IF I CAN JUST FLY IT TO US IN TIME...
ITS BAT-LADDER WILL STILL BE UNFURLED...
HERE IT COMES, BATMAN!
WHUP-WHUP-WHUP-WHUP-

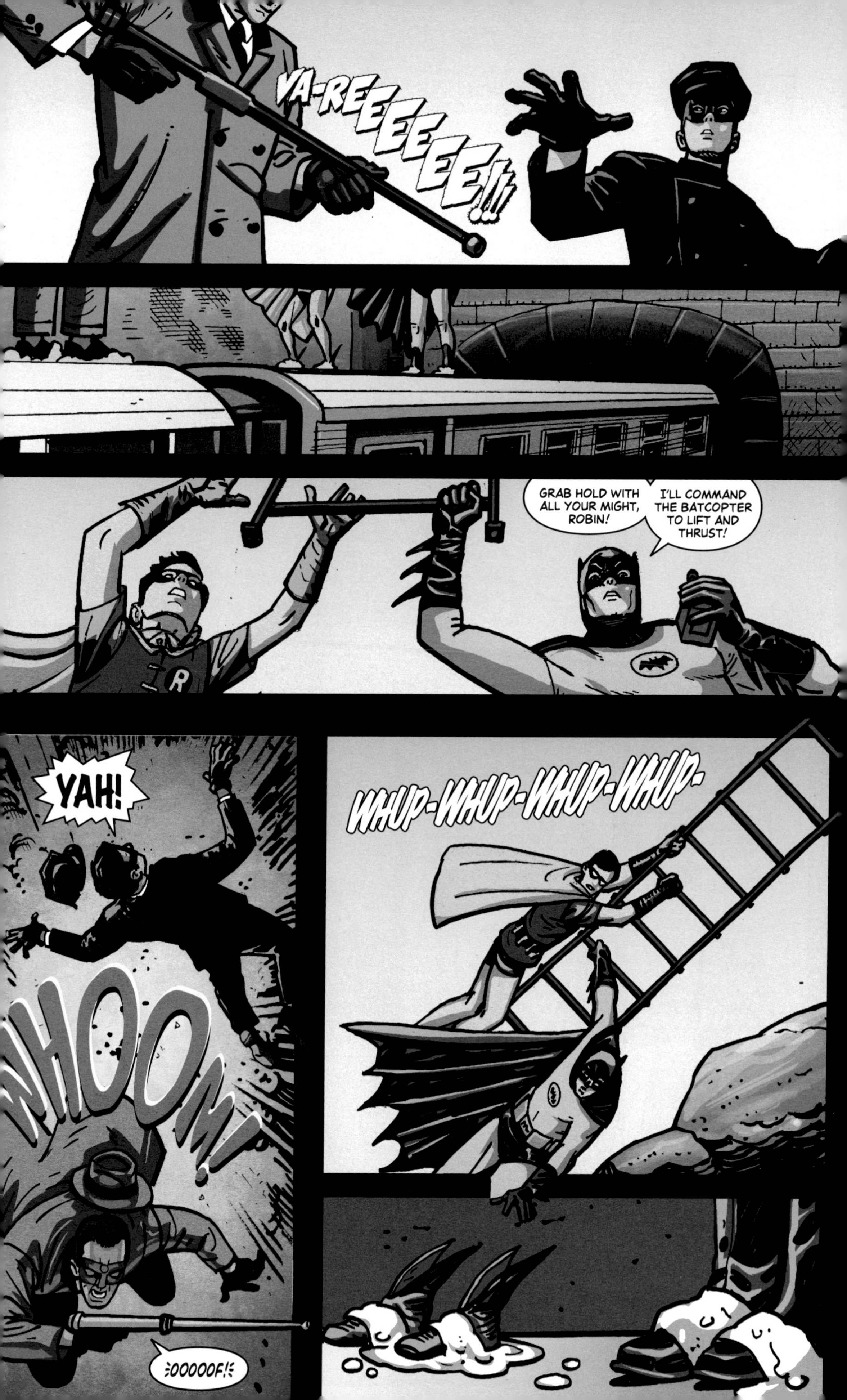
VA-REEEEEEE!!!
GRAB HOLD WITH ALL YOUR MIGHT, ROBIN!
I'LL COMMAND THE BATCOPTER TO LIFT AND THRUST!
YAH!
WHOOM!
OOOOOF!
WHUP-WHUP-WHUP-WHUP-

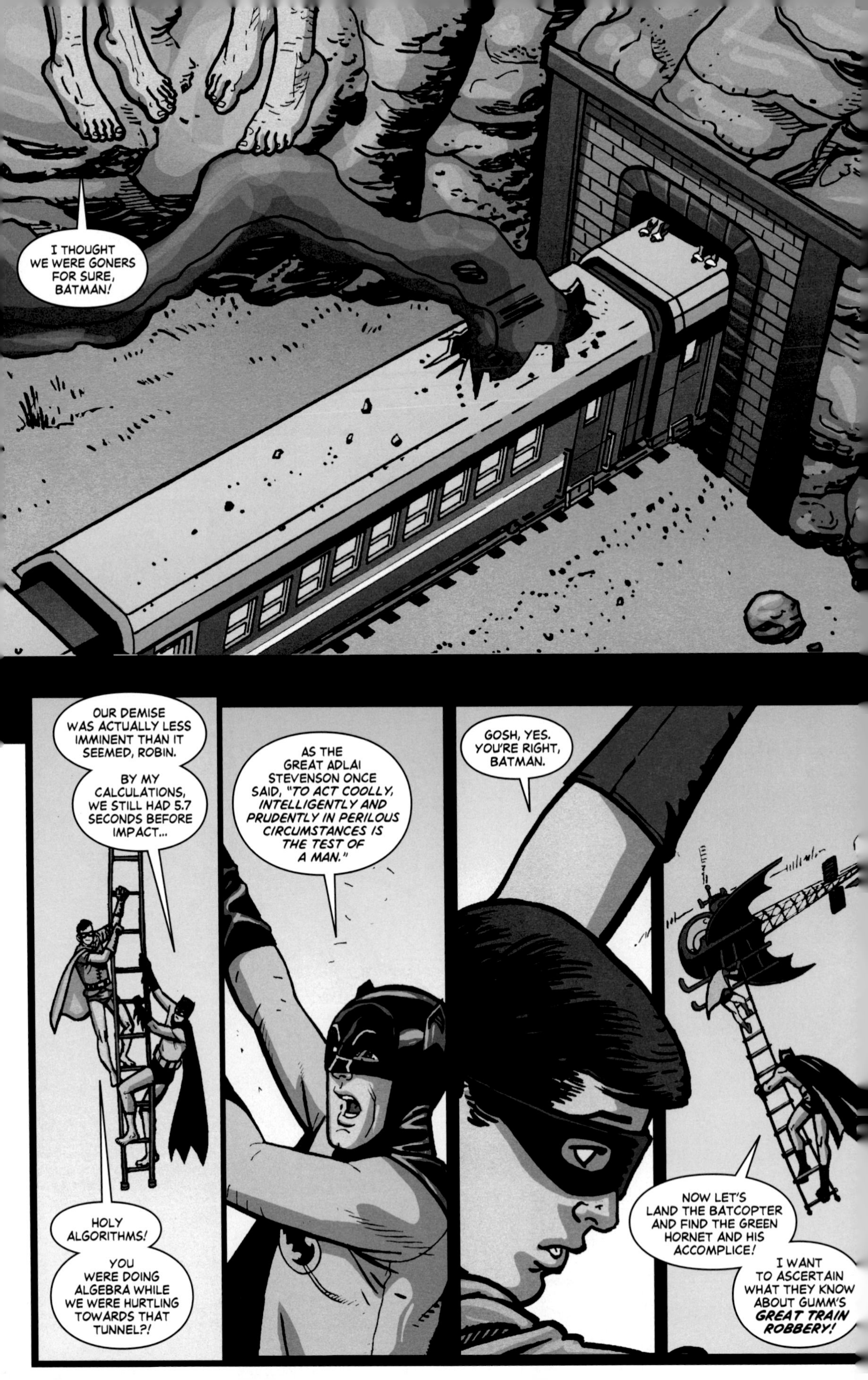
I THOUGHT WE WERE GONERS FOR SURE, BATMAN!
OUR DEMISE WAS ACTUALLY LESS IMMINENT THAN IT SEEMED, ROBIN.
BY MY CALCULATIONS, WE STILL HAD 5.7 SECONDS BEFORE IMPACT...
HOLY ALGORITHMS!
YOU WERE DOING ALGEBRA WHILE WE WERE HURTLING TOWARDS THAT TUNNEL?!
AS THE GREAT ADLAI STEVENSON ONCE SAID, "TO ACT COOLLY, INTELLIGENTLY AND PRUDENTLY IN PERILOUS CIRCUMSTANCES IS THE TEST OF A MAN."
GOSH, YES. YOU'RE RIGHT, BATMAN.
NOW LET'S LAND THE BATCOPTER AND FIND THE GREEN HORNET AND HIS ACCOMPLICE!
I WANT TO ASCERTAIN WHAT THEY KNOW ABOUT GUMM'S GREAT TRAIN ROBBERY!

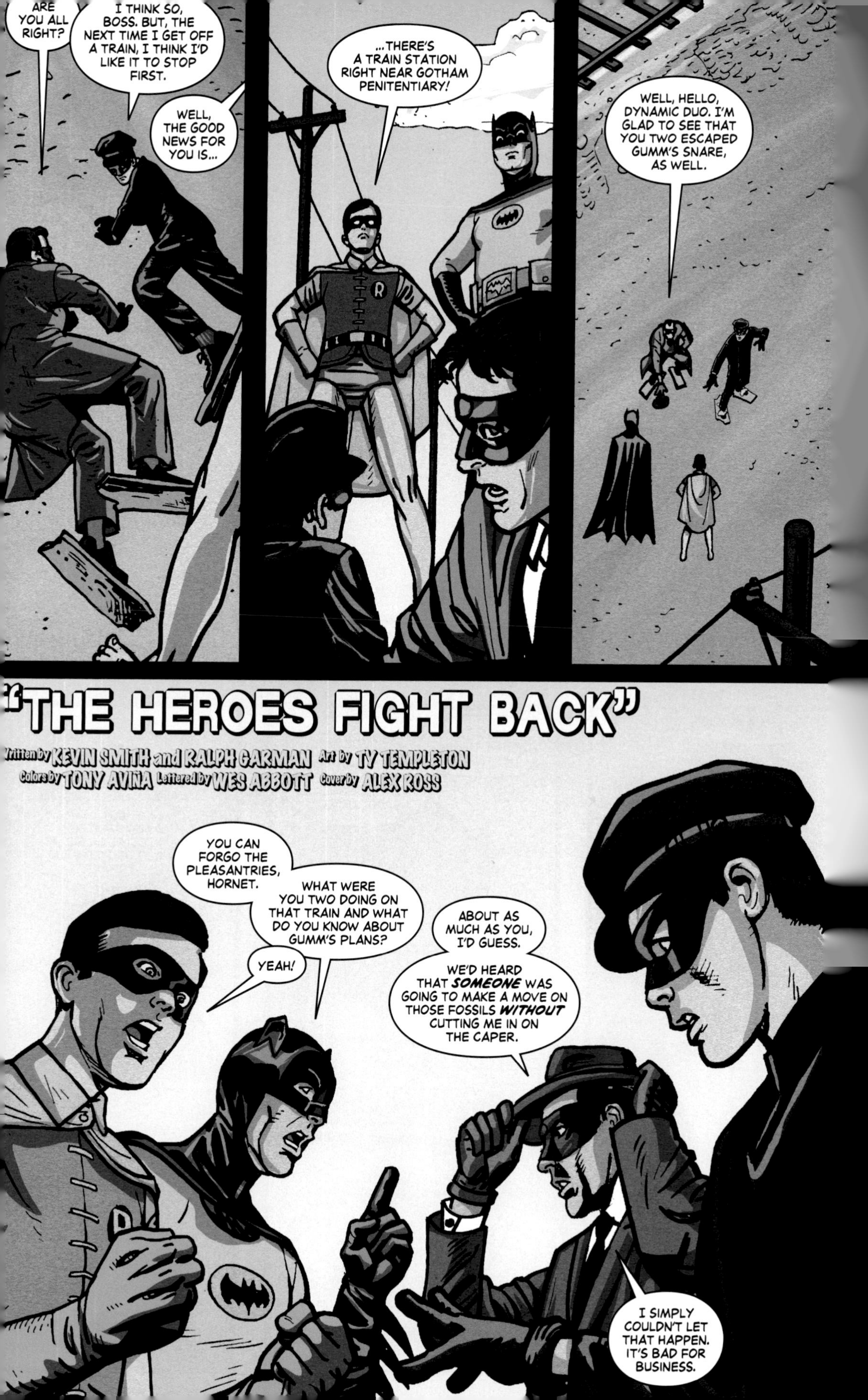
ARE YOU ALL RIGHT?
I THINK SO, BOSS. BUT, THE NEXT TIME I GET OFF A TRAIN, I THINK I'D LIKE IT TO STOP FIRST.
WELL, THE GOOD NEWS FOR YOU IS...
...THERE'S A TRAIN STATION RIGHT NEAR GOTHAM PENITENTIARY!
WELL, HELLO, DYNAMIC DUO. I'M GLAD TO SEE THAT YOU TWO ESCAPED GUMM'S SNARE, AS WELL.
"THE HEROES FIGHT BACK"
Written by KEVIN SMITH and RALPH GARMAN Art by TY TEMPLETON
Colors by TONY AVIÑA Lettered by WES ABBOTT Cover by ALEX ROSS
YOU CAN FORGO THE PLEASANTRIES, HORNET.
WHAT WERE YOU TWO DOING ON THAT TRAIN AND WHAT DO YOU KNOW ABOUT GUMM'S PLANS?
YEAH!
ABOUT AS MUCH AS YOU, I'D GUESS.
WE'D HEARD THAT SOMEONE WAS GOING TO MAKE A MOVE ON THOSE FOSSILS WITHOUT CUTTING ME IN ON THE CAPER.
I SIMPLY COULDN'T LET THAT HAPPEN. IT'S BAD FOR BUSINESS.

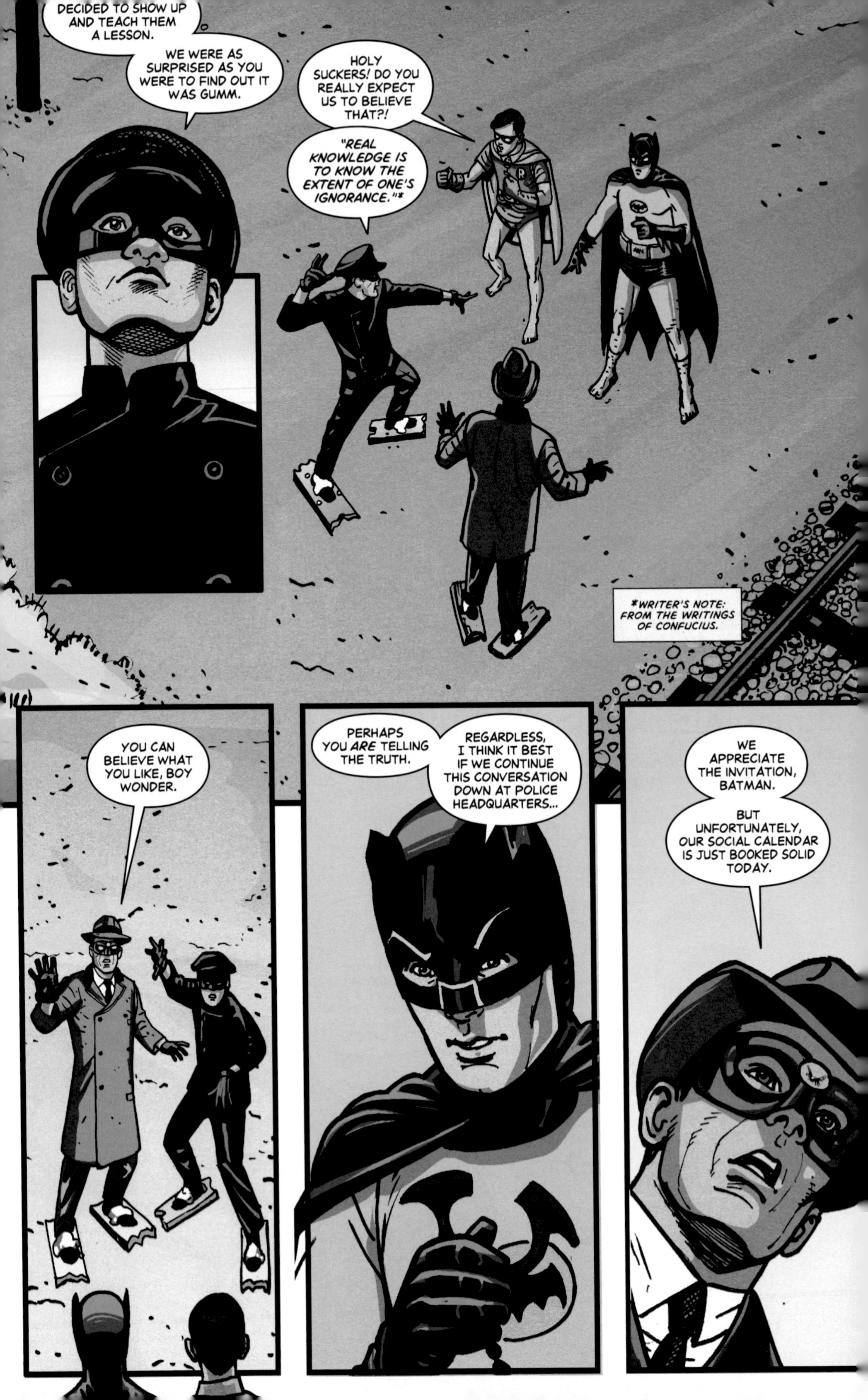
DECIDED TO SHOW UP AND TEACH THEM A LESSON.
WE WERE AS SURPRISED AS YOU WERE TO FIND OUT IT WAS GUMM.
HOLY SUCKERS! DO YOU REALLY EXPECT US TO BELIEVE THAT?!
"REAL KNOWLEDGE IS TO KNOW THE EXTENT OF ONE'S IGNORANCE."*
*WRITER'S NOTE: FROM THE WRITINGS OF CONFUCIUS.
YOU CAN BELIEVE WHAT YOU LIKE, BOY WONDER.
PERHAPS YOU ARE TELLING THE TRUTH.
REGARDLESS, I THINK IT BEST IF WE CONTINUE THIS CONVERSATION DOWN AT POLICE HEADQUARTERS...
WE APPRECIATE THE INVITATION, BATMAN.
BUT UNFORTUNATELY, OUR SOCIAL CALENDAR IS JUST BOOKED SOLID TODAY.

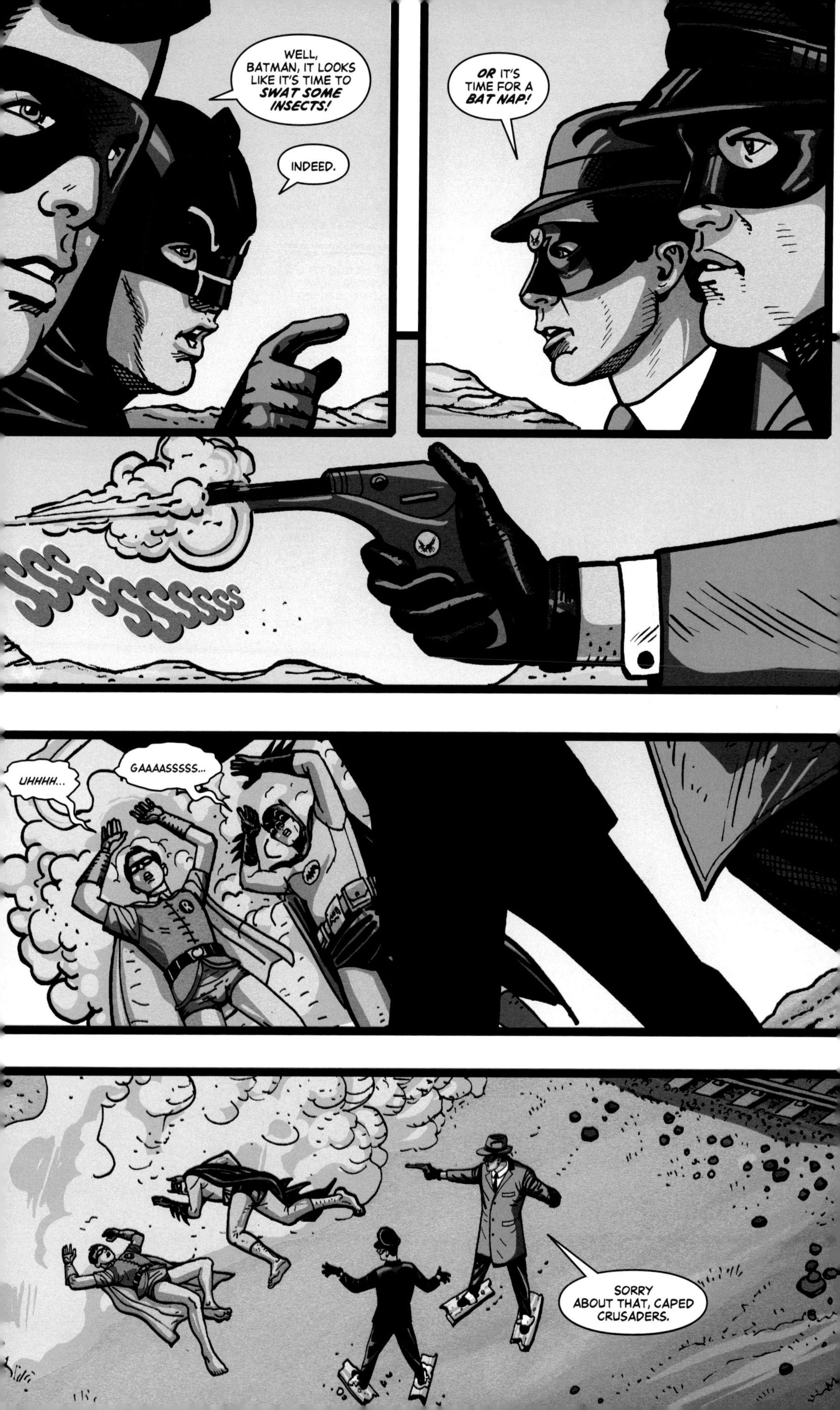
WELL, BATMAN, IT LOOKS LIKE IT'S TIME TO SWAT SOME INSECTS!
INDEED.
OR IT'S TIME FOR A BAT NAP!
SSSSSSSSSSS
UHHHH...
GAAAASSSSS...
SORRY ABOUT THAT, CAPED CRUSADERS.

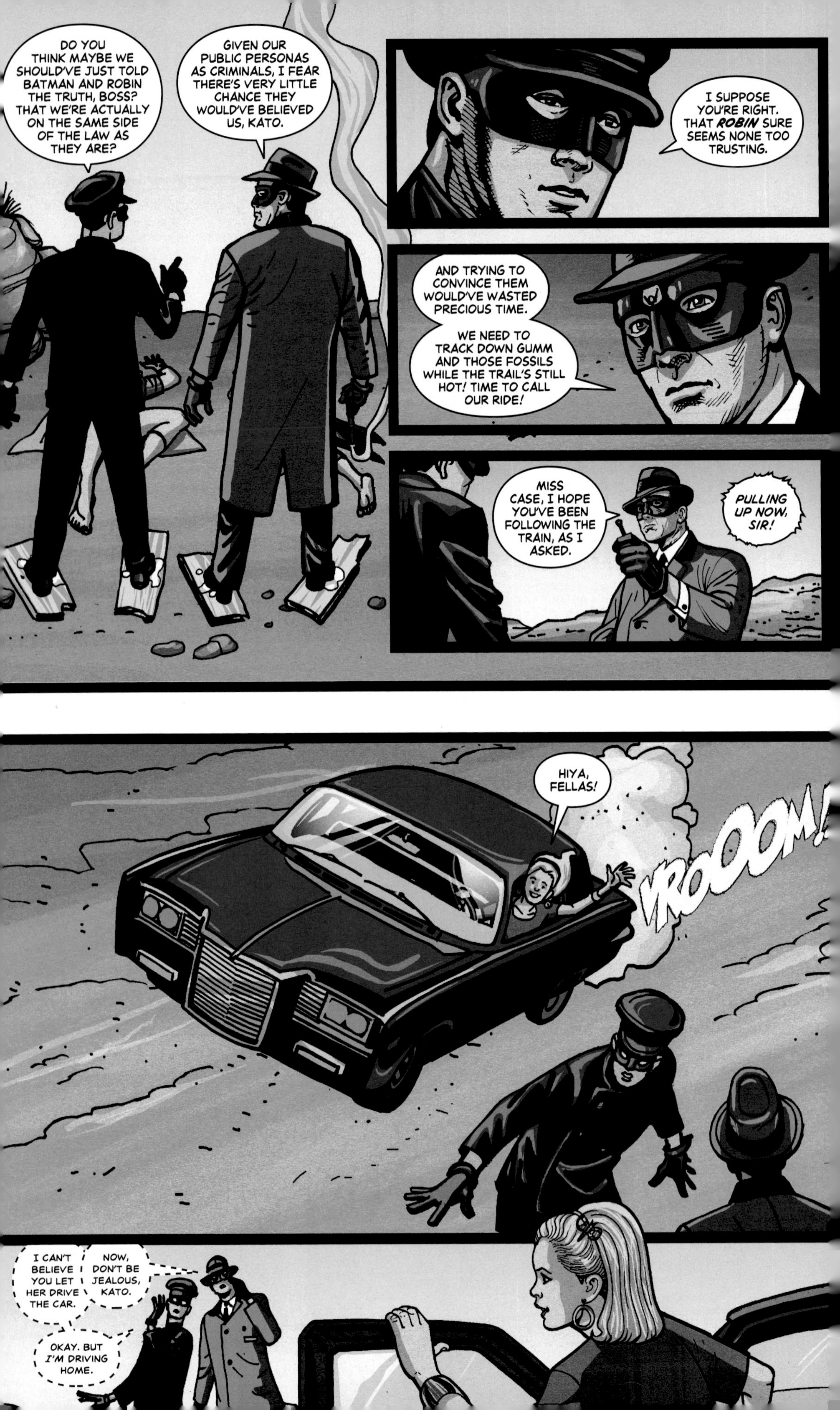
DO YOU THINK MAYBE WE SHOULD'VE JUST TOLD BATMAN AND ROBIN THE TRUTH, BOSS? THAT WE'RE ACTUALLY ON THE SAME SIDE OF THE LAW AS THEY ARE?
GIVEN OUR PUBLIC PERSONAS AS CRIMINALS, I FEAR THERE'S VERY LITTLE CHANCE THEY WOULD'VE BELIEVED US, KATO.
I SUPPOSE YOU'RE RIGHT. THAT ROBIN SURE SEEMS NONE TOO TRUSTING.
AND TRYING TO CONVINCE THEM WOULD'VE WASTED PRECIOUS TIME.
WE NEED TO TRACK DOWN GUMM AND THOSE FOSSILS WHILE THE TRAIL'S STILL HOT! TIME TO CALL OUR RIDE!
MISS CASE, I HOPE YOU'VE BEEN FOLLOWING THE TRAIN, AS I ASKED.
PULLING UP NOW, SIR!
HIYA, FELLAS!
VROOOOM!
I CAN'T BELIEVE YOU LET HER DRIVE THE CAR.
NOW, DON'T BE JEALOUS, KATO.
OKAY. BUT I'M DRIVING HOME.

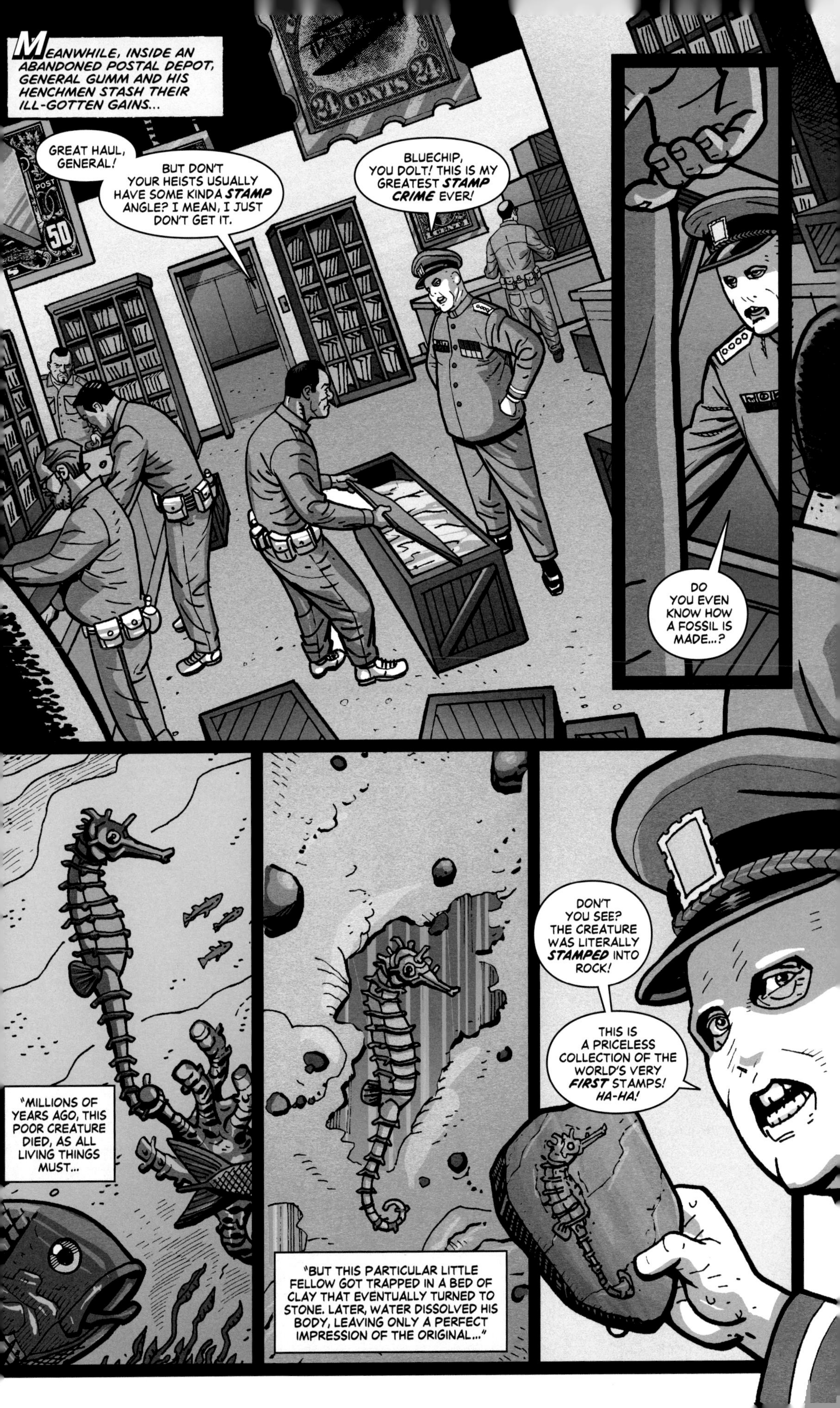
MEANWHILE, INSIDE AN ABANDONED POSTAL DEPOT, GENERAL GUMM AND HIS HENCHMEN STASH THEIR ILL-GOTTEN GAINS...
GREAT HAUL, GENERAL!
BUT DON'T YOUR HEISTS USUALLY HAVE SOME KINDA STAMP ANGLE? I MEAN, I JUST DON'T GET IT.
BLUECHIP, YOU DOLT! THIS IS MY GREATEST STAMP CRIME EVER!
DO YOU EVEN KNOW HOW A FOSSIL IS MADE...?
"MILLIONS OF YEARS AGO, THIS POOR CREATURE DIED, AS ALL LIVING THINGS MUST...
"BUT THIS PARTICULAR LITTLE FELLOW GOT TRAPPED IN A BED OF CLAY THAT EVENTUALLY TURNED TO STONE. LATER, WATER DISSOLVED HIS BODY, LEAVING ONLY A PERFECT IMPRESSION OF THE ORIGINAL..."
DON'T YOU SEE? THE CREATURE WAS LITERALLY STAMPED INTO ROCK!
THIS IS A PRICELESS COLLECTION OF THE WORLD'S VERY FIRST STAMPS! HA-HA!

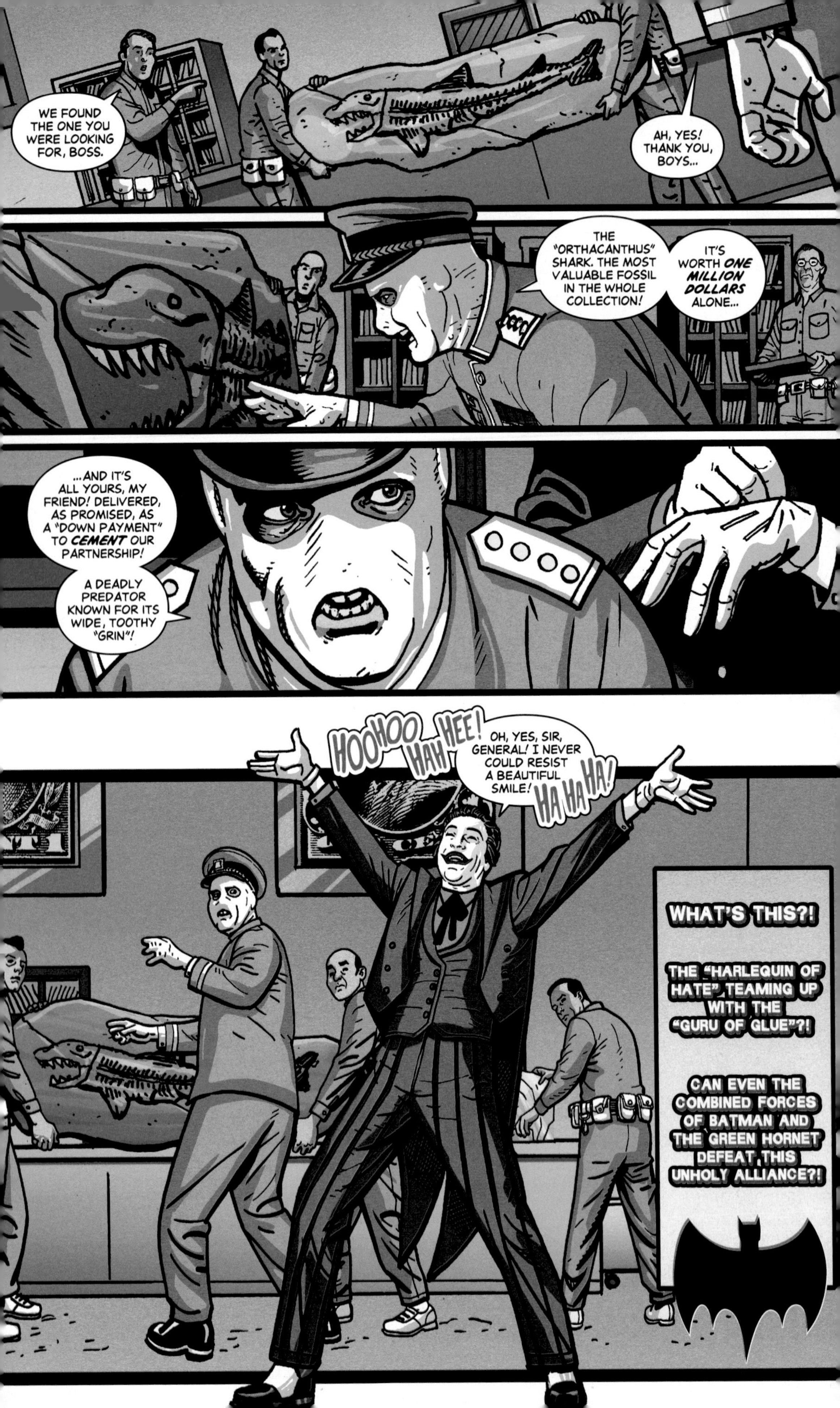
WE FOUND THE ONE YOU WERE LOOKING FOR, BOSS.
AH, YES! THANK YOU, BOYS...
THE "ORTHACANTHUS" SHARK. THE MOST VALUABLE FOSSIL IN THE WHOLE COLLECTION!
IT'S WORTH ONE MILLION DOLLARS ALONE...
...AND IT'S ALL YOURS, MY FRIEND! DELIVERED, AS PROMISED, AS A "DOWN PAYMENT" TO CEMENT OUR PARTNERSHIP!
A DEADLY PREDATOR KNOWN FOR ITS WIDE, TOOTHY "GRIN"!
HOOHOO HAH HEE!
OH, YES, SIR, GENERAL! I NEVER COULD RESIST A BEAUTIFUL SMILE!
HA HA HA!
WHAT'S THIS?!
THE "HARLEQUIN OF HATE" TEAMING UP WITH THE "GURU OF GLUE"?!
CAN EVEN THE COMBINED FORCES OF BATMAN AND THE GREEN HORNET DEFEAT THIS UNHOLY ALLIANCE?!

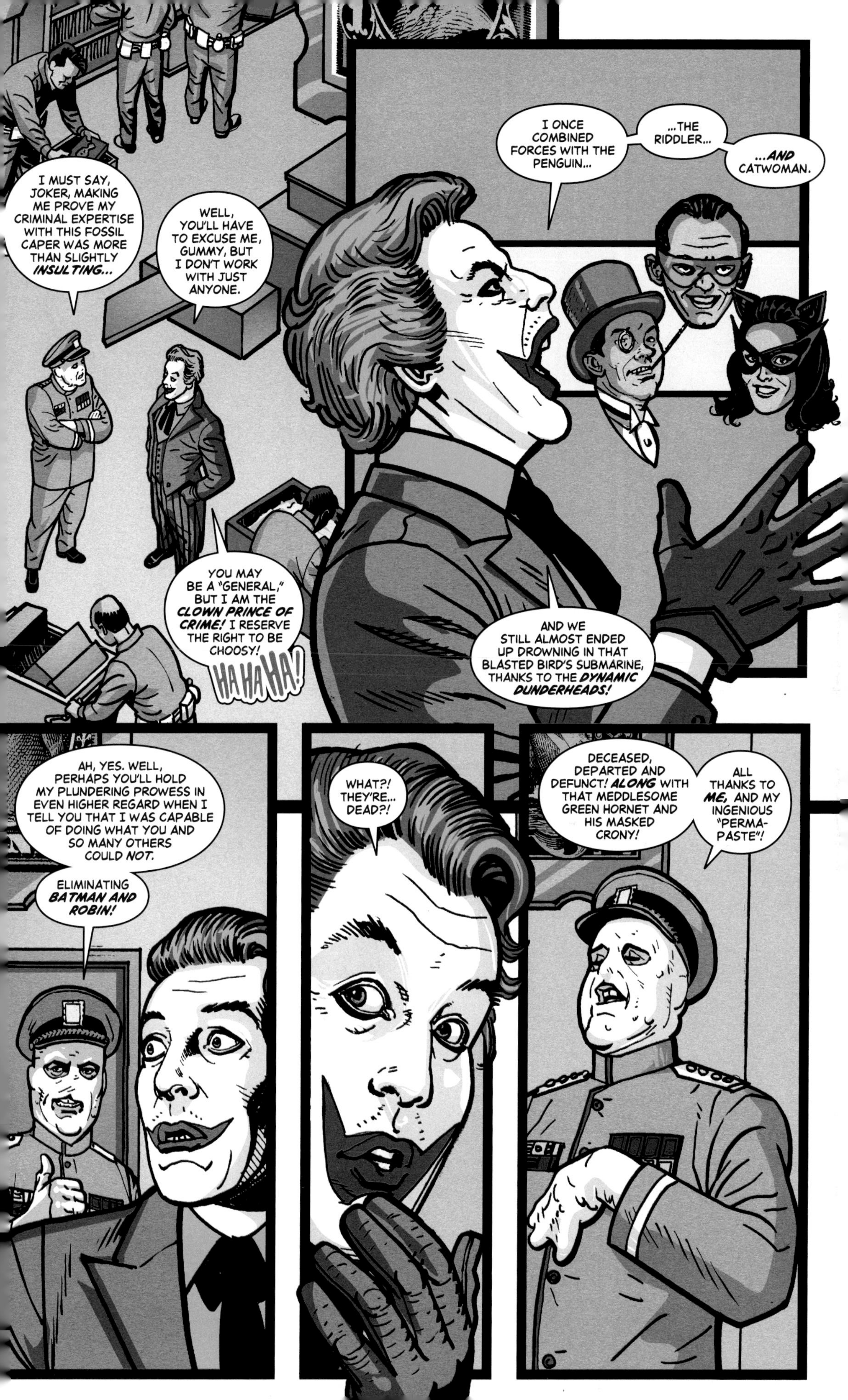
I MUST SAY, JOKER, MAKING ME PROVE MY CRIMINAL EXPERTISE WITH THIS FOSSIL CAPER WAS MORE THAN SLIGHTLY INSULTING...
WELL, YOU'LL HAVE TO EXCUSE ME, GUMMY, BUT I DON'T WORK WITH JUST ANYONE.
YOU MAY BE A "GENERAL," BUT I AM THE CLOWN PRINCE OF CRIME! I RESERVE THE RIGHT TO BE CHOOSY!
HA HA HA!
I ONCE COMBINED FORCES WITH THE PENGUIN...
...THE RIDDLER...
...AND CATWOMAN.
AND WE STILL ALMOST ENDED UP DROWNING IN THAT BLASTED BIRD'S SUBMARINE, THANKS TO THE DYNAMIC DUNDERHEADS!
AH, YES. WELL, PERHAPS YOU'LL HOLD MY PLUNDERING PROWESS IN EVEN HIGHER REGARD WHEN I TELL YOU THAT I WAS CAPABLE OF DOING WHAT YOU AND SO MANY OTHERS COULD NOT.
ELIMINATING BATMAN AND ROBIN!
WHAT?! THEY'RE... DEAD?!
DECEASED, DEPARTED AND DEFUNCT! ALONG WITH THAT MEDDLESOME GREEN HORNET AND HIS MASKED CRONY!
ALL THANKS TO ME, AND MY INGENIOUS "PERMA-PASTE"!

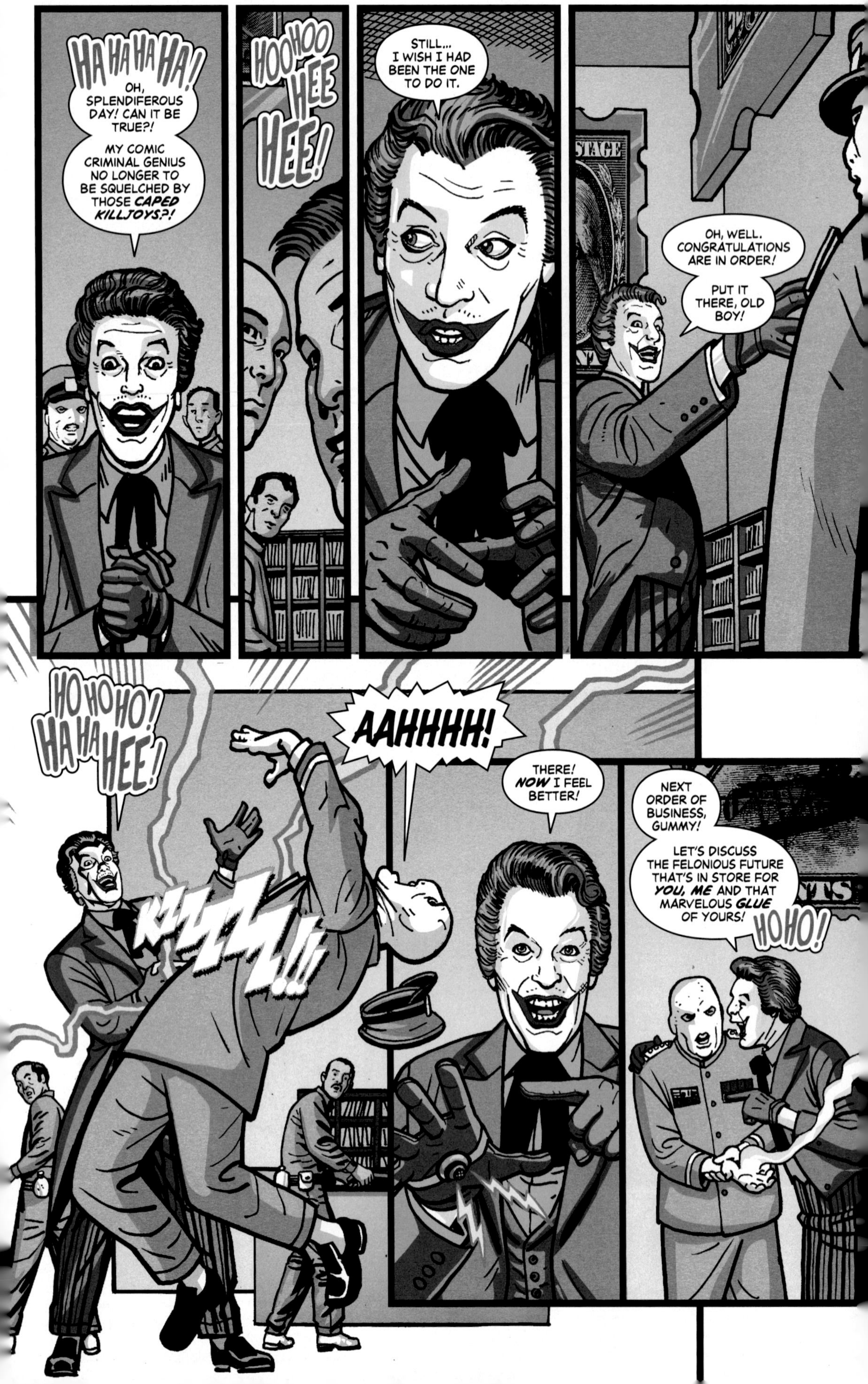
HA HA HA HA!
OH, SPLENDIFEROUS DAY! CAN IT BE TRUE?!
MY COMIC CRIMINAL GENIUS NO LONGER TO BE SQUELCHED BY THOSE CAPED KILLJOYS?!
HOO HOO HEE HEE!
STILL... I WISH I HAD BEEN THE ONE TO DO IT.
OH, WELL. CONGRATULATIONS ARE IN ORDER!
PUT IT THERE, OLD BOY!
HO HO HO! HA HA HEE!
AAHHHH!
KZZZZZ...!!
THERE! NOW I FEEL BETTER!
NEXT ORDER OF BUSINESS, GUMMY!
LET'S DISCUSS THE FELONIOUS FUTURE THAT'S IN STORE FOR YOU, ME AND THAT MARVELOUS GLUE OF YOURS!
HOHO!

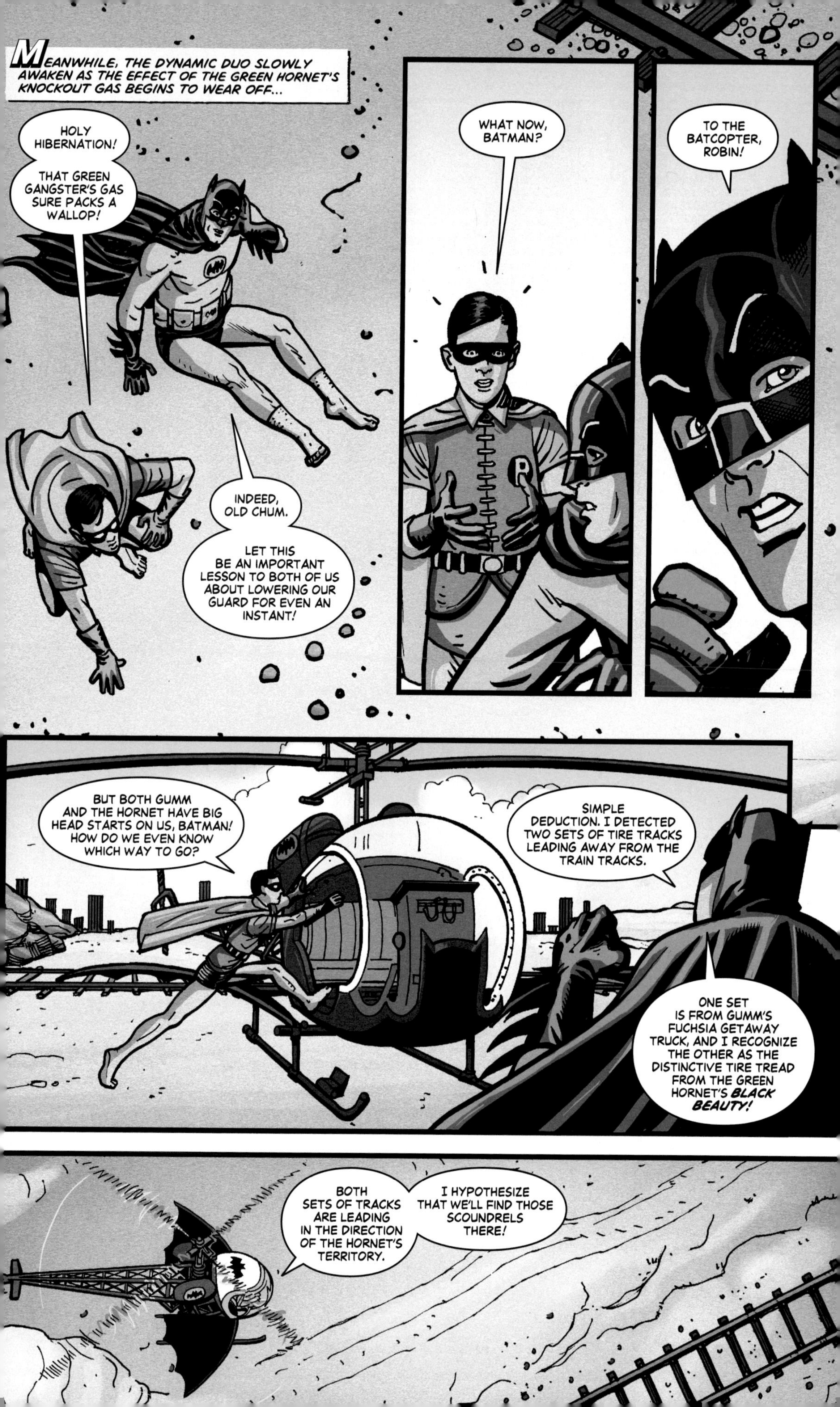
MEANWHILE, THE DYNAMIC DUO SLOWLY AWAKEN AS THE EFFECT OF THE GREEN HORNET'S KNOCKOUT GAS BEGINS TO WEAR OFF...
HOLY HIBERNATION!
THAT GREEN GANGSTER'S GAS SURE PACKS A WALLOP!
INDEED, OLD CHUM.
LET THIS BE AN IMPORTANT LESSON TO BOTH OF US ABOUT LOWERING OUR GUARD FOR EVEN AN INSTANT!
WHAT NOW, BATMAN?
TO THE BATCOPTER, ROBIN!
BUT BOTH GUMM AND THE HORNET HAVE BIG HEAD STARTS ON US, BATMAN! HOW DO WE EVEN KNOW WHICH WAY TO GO?
SIMPLE DEDUCTION. I DETECTED TWO SETS OF TIRE TRACKS LEADING AWAY FROM THE TRAIN TRACKS.
ONE SET IS FROM GUMM'S FUCHSIA GETAWAY TRUCK, AND I RECOGNIZE THE OTHER AS THE DISTINCTIVE TIRE TREAD FROM THE GREEN HORNET'S BLACK BEAUTY!
BOTH SETS OF TRACKS ARE LEADING IN THE DIRECTION OF THE HORNET'S TERRITORY.
I HYPOTHESIZE THAT WE'LL FIND THOSE SCOUNDRELS THERE!

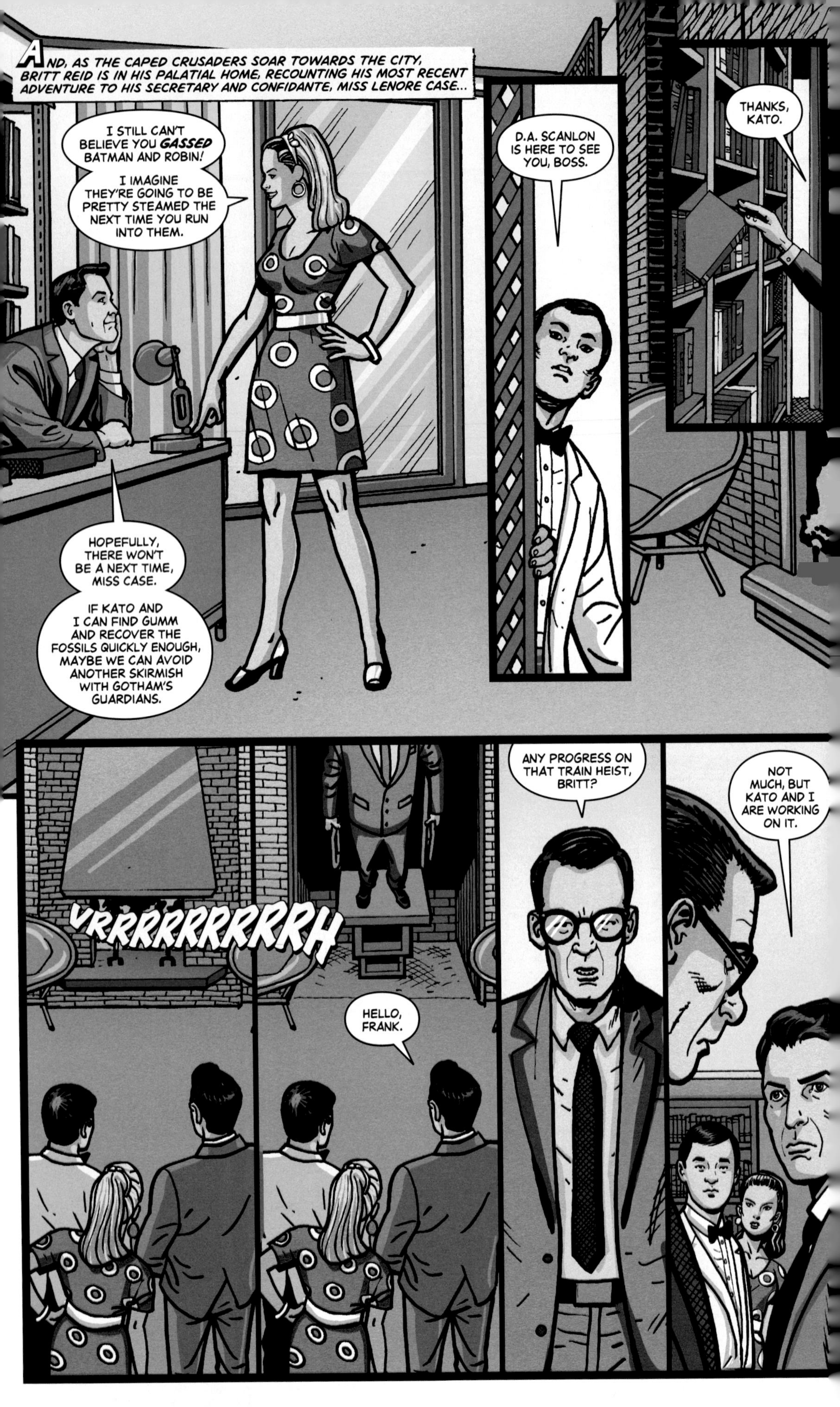
AND, AS THE CAPED CRUSADERS SOAR TOWARDS THE CITY, BRITT REID IS IN HIS PALATIAL HOME, RECOUNTING HIS MOST RECENT ADVENTURE TO HIS SECRETARY AND CONFIDANTE, MISS LENORE CASE...
I STILL CAN'T BELIEVE YOU GASSED BATMAN AND ROBIN!
I IMAGINE THEY'RE GOING TO BE PRETTY STEAMED THE NEXT TIME YOU RUN INTO THEM.
HOPEFULLY, THERE WON'T BE A NEXT TIME, MISS CASE.
IF KATO AND I CAN FIND GUMM AND RECOVER THE FOSSILS QUICKLY ENOUGH, MAYBE WE CAN AVOID ANOTHER SKIRMISH WITH GOTHAM'S GUARDIANS.
D.A. SCANLON IS HERE TO SEE YOU, BOSS.
THANKS, KATO.
VRRRRRRRRRH
HELLO, FRANK.
ANY PROGRESS ON THAT TRAIN HEIST, BRITT?
NOT MUCH, BUT KATO AND I ARE WORKING ON IT.

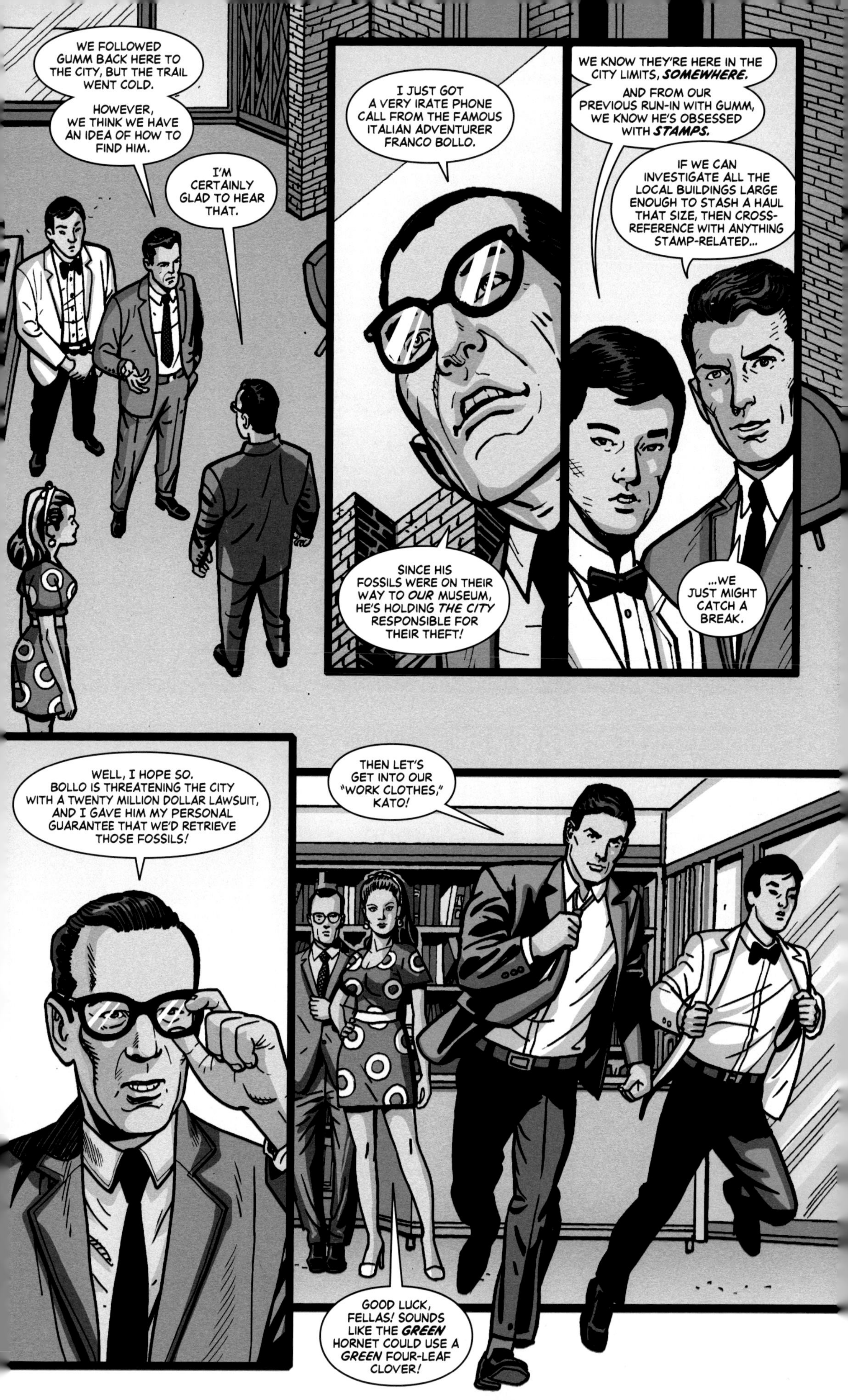
WE FOLLOWED GUMM BACK HERE TO THE CITY, BUT THE TRAIL WENT COLD.
HOWEVER, WE THINK WE HAVE AN IDEA OF HOW TO FIND HIM.
I'M CERTAINLY GLAD TO HEAR THAT.
I JUST GOT A VERY IRATE PHONE CALL FROM THE FAMOUS ITALIAN ADVENTURER FRANCO BOLLO.
SINCE HIS FOSSILS WERE ON THEIR WAY TO *OUR* MUSEUM, HE'S HOLDING *THE CITY* RESPONSIBLE FOR THEIR THEFT!
WE KNOW THEY'RE HERE IN THE CITY LIMITS, ***SOMEWHERE.***
AND FROM OUR PREVIOUS RUN-IN WITH GUMM, WE KNOW HE'S OBSESSED WITH ***STAMPS.***
IF WE CAN INVESTIGATE ALL THE LOCAL BUILDINGS LARGE ENOUGH TO STASH A HAUL THAT SIZE, THEN CROSS-REFERENCE WITH ANYTHING STAMP-RELATED...
...WE JUST MIGHT CATCH A BREAK.
WELL, I HOPE SO. BOLLO IS THREATENING THE CITY WITH A TWENTY MILLION DOLLAR LAWSUIT, AND I GAVE HIM MY PERSONAL GUARANTEE THAT WE'D RETRIEVE THOSE FOSSILS!
THEN LET'S GET INTO OUR "WORK CLOTHES," KATO!
GOOD LUCK, FELLAS! SOUNDS LIKE THE ***GREEN*** HORNET COULD USE A ***GREEN*** FOUR-LEAF CLOVER!

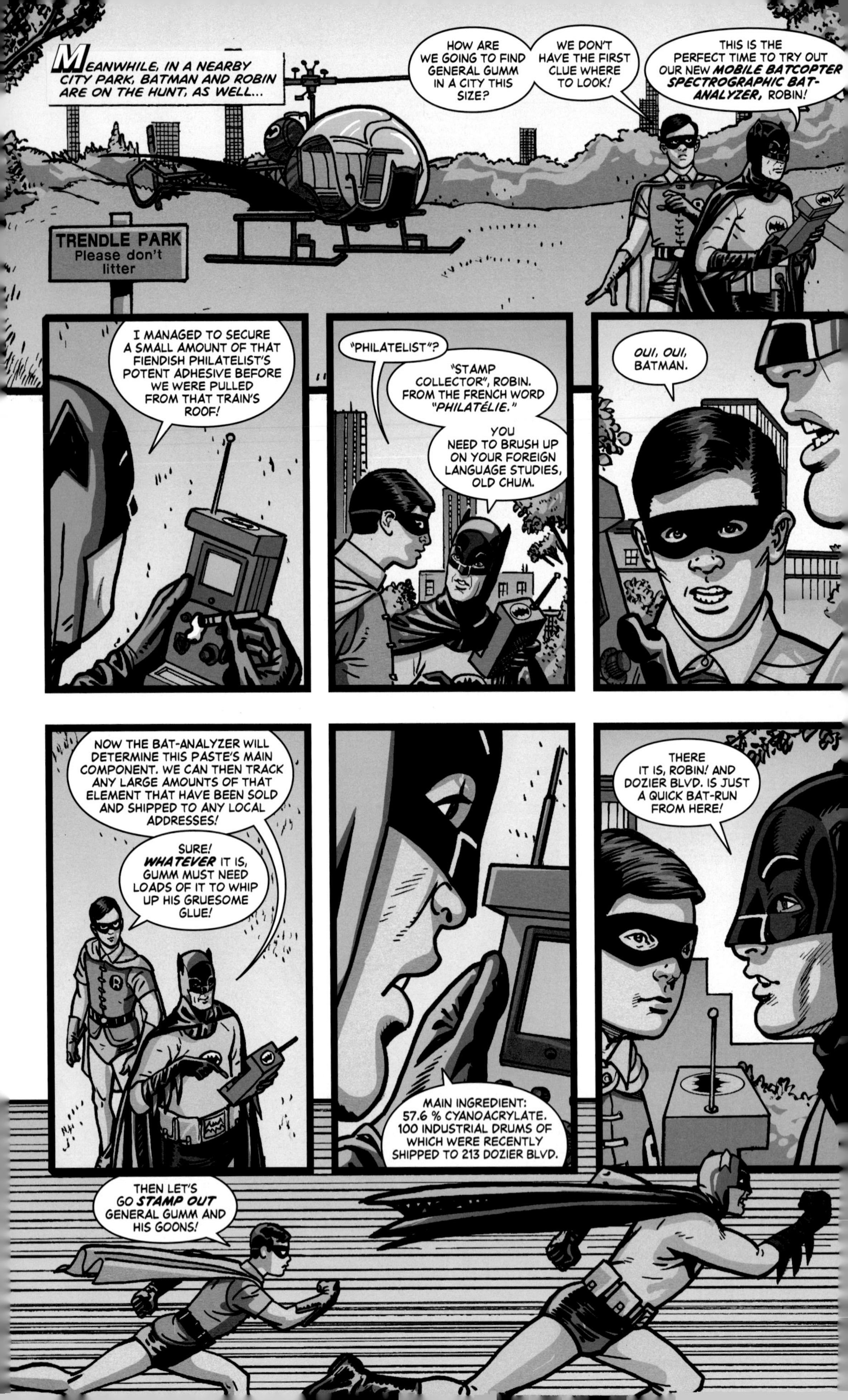
MEANWHILE, IN A NEARBY CITY PARK, BATMAN AND ROBIN ARE ON THE HUNT, AS WELL...
HOW ARE WE GOING TO FIND GENERAL GUMM IN A CITY THIS SIZE?
WE DON'T HAVE THE FIRST CLUE WHERE TO LOOK!
THIS IS THE PERFECT TIME TO TRY OUT OUR NEW MOBILE BATCOPTER SPECTROGRAPHIC BAT-ANALYZER, ROBIN!
TRENDLE PARK Please don't litter
I MANAGED TO SECURE A SMALL AMOUNT OF THAT FIENDISH PHILATELIST'S POTENT ADHESIVE BEFORE WE WERE PULLED FROM THAT TRAIN'S ROOF!
"PHILATELIST"?
"STAMP COLLECTOR", ROBIN. FROM THE FRENCH WORD "PHILATÉLIE."
YOU NEED TO BRUSH UP ON YOUR FOREIGN LANGUAGE STUDIES, OLD CHUM.
OUI, OUI, BATMAN.
NOW THE BAT-ANALYZER WILL DETERMINE THIS PASTE'S MAIN COMPONENT. WE CAN THEN TRACK ANY LARGE AMOUNTS OF THAT ELEMENT THAT HAVE BEEN SOLD AND SHIPPED TO ANY LOCAL ADDRESSES!
SURE! WHATEVER IT IS, GUMM MUST NEED LOADS OF IT TO WHIP UP HIS GRUESOME GLUE!
MAIN INGREDIENT: 57.6 % CYANOACRYLATE. 100 INDUSTRIAL DRUMS OF WHICH WERE RECENTLY SHIPPED TO 213 DOZIER BLVD.
THERE IT IS, ROBIN! AND DOZIER BLVD. IS JUST A QUICK BAT-RUN FROM HERE!
THEN LET'S GO STAMP OUT GENERAL GUMM AND HIS GOONS!

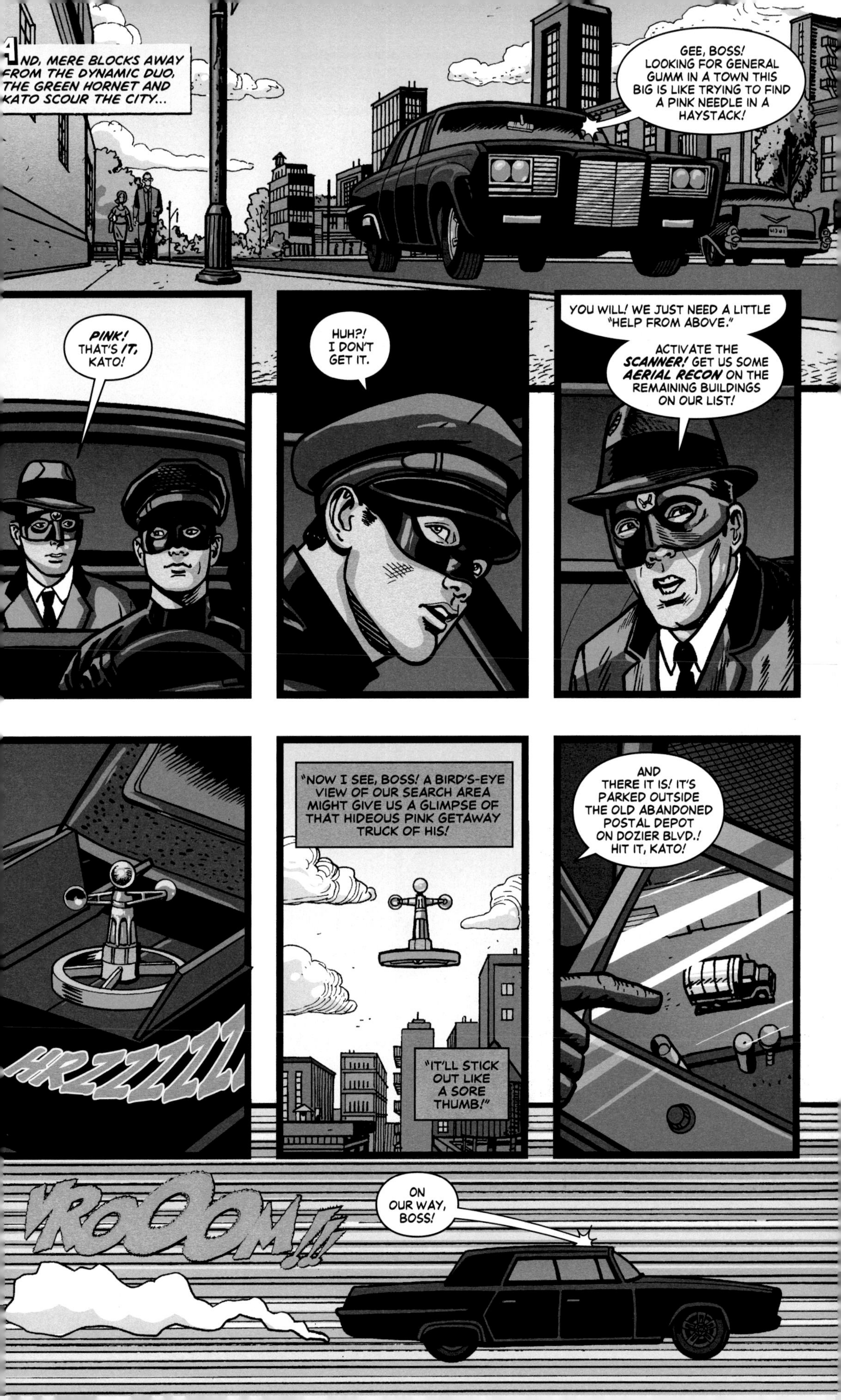
AND, MERE BLOCKS AWAY FROM THE DYNAMIC DUO, THE GREEN HORNET AND KATO SCOUR THE CITY...
GEE, BOSS! LOOKING FOR GENERAL GUMM IN A TOWN THIS BIG IS LIKE TRYING TO FIND A PINK NEEDLE IN A HAYSTACK!
PINK! THAT'S IT, KATO!
HUH?! I DON'T GET IT.
YOU WILL! WE JUST NEED A LITTLE "HELP FROM ABOVE."
ACTIVATE THE SCANNER! GET US SOME AERIAL RECON ON THE REMAINING BUILDINGS ON OUR LIST!
HRZZZZZZ
"NOW I SEE, BOSS! A BIRD'S-EYE VIEW OF OUR SEARCH AREA MIGHT GIVE US A GLIMPSE OF THAT HIDEOUS PINK GETAWAY TRUCK OF HIS!
"IT'LL STICK OUT LIKE A SORE THUMB!"
AND THERE IT IS! IT'S PARKED OUTSIDE THE OLD ABANDONED POSTAL DEPOT ON DOZIER BLVD.! HIT IT, KATO!
VROOOOM!!!
ON OUR WAY, BOSS!

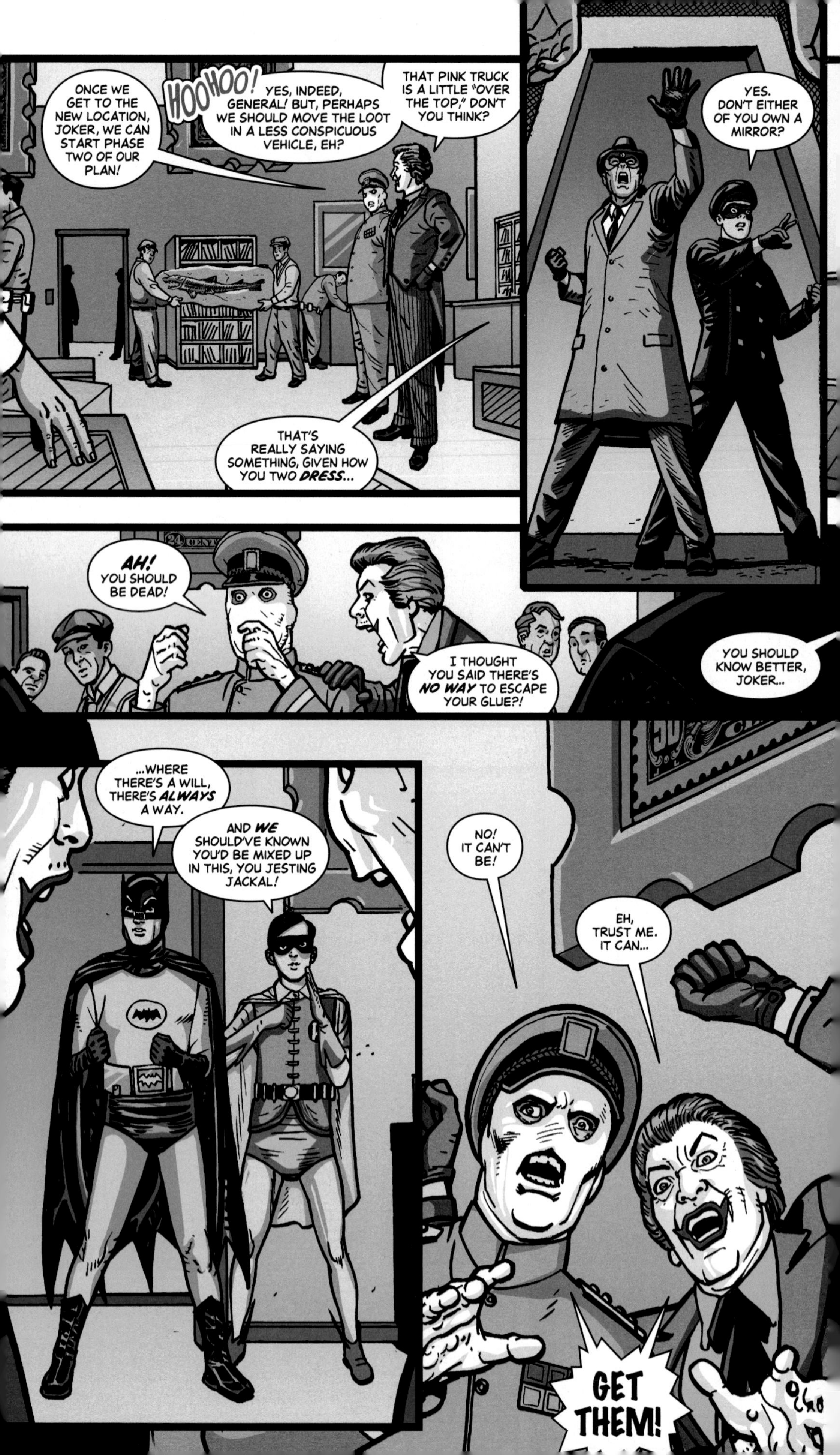

ONCE WE GET TO THE NEW LOCATION, JOKER, WE CAN START PHASE TWO OF OUR PLAN!
HOOHOO!
YES, INDEED, GENERAL! BUT, PERHAPS WE SHOULD MOVE THE LOOT IN A LESS CONSPICUOUS VEHICLE, EH?
THAT PINK TRUCK IS A LITTLE "OVER THE TOP," DON'T YOU THINK?
THAT'S REALLY SAYING SOMETHING, GIVEN HOW YOU TWO DRESS...
YES. DON'T EITHER OF YOU OWN A MIRROR?
AH! YOU SHOULD BE DEAD!
I THOUGHT YOU SAID THERE'S NO WAY TO ESCAPE YOUR GLUE?!
YOU SHOULD KNOW BETTER, JOKER...
...WHERE THERE'S A WILL, THERE'S ALWAYS A WAY.
AND WE SHOULD'VE KNOWN YOU'D BE MIXED UP IN THIS, YOU JESTING JACKAL!
NO! IT CAN'T BE!
EH, TRUST ME. IT CAN...
GET THEM!

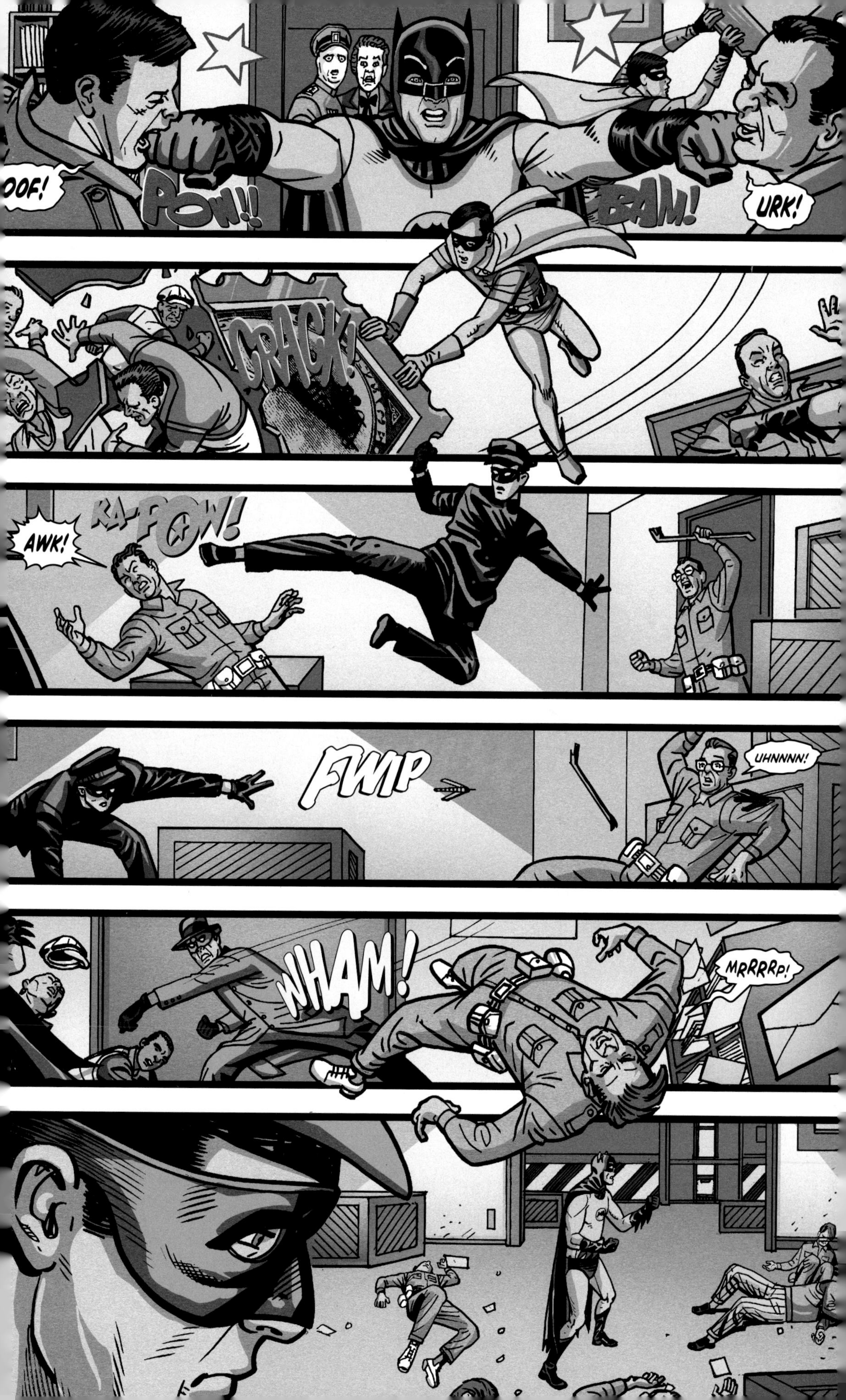
OOF!
POW!!
BAM!
URK!
CRACK!
KA-POW!
AWK!
FWIP
UHNNNN!
WHAM!
MRRRRP!

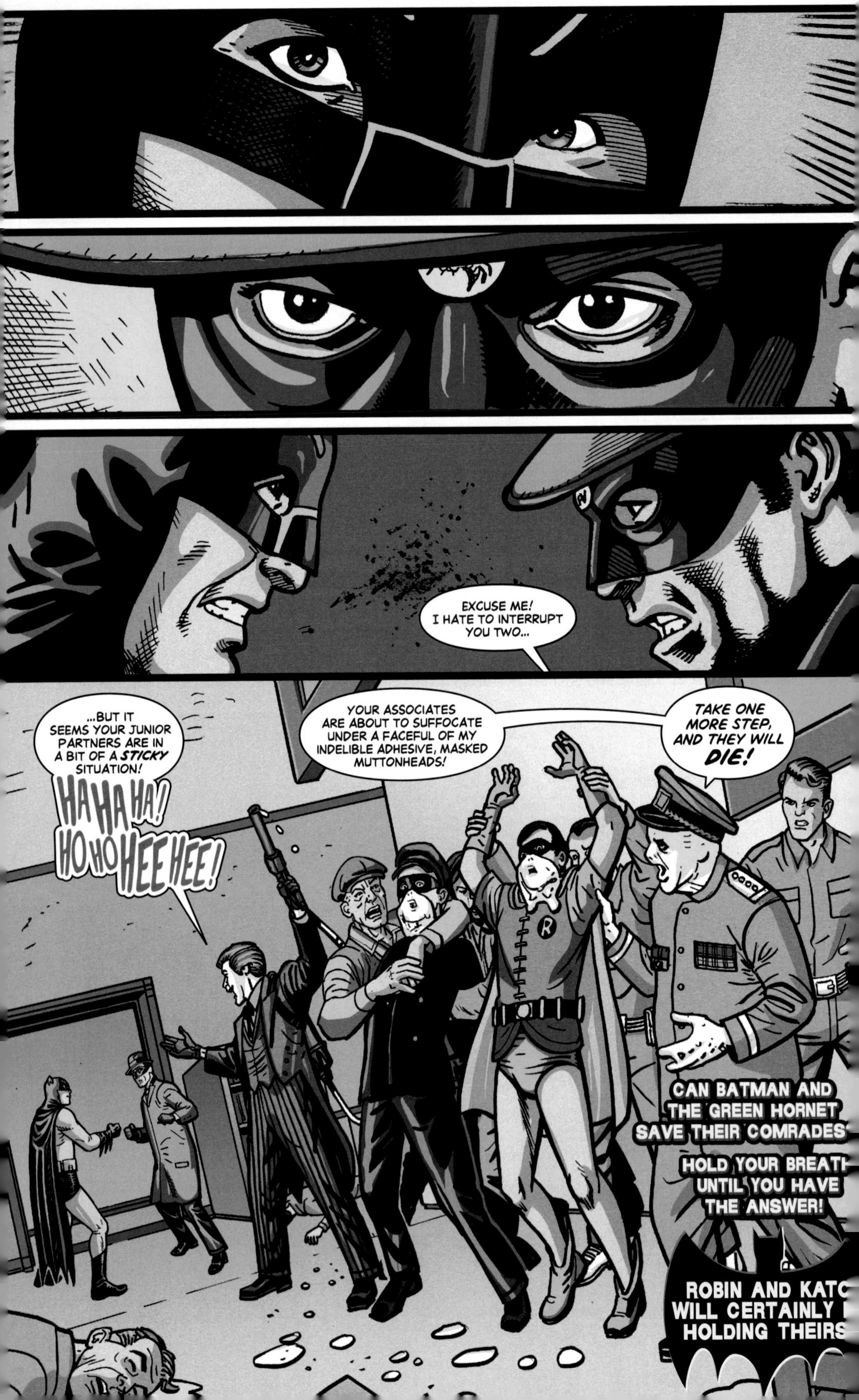
EXCUSE ME! I HATE TO INTERRUPT YOU TWO...
...BUT IT SEEMS YOUR JUNIOR PARTNERS ARE IN A BIT OF A STICKY SITUATION!
HA HA HA! HO HO HEE HEE!
YOUR ASSOCIATES ARE ABOUT TO SUFFOCATE UNDER A FACEFUL OF MY INDELIBLE ADHESIVE, MASKED MUTTONHEADS!
TAKE ONE MORE STEP, AND THEY WILL DIE!
CAN BATMAN AND THE GREEN HORNET SAVE THEIR COMRADES
HOLD YOUR BREATH UNTIL YOU HAVE THE ANSWER!
ROBIN AND KATO WILL CERTAINLY HOLDING THEIRS

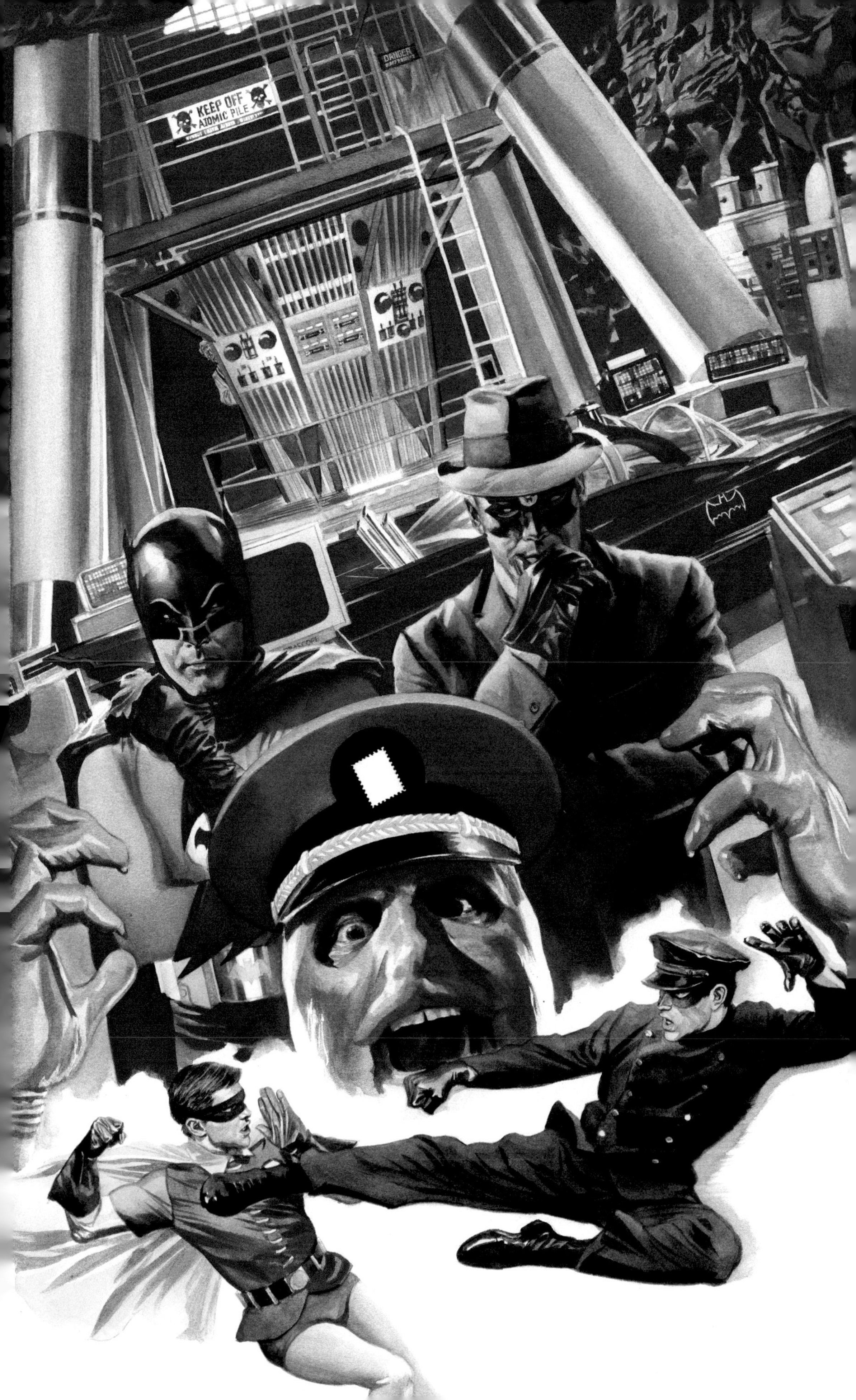
KEEP OFF
ATOMIC PILE
DANGER

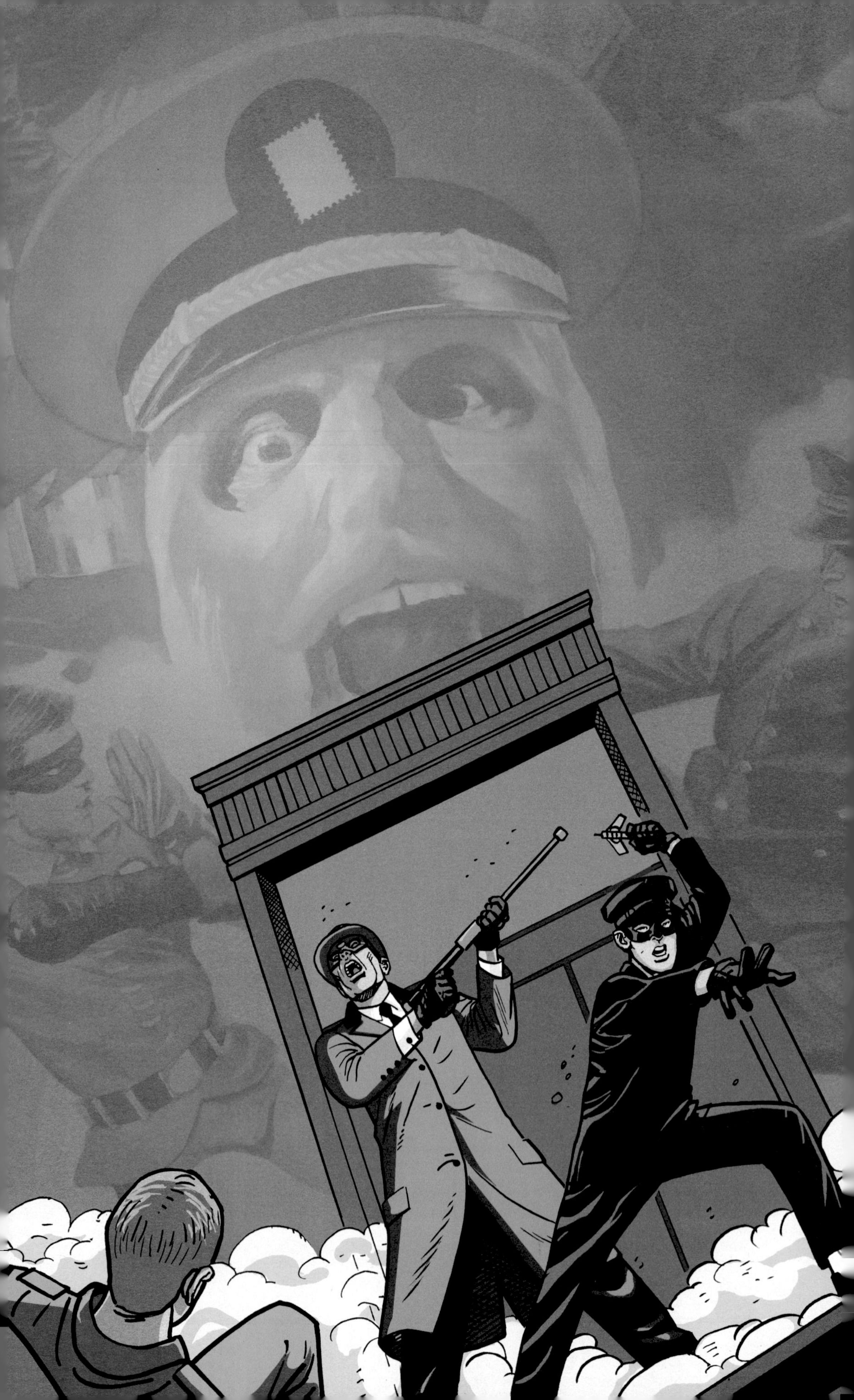

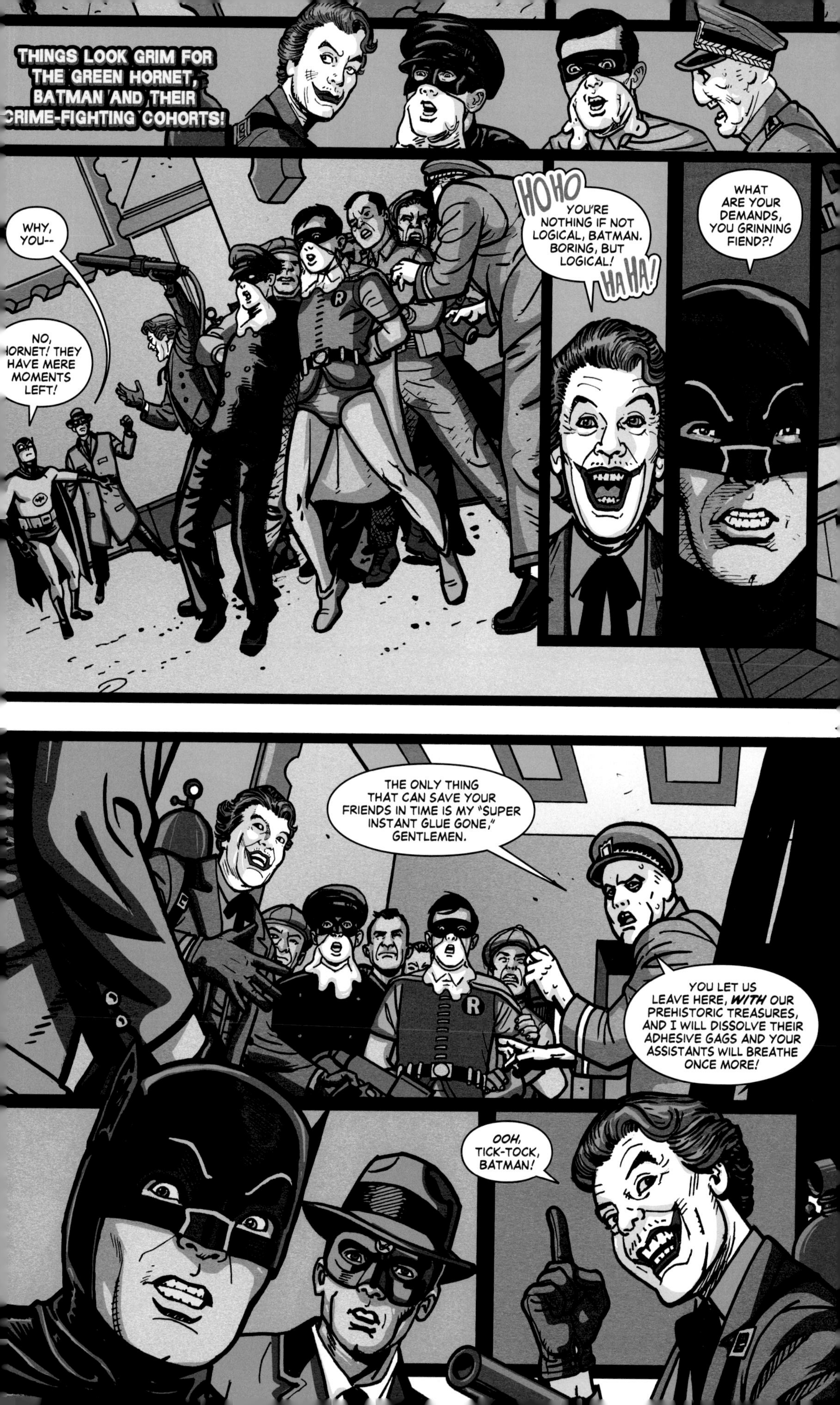

THINGS LOOK GRIM FOR THE GREEN HORNET, BATMAN AND THEIR CRIME-FIGHTING COHORTS!
WHY, YOU--
NO, HORNET! THEY HAVE MERE MOMENTS LEFT!
HOHO
YOU'RE NOTHING IF NOT LOGICAL, BATMAN. BORING, BUT LOGICAL!
HAHA!
WHAT ARE YOUR DEMANDS, YOU GRINNING FIEND?!
THE ONLY THING THAT CAN SAVE YOUR FRIENDS IN TIME IS MY "SUPER INSTANT GLUE GONE," GENTLEMEN.
YOU LET US LEAVE HERE, *WITH* OUR PREHISTORIC TREASURES, AND I WILL DISSOLVE THEIR ADHESIVE GAGS AND YOUR ASSISTANTS WILL BREATHE ONCE MORE!
OOH, TICK-TOCK, BATMAN!

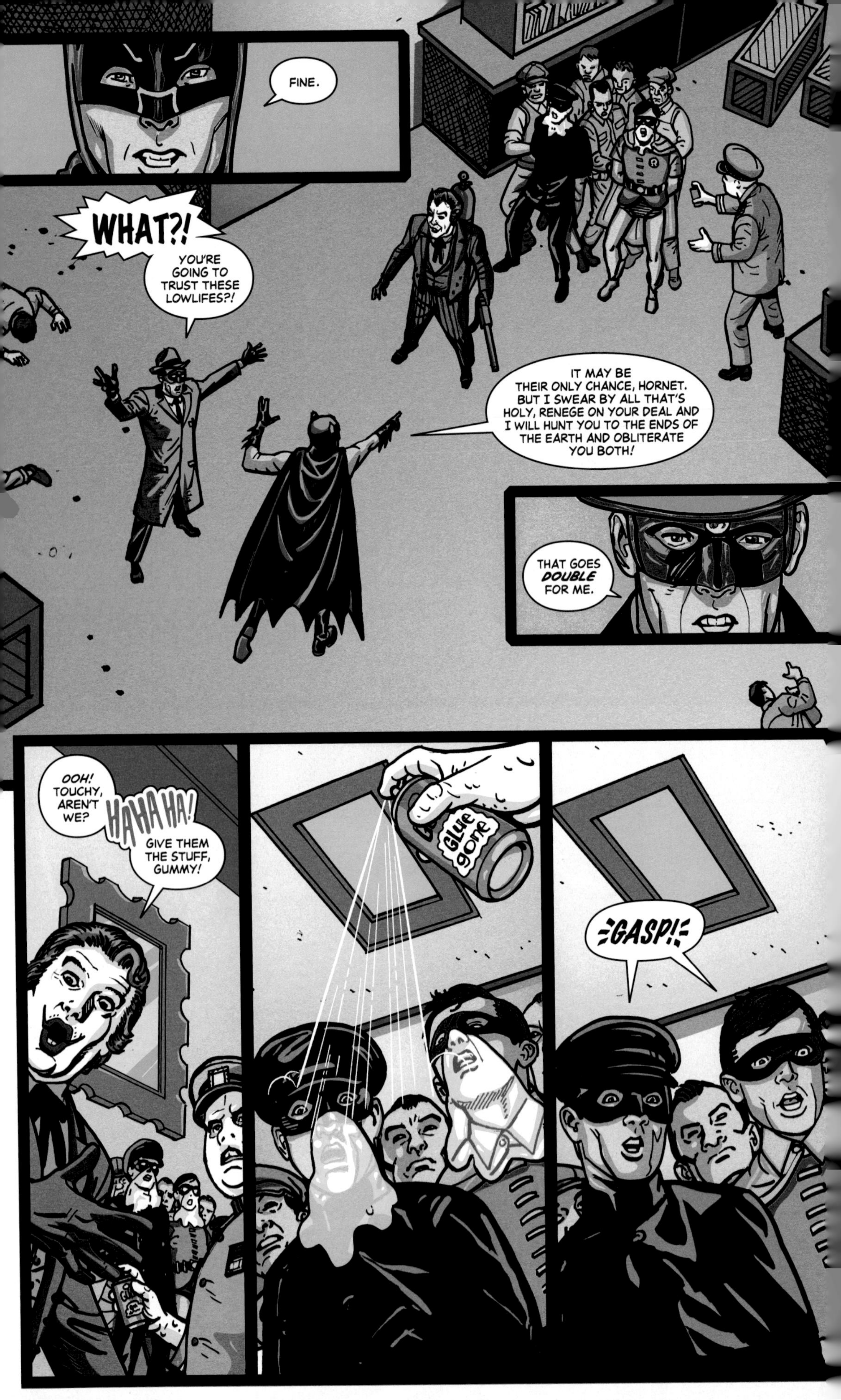
FINE.
WHAT?!
YOU'RE GOING TO TRUST THESE LOWLIFES?!
IT MAY BE THEIR ONLY CHANCE, HORNET. BUT I SWEAR BY ALL THAT'S HOLY, RENEGE ON YOUR DEAL AND I WILL HUNT YOU TO THE ENDS OF THE EARTH AND OBLITERATE YOU BOTH!
THAT GOES *DOUBLE* FOR ME.
OOH! TOUCHY, AREN'T WE?
HAHAHA!
GIVE THEM THE STUFF, GUMMY!
GLUE GONE
GASP!

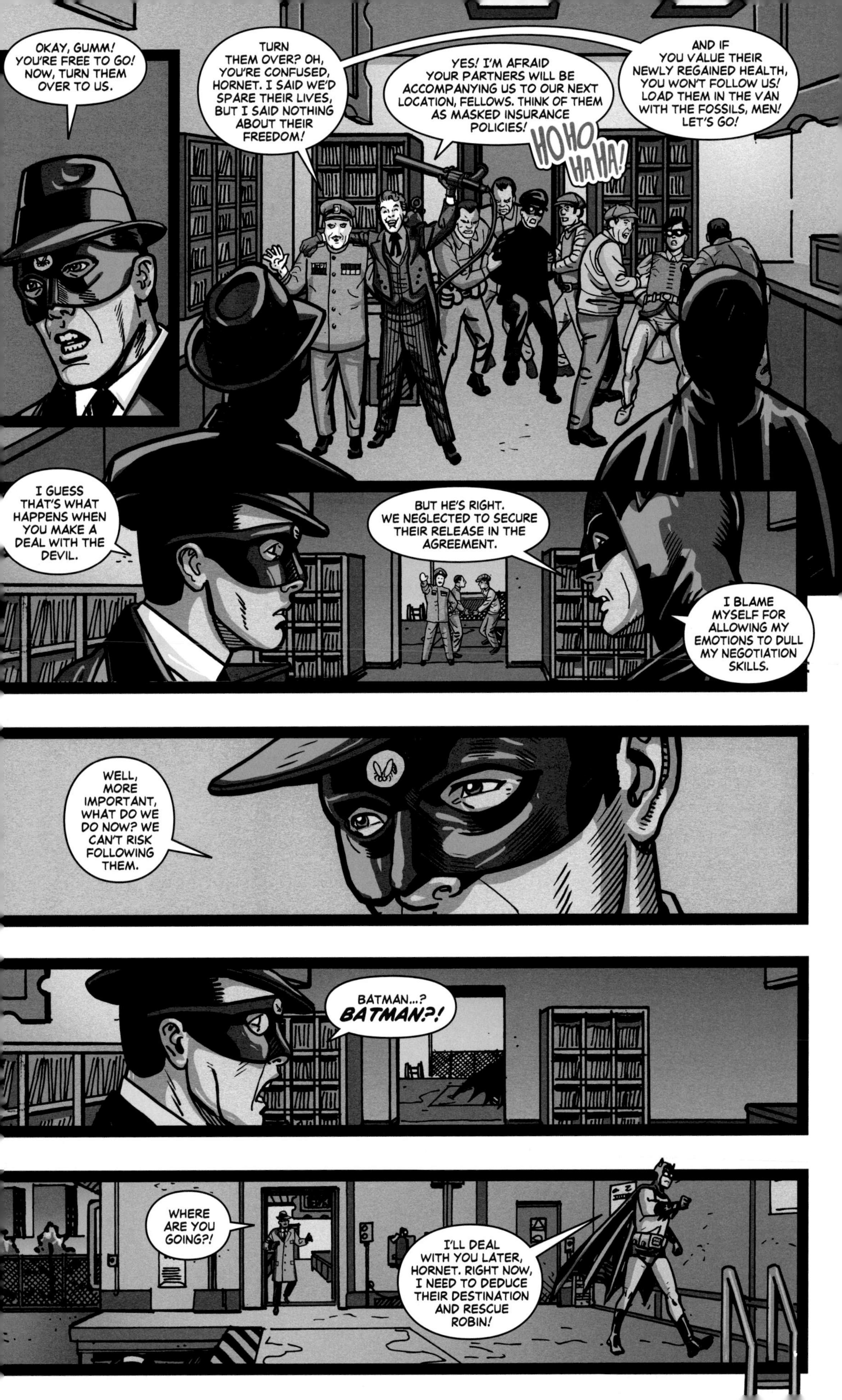
OKAY, GUMM! YOU'RE FREE TO GO! NOW, TURN THEM OVER TO US.
TURN THEM OVER? OH, YOU'RE CONFUSED, HORNET. I SAID WE'D SPARE THEIR LIVES, BUT I SAID NOTHING ABOUT THEIR FREEDOM!
YES! I'M AFRAID YOUR PARTNERS WILL BE ACCOMPANYING US TO OUR NEXT LOCATION, FELLOWS. THINK OF THEM AS MASKED INSURANCE POLICIES!
HOHO HAHA!
AND IF YOU VALUE THEIR NEWLY REGAINED HEALTH, YOU WON'T FOLLOW US! LOAD THEM IN THE VAN WITH THE FOSSILS, MEN! LET'S GO!
I GUESS THAT'S WHAT HAPPENS WHEN YOU MAKE A DEAL WITH THE DEVIL.
BUT HE'S RIGHT. WE NEGLECTED TO SECURE THEIR RELEASE IN THE AGREEMENT.
I BLAME MYSELF FOR ALLOWING MY EMOTIONS TO DULL MY NEGOTIATION SKILLS.
WELL, MORE IMPORTANT, WHAT DO WE DO NOW? WE CAN'T RISK FOLLOWING THEM.
BATMAN...? BATMAN?!
WHERE ARE YOU GOING?!
I'LL DEAL WITH YOU LATER, HORNET. RIGHT NOW, I NEED TO DEDUCE THEIR DESTINATION AND RESCUE ROBIN!

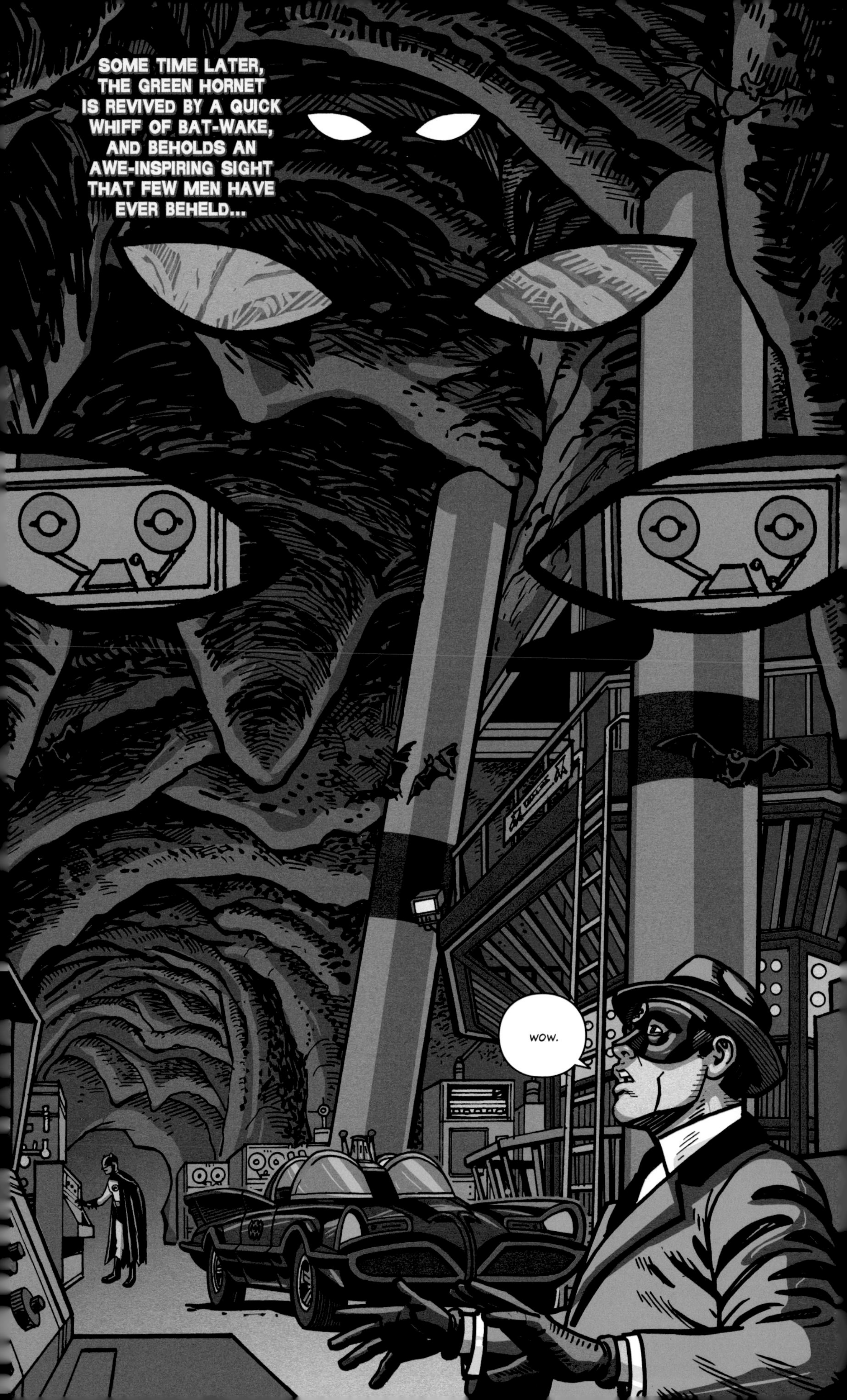
SOME TIME LATER, THE GREEN HORNET IS REVIVED BY A QUICK WHIFF OF BAT-WAKE, AND BEHOLDS AN AWE-INSPIRING SIGHT THAT FEW MEN HAVE EVER BEHELD...
WOW.

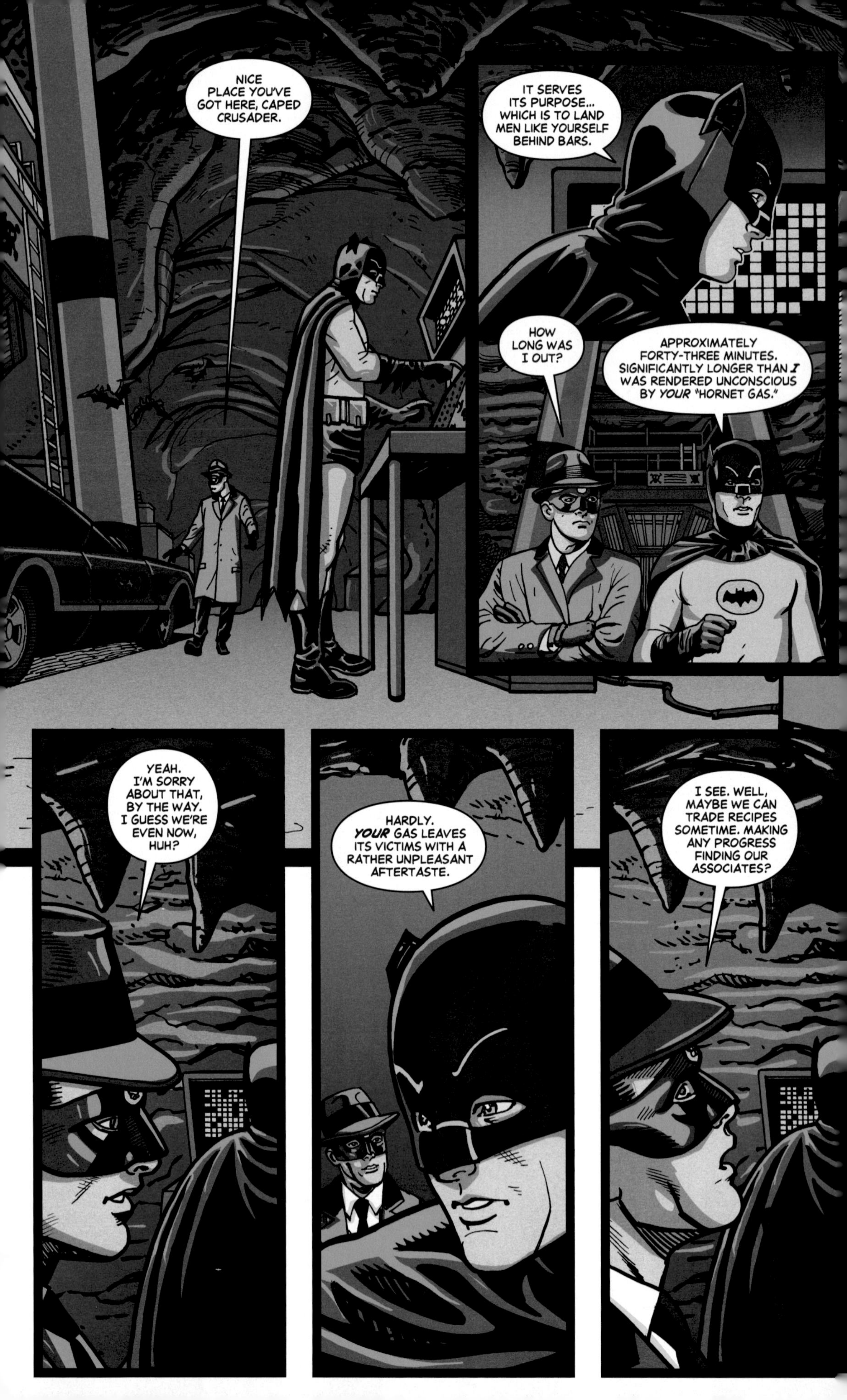
NICE PLACE YOU'VE GOT HERE, CAPED CRUSADER.
IT SERVES ITS PURPOSE... WHICH IS TO LAND MEN LIKE YOURSELF BEHIND BARS.
HOW LONG WAS I OUT?
APPROXIMATELY FORTY-THREE MINUTES. SIGNIFICANTLY LONGER THAN *I* WAS RENDERED UNCONSCIOUS BY *YOUR* "HORNET GAS."
YEAH. I'M SORRY ABOUT THAT, BY THE WAY. I GUESS WE'RE EVEN NOW, HUH?
HARDLY. ***YOUR*** GAS LEAVES ITS VICTIMS WITH A RATHER UNPLEASANT AFTERTASTE.
I SEE. WELL, MAYBE WE CAN TRADE RECIPES SOMETIME. MAKING ANY PROGRESS FINDING OUR ASSOCIATES?

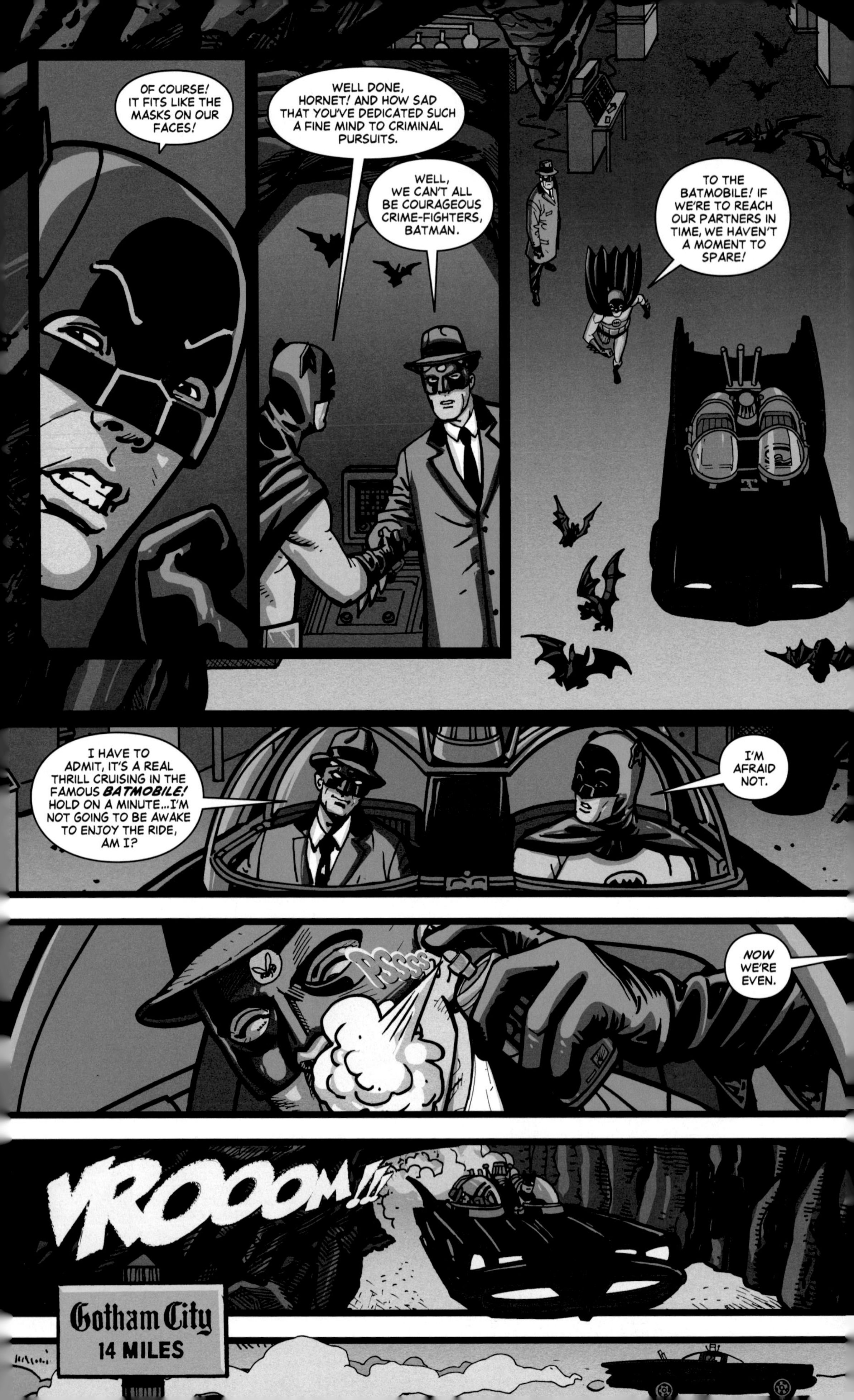
OF COURSE! IT FITS LIKE THE MASKS ON OUR FACES!
WELL DONE, HORNET! AND HOW SAD THAT YOU'VE DEDICATED SUCH A FINE MIND TO CRIMINAL PURSUITS.
WELL, WE CAN'T ALL BE COURAGEOUS CRIME-FIGHTERS, BATMAN.
TO THE BATMOBILE! IF WE'RE TO REACH OUR PARTNERS IN TIME, WE HAVEN'T A MOMENT TO SPARE!
I HAVE TO ADMIT, IT'S A REAL THRILL CRUISING IN THE FAMOUS BATMOBILE! HOLD ON A MINUTE...I'M NOT GOING TO BE AWAKE TO ENJOY THE RIDE, AM I?
I'M AFRAID NOT.
PSSSS
NOW WE'RE EVEN.
VROOOM!!!
Gotham City
14 MILES

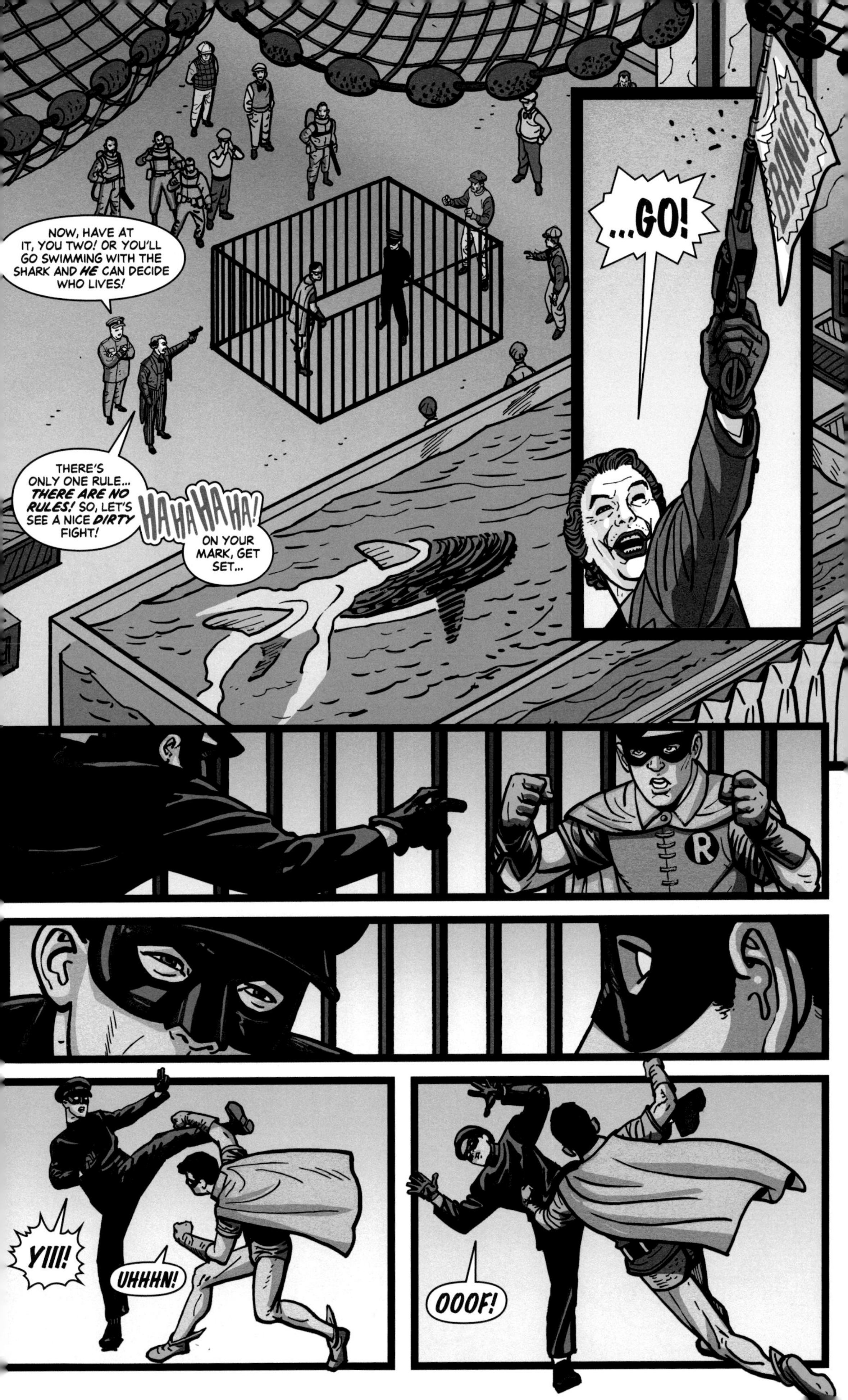
NOW, HAVE AT IT, YOU TWO! OR YOU'LL GO SWIMMING WITH THE SHARK AND HE CAN DECIDE WHO LIVES!
THERE'S ONLY ONE RULE... THERE ARE NO RULES! SO, LET'S SEE A NICE DIRTY FIGHT!
HAHAHAHA!
ON YOUR MARK, GET SET...
...GO!
BANG!
YIII!
UHHHN!
OOOF!

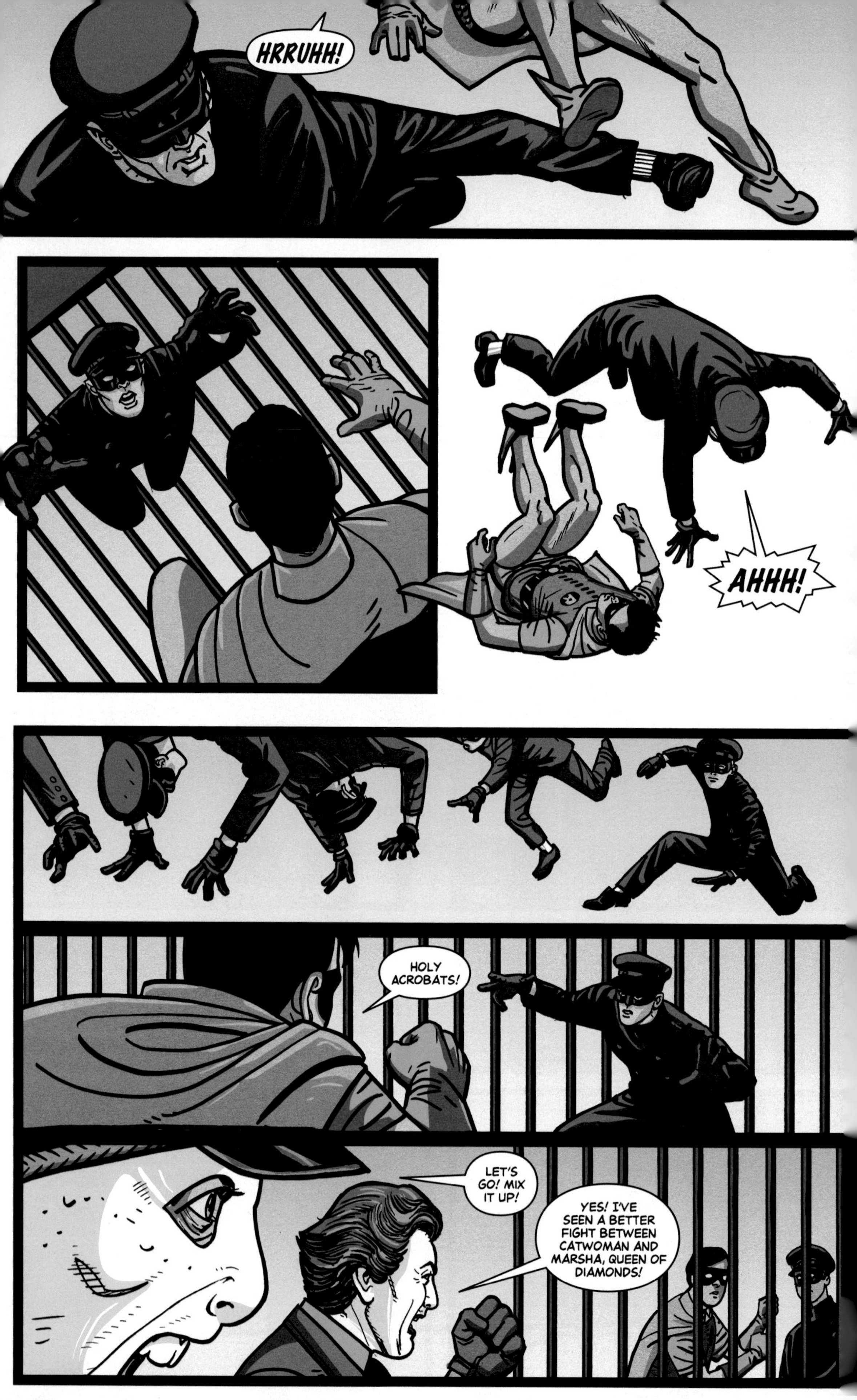
HRRUHH!
AHHH!
HOLY ACROBATS!
LET'S GO! MIX IT UP!
YES! I'VE SEEN A BETTER FIGHT BETWEEN CATWOMAN AND MARSHA, QUEEN OF DIAMONDS!

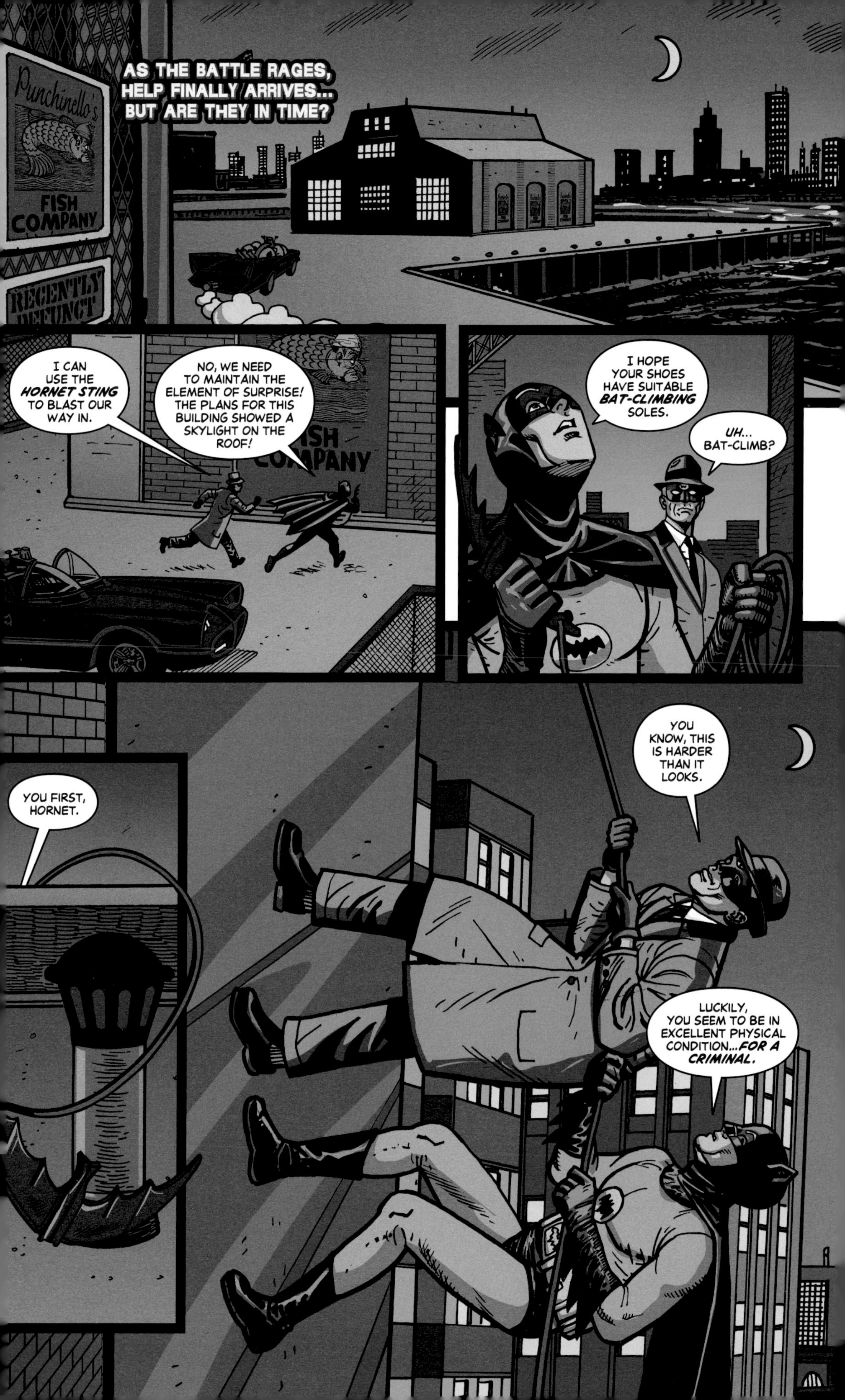
AS THE BATTLE RAGES, HELP FINALLY ARRIVES... BUT ARE THEY IN TIME?
Punchinello's FISH COMPANY
RECENTLY DEFUNCT
I CAN USE THE HORNET STING TO BLAST OUR WAY IN.
NO, WE NEED TO MAINTAIN THE ELEMENT OF SURPRISE! THE PLANS FOR THIS BUILDING SHOWED A SKYLIGHT ON THE ROOF!
I HOPE YOUR SHOES HAVE SUITABLE BAT-CLIMBING SOLES.
UH... BAT-CLIMB?
YOU FIRST, HORNET.
YOU KNOW, THIS IS HARDER THAN IT LOOKS.
LUCKILY, YOU SEEM TO BE IN EXCELLENT PHYSICAL CONDITION...FOR A CRIMINAL.

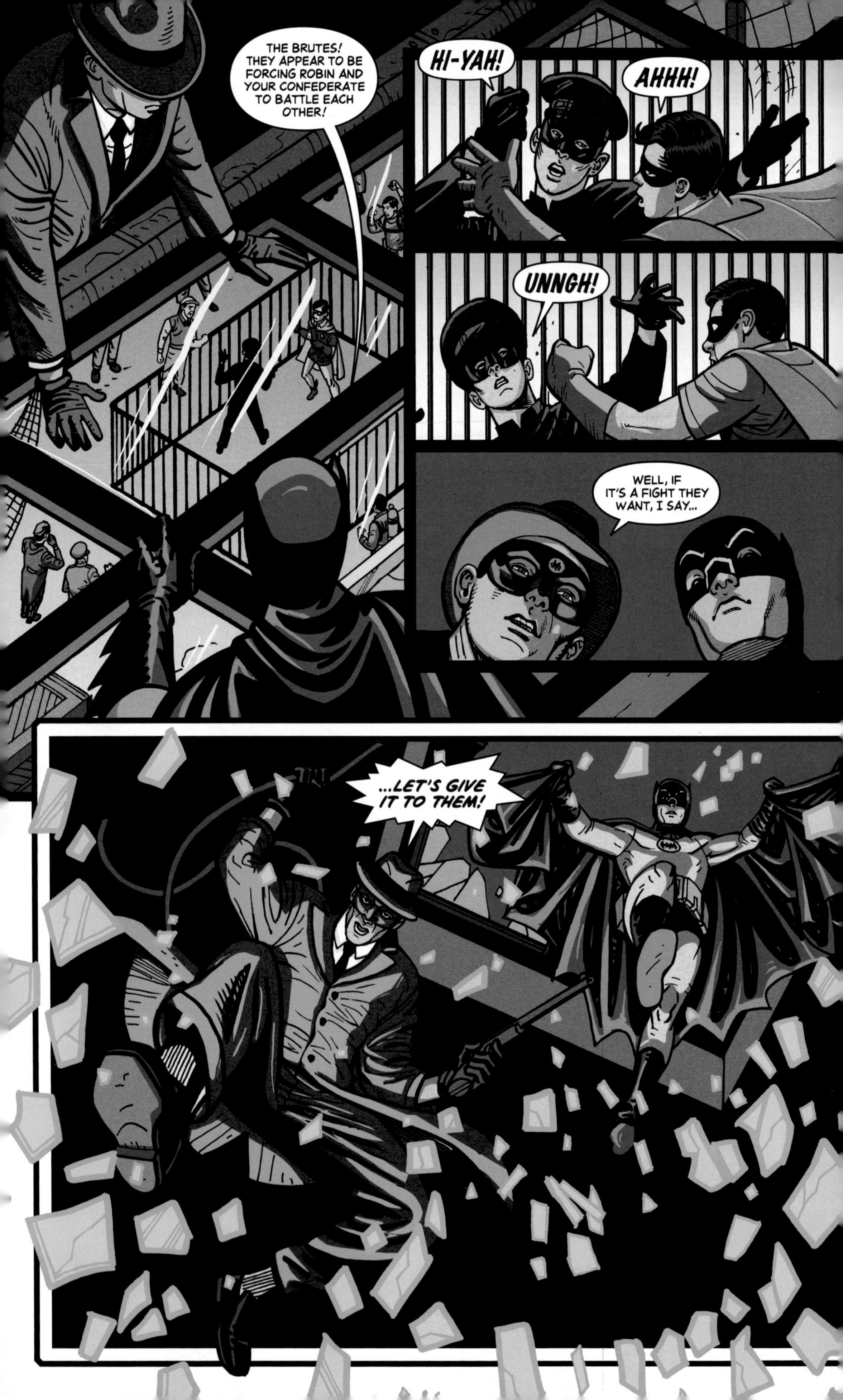
THE BRUTES! THEY APPEAR TO BE FORCING ROBIN AND YOUR CONFEDERATE TO BATTLE EACH OTHER!
HI-YAH!
AHHH!
UNNGH!
WELL, IF IT'S A FIGHT THEY WANT, I SAY...
...LET'S GIVE IT TO THEM!

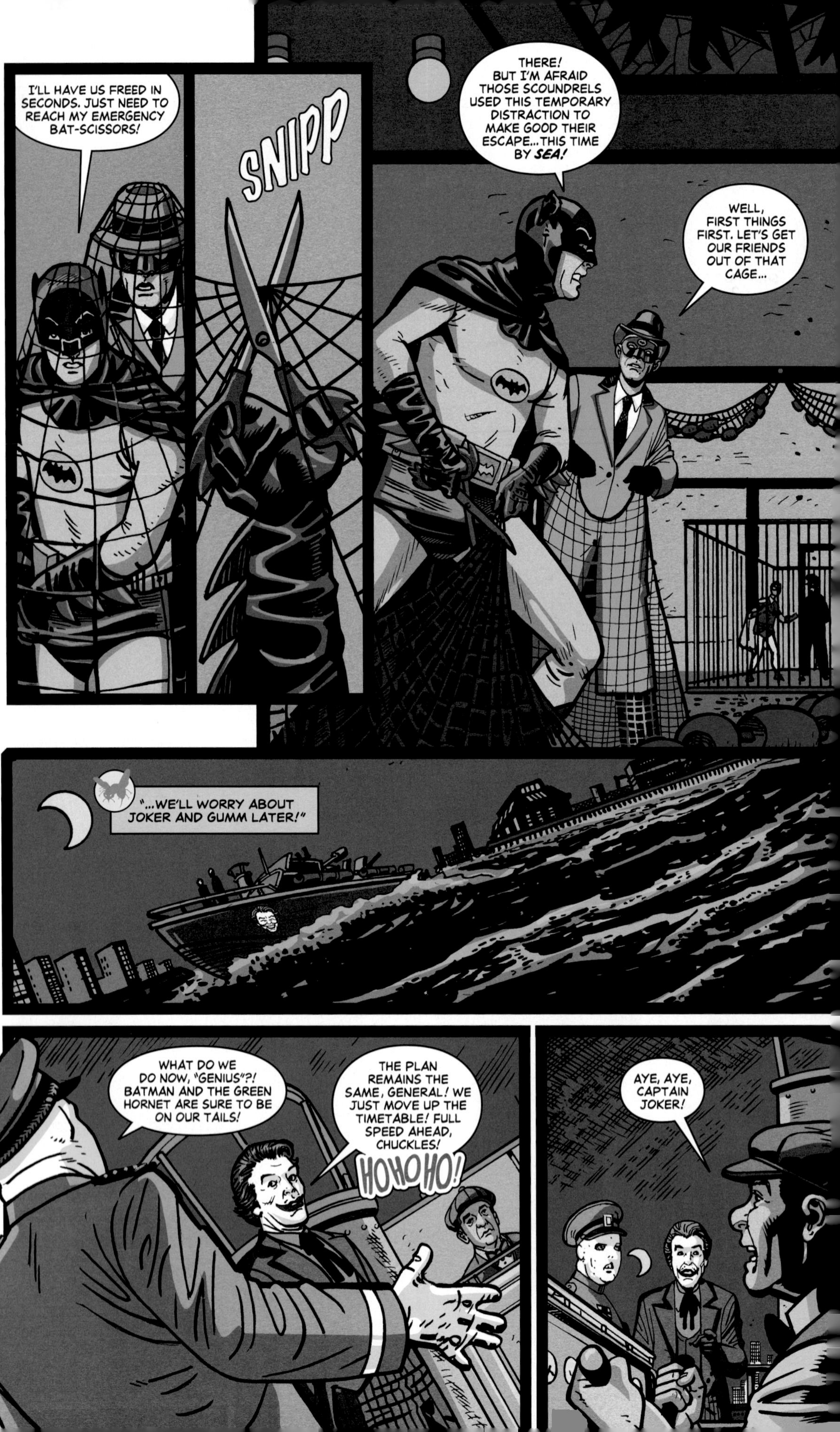
I'LL HAVE US FREED IN SECONDS. JUST NEED TO REACH MY EMERGENCY BAT-SCISSORS!
SNIPP
THERE! BUT I'M AFRAID THOSE SCOUNDRELS USED THIS TEMPORARY DISTRACTION TO MAKE GOOD THEIR ESCAPE...THIS TIME BY SEA!
WELL, FIRST THINGS FIRST. LET'S GET OUR FRIENDS OUT OF THAT CAGE...
"...WE'LL WORRY ABOUT JOKER AND GUMM LATER!"
WHAT DO WE DO NOW, "GENIUS"?! BATMAN AND THE GREEN HORNET ARE SURE TO BE ON OUR TAILS!
THE PLAN REMAINS THE SAME, GENERAL! WE JUST MOVE UP THE TIMETABLE! FULL SPEED AHEAD, CHUCKLES!
HOHOHO!
AYE, AYE, CAPTAIN JOKER!

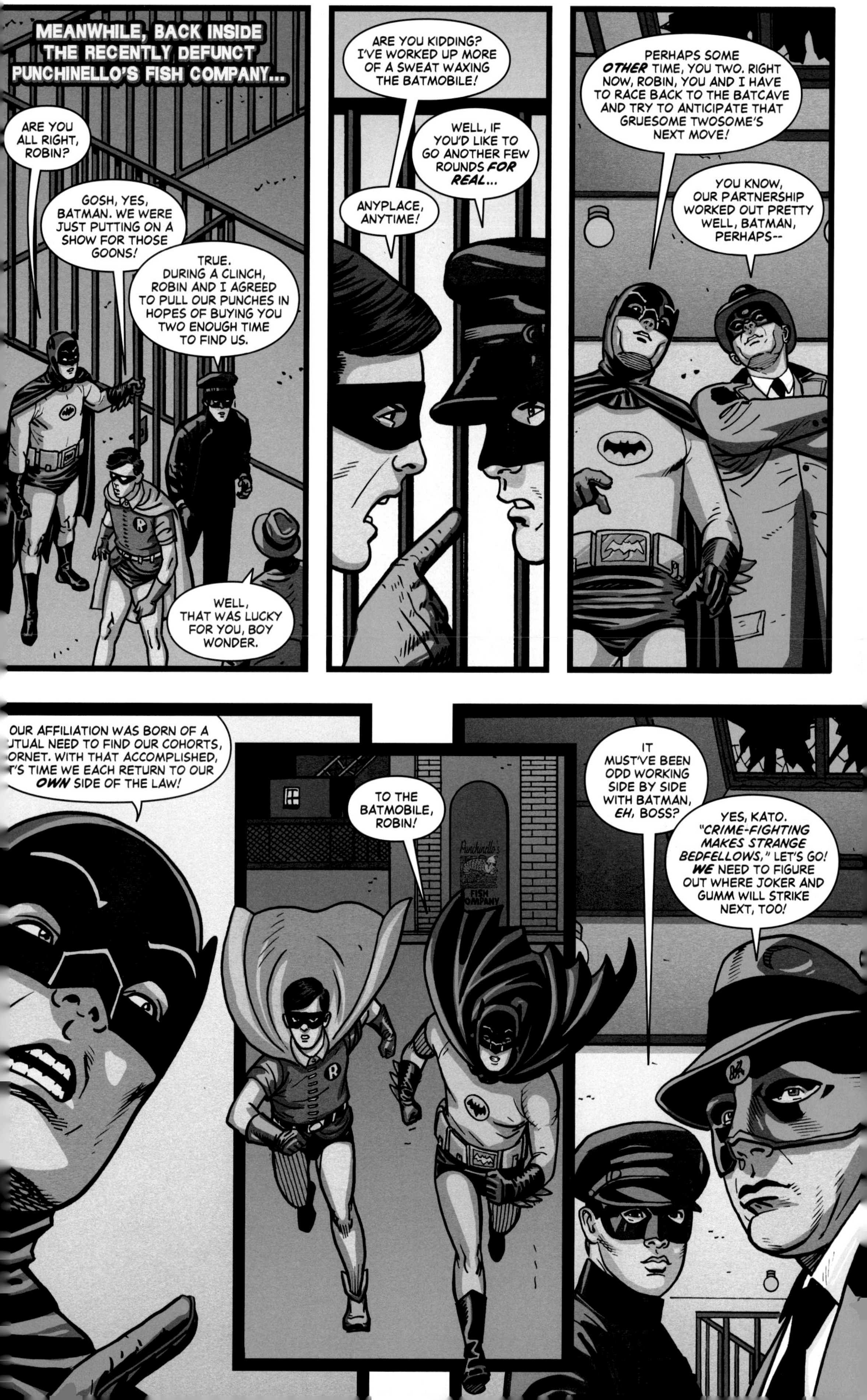
MEANWHILE, BACK INSIDE THE RECENTLY DEFUNCT PUNCHINELLO'S FISH COMPANY...
ARE YOU ALL RIGHT, ROBIN?
GOSH, YES, BATMAN. WE WERE JUST PUTTING ON A SHOW FOR THOSE GOONS!
TRUE. DURING A CLINCH, ROBIN AND I AGREED TO PULL OUR PUNCHES IN HOPES OF BUYING YOU TWO ENOUGH TIME TO FIND US.
WELL, THAT WAS LUCKY FOR YOU, BOY WONDER.
ARE YOU KIDDING? I'VE WORKED UP MORE OF A SWEAT WAXING THE BATMOBILE!
WELL, IF YOU'D LIKE TO GO ANOTHER FEW ROUNDS *FOR REAL*...
ANYPLACE, ANYTIME!
PERHAPS SOME *OTHER* TIME, YOU TWO. RIGHT NOW, ROBIN, YOU AND I HAVE TO RACE BACK TO THE BATCAVE AND TRY TO ANTICIPATE THAT GRUESOME TWOSOME'S NEXT MOVE!
YOU KNOW, OUR PARTNERSHIP WORKED OUT PRETTY WELL, BATMAN, PERHAPS--
OUR AFFILIATION WAS BORN OF A UTUAL NEED TO FIND OUR COHORTS, ORNET. WITH THAT ACCOMPLISHED, T'S TIME WE EACH RETURN TO OUR *OWN* SIDE OF THE LAW!
TO THE BATMOBILE, ROBIN!
Punchinello's FISH OMPANY
IT MUST'VE BEEN ODD WORKING SIDE BY SIDE WITH BATMAN, *EH*, BOSS?
YES, KATO. *"CRIME-FIGHTING MAKES STRANGE BEDFELLOWS,"* LET'S GO! *WE* NEED TO FIGURE OUT WHERE JOKER AND GUMM WILL STRIKE NEXT, TOO!

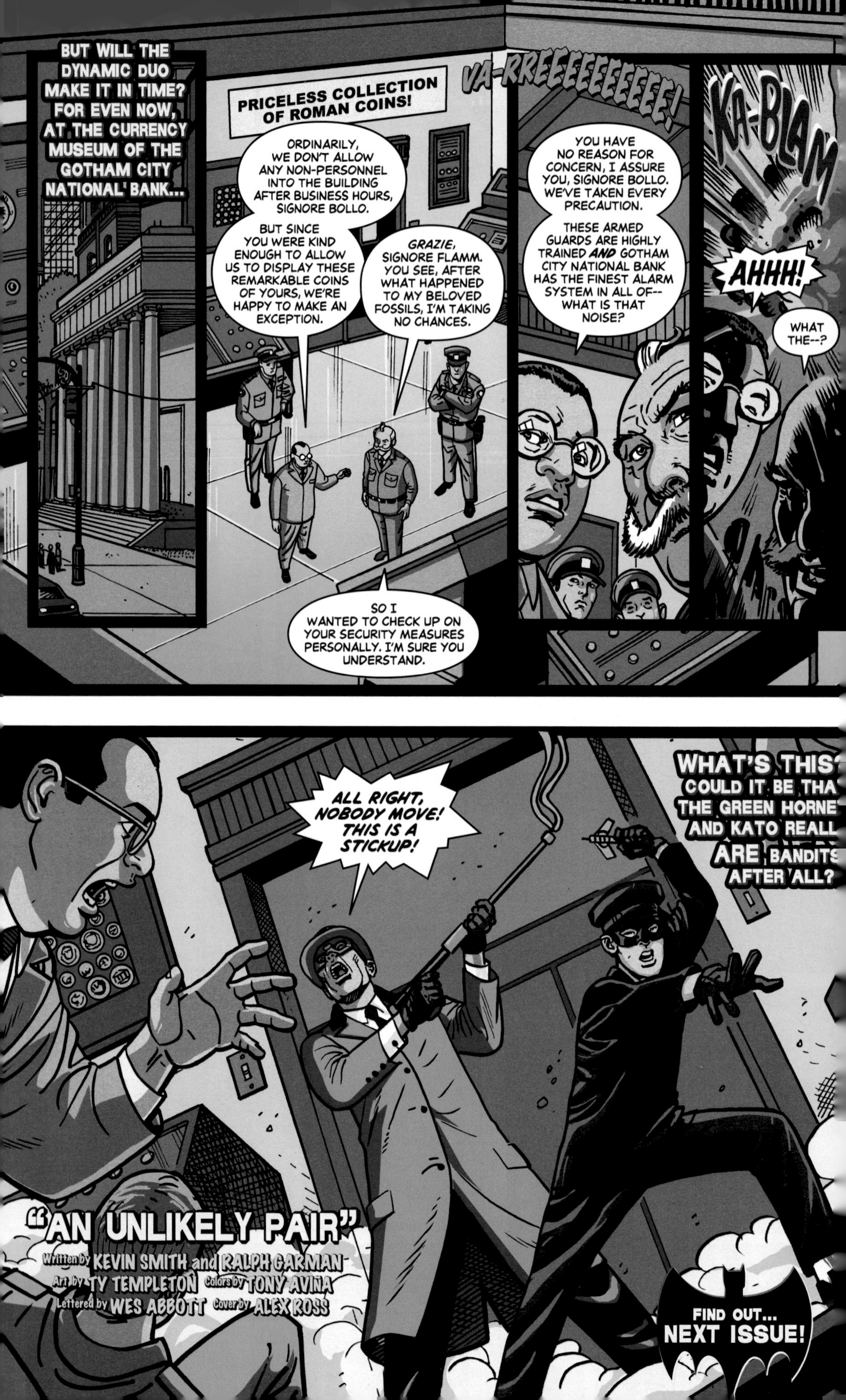

BUT WILL THE DYNAMIC DUO MAKE IT IN TIME? FOR EVEN NOW, AT THE CURRENCY MUSEUM OF THE GOTHAM CITY NATIONAL BANK...
PRICELESS COLLECTION OF ROMAN COINS!
ORDINARILY, WE DON'T ALLOW ANY NON-PERSONNEL INTO THE BUILDING AFTER BUSINESS HOURS, SIGNORE BOLLO.
BUT SINCE YOU WERE KIND ENOUGH TO ALLOW US TO DISPLAY THESE REMARKABLE COINS OF YOURS, WE'RE HAPPY TO MAKE AN EXCEPTION.
GRAZIE, SIGNORE FLAMM. YOU SEE, AFTER WHAT HAPPENED TO MY BELOVED FOSSILS, I'M TAKING NO CHANCES.
SO I WANTED TO CHECK UP ON YOUR SECURITY MEASURES PERSONALLY. I'M SURE YOU UNDERSTAND.
VA-RREEEEEEEEEEE!
YOU HAVE NO REASON FOR CONCERN, I ASSURE YOU, SIGNORE BOLLO. WE'VE TAKEN EVERY PRECAUTION.
THESE ARMED GUARDS ARE HIGHLY TRAINED AND GOTHAM CITY NATIONAL BANK HAS THE FINEST ALARM SYSTEM IN ALL OF-- WHAT IS THAT NOISE?
KA-BLAM
AHHH!
WHAT THE--?
ALL RIGHT, NOBODY MOVE! THIS IS A STICKUP!
WHAT'S THIS? COULD IT BE THA THE GREEN HORNE AND KATO REALL ARE BANDITS AFTER ALL?
"AN UNLIKELY PAIR"
Written by KEVIN SMITH and RALPH GARMAN
Art by TY TEMPLETON Colors by TONY AVIÑA
Lettered by WES ABBOTT Cover by ALEX ROSS
FIND OUT... NEXT ISSUE!

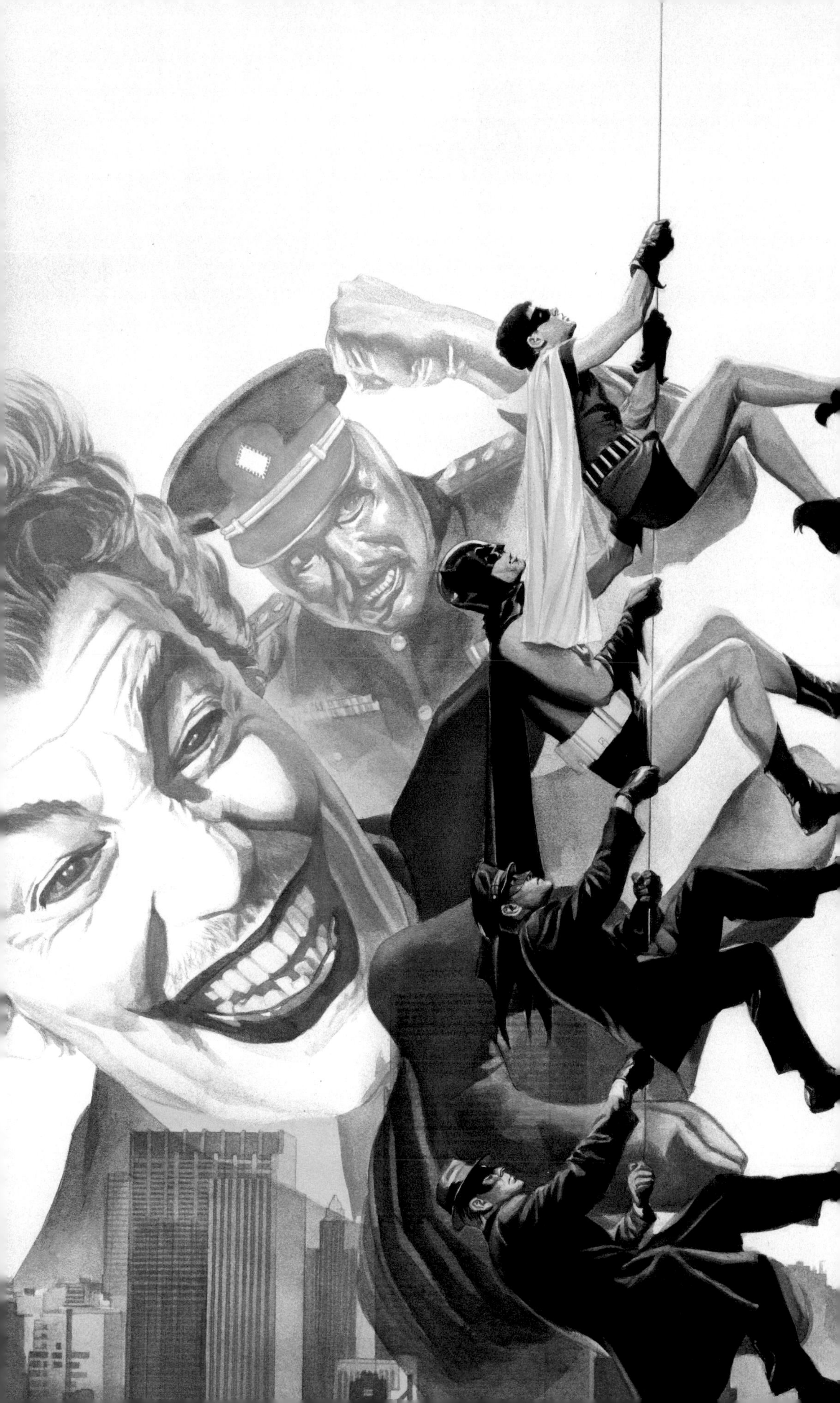

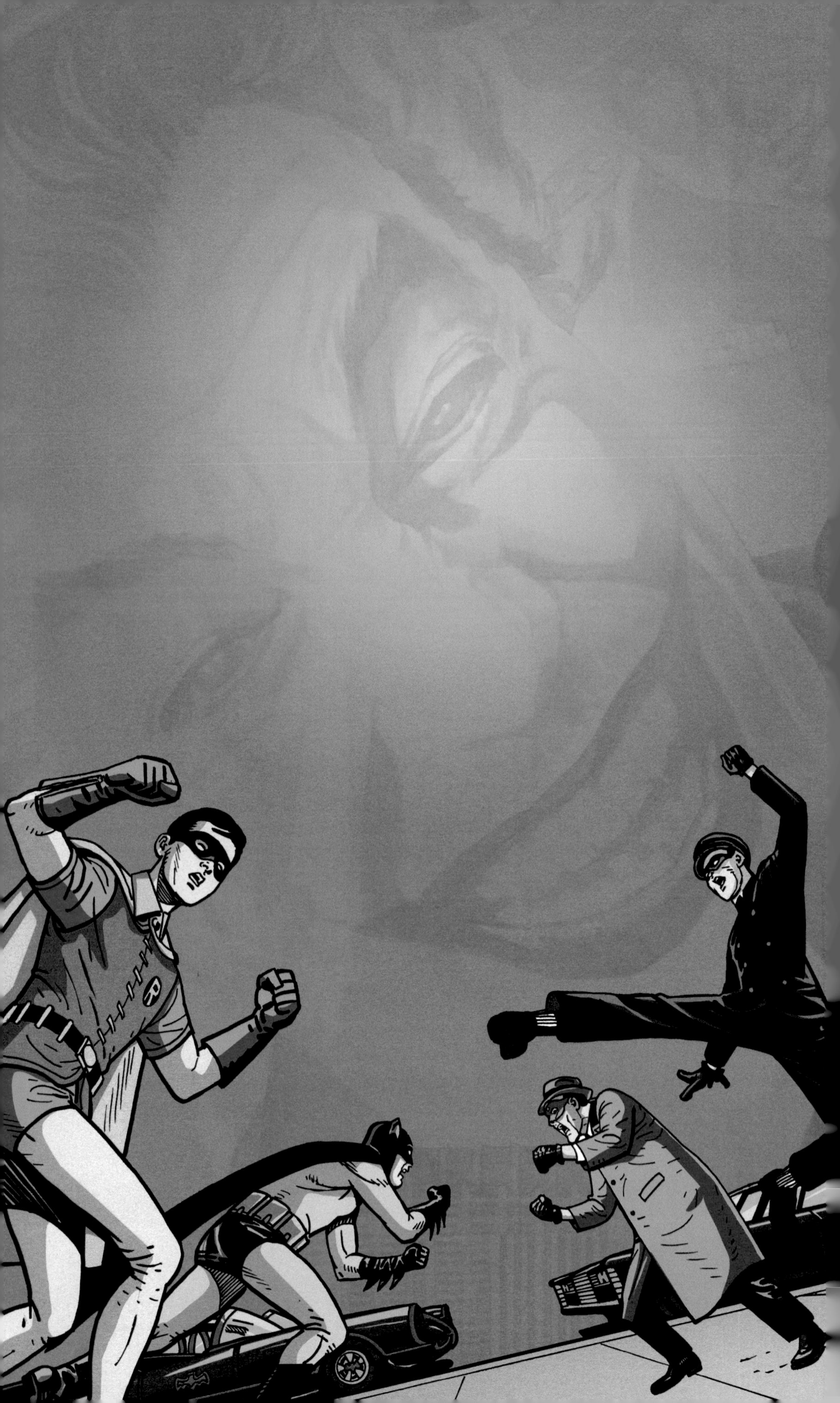

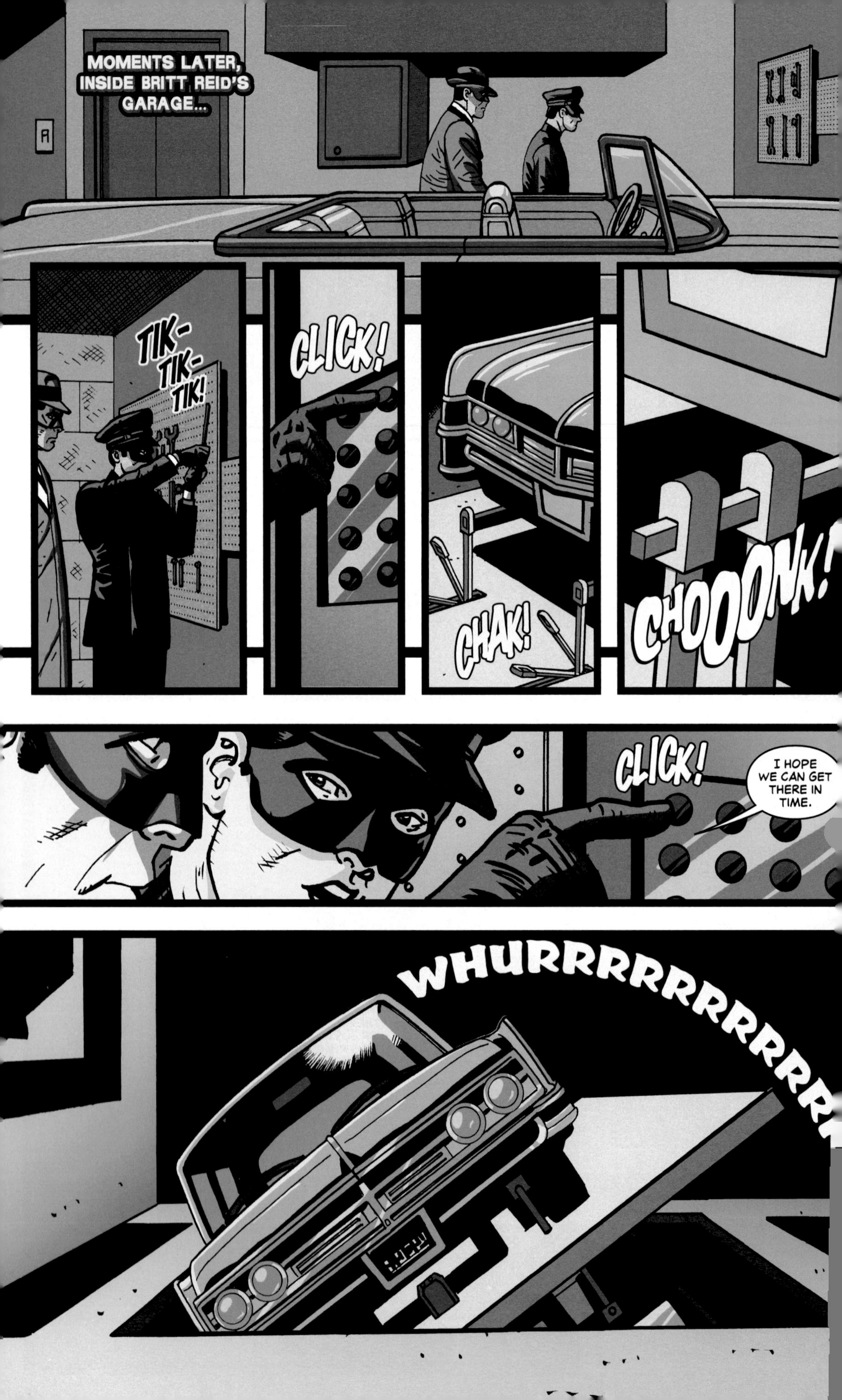
MOMENTS LATER, INSIDE BRITT REID'S GARAGE...
TIK-TIK-TIK!
CLICK!
CHAK!
CHOOONK!
CLICK!
I HOPE WE CAN GET THERE IN TIME.
WHURRRRRRRRRRR

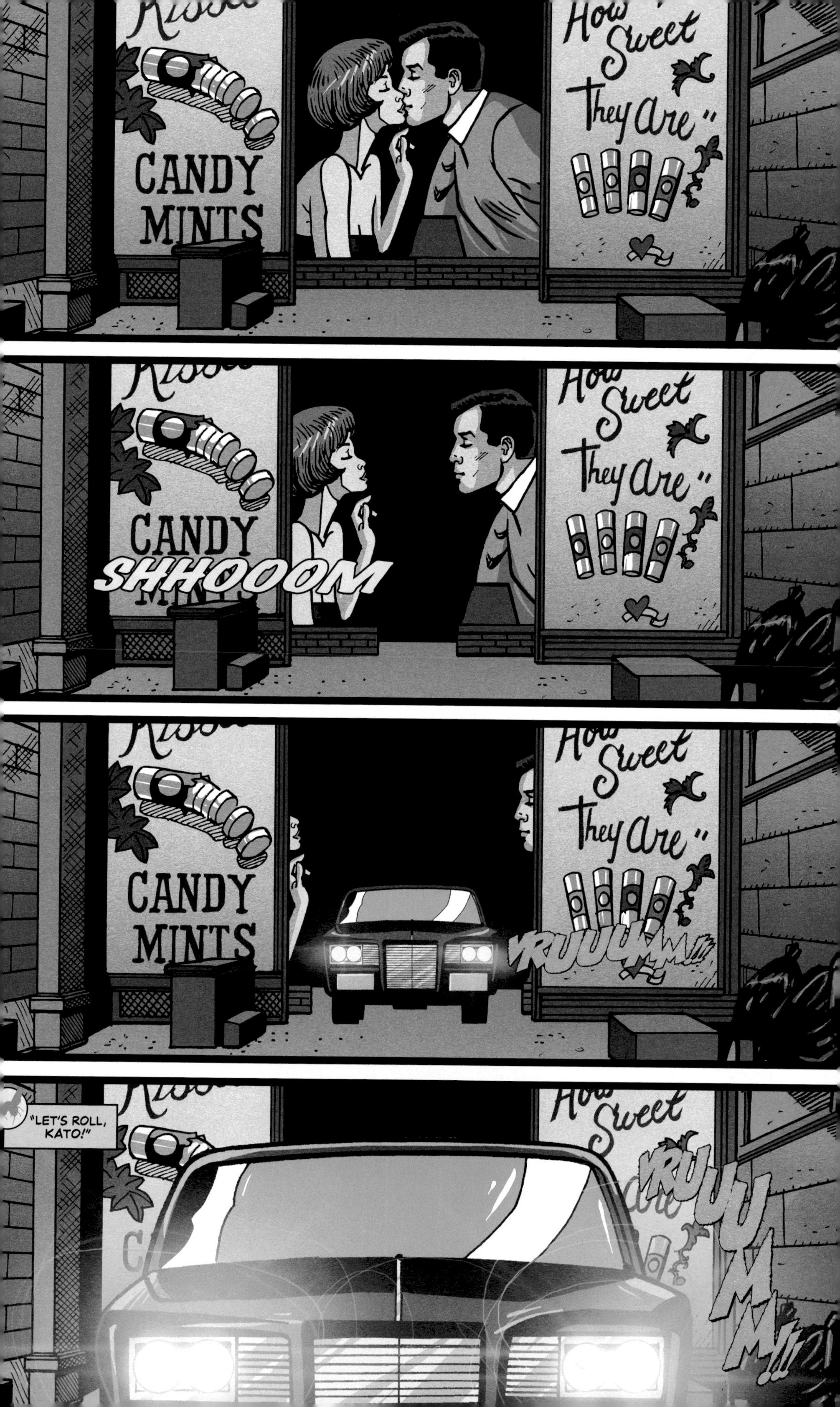
CANDY
MINTS
Sweet
They Are"
SHHOOOM
VRUUUMM!!
"LET'S ROLL, KATO!"
VRUUUMMM!!

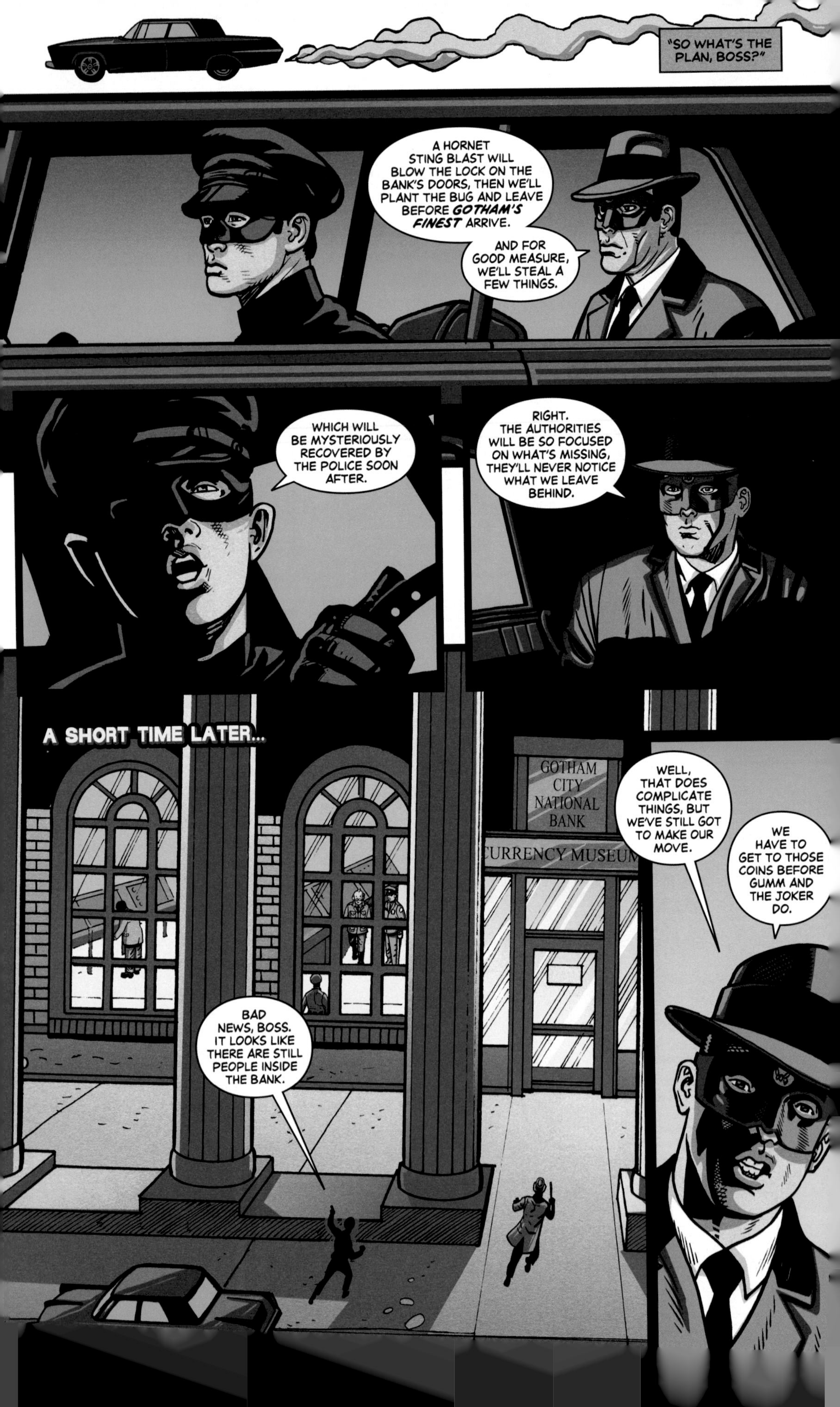
"SO WHAT'S THE PLAN, BOSS?"
A HORNET STING BLAST WILL BLOW THE LOCK ON THE BANK'S DOORS, THEN WE'LL PLANT THE BUG AND LEAVE BEFORE GOTHAM'S FINEST ARRIVE.
AND FOR GOOD MEASURE, WE'LL STEAL A FEW THINGS.
WHICH WILL BE MYSTERIOUSLY RECOVERED BY THE POLICE SOON AFTER.
RIGHT. THE AUTHORITIES WILL BE SO FOCUSED ON WHAT'S MISSING, THEY'LL NEVER NOTICE WHAT WE LEAVE BEHIND.
A SHORT TIME LATER...
GOTHAM CITY NATIONAL BANK
CURRENCY MUSEUM
BAD NEWS, BOSS. IT LOOKS LIKE THERE ARE STILL PEOPLE INSIDE THE BANK.
WELL, THAT DOES COMPLICATE THINGS, BUT WE'VE STILL GOT TO MAKE OUR MOVE.
WE HAVE TO GET TO THOSE COINS BEFORE GUMM AND THE JOKER DO.

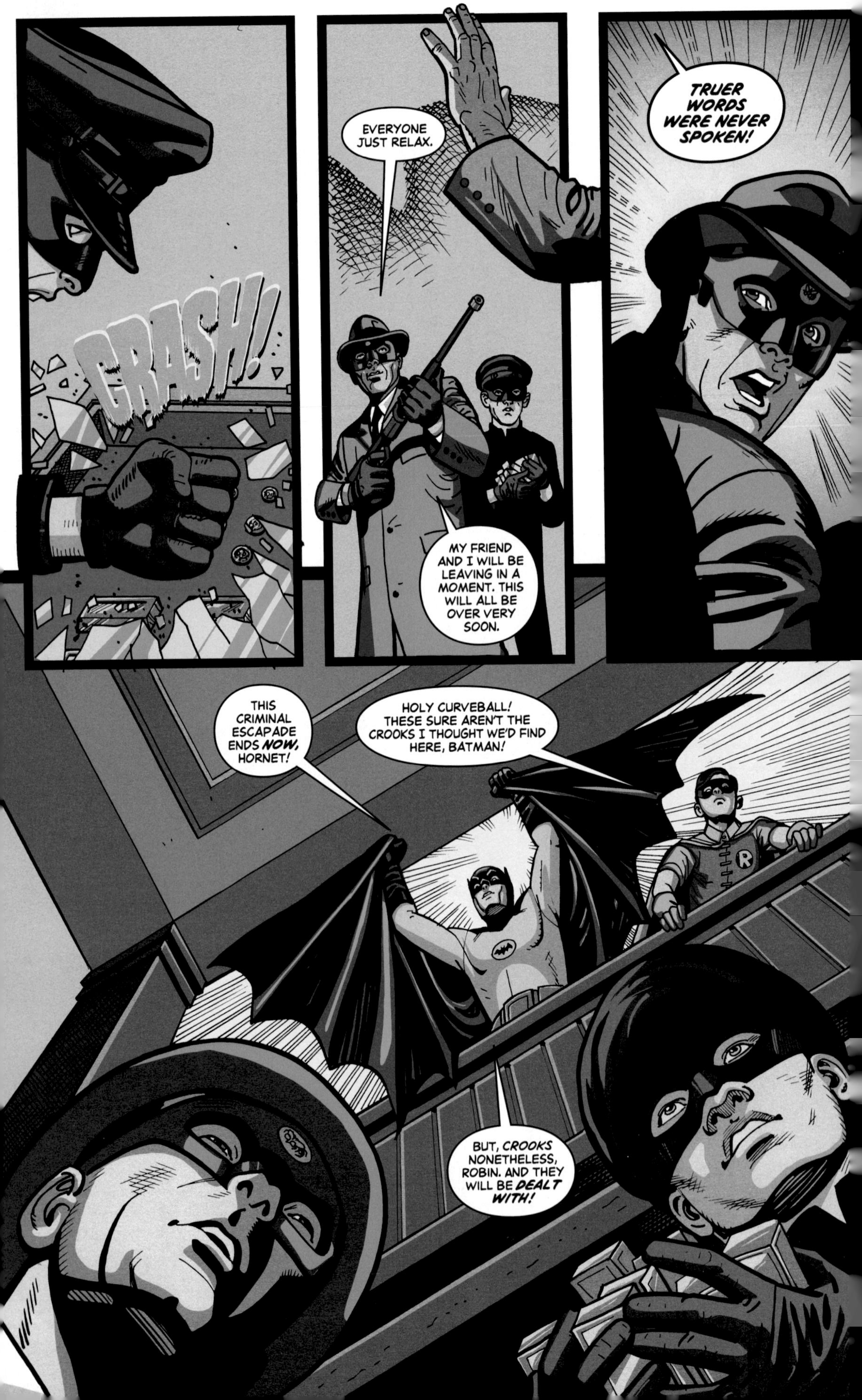
CRASH!
EVERYONE JUST RELAX.
MY FRIEND AND I WILL BE LEAVING IN A MOMENT. THIS WILL ALL BE OVER VERY SOON.
TRUER WORDS WERE NEVER SPOKEN!
THIS CRIMINAL ESCAPADE ENDS *NOW*, HORNET!
HOLY CURVEBALL! THESE SURE AREN'T THE CROOKS I THOUGHT WE'D FIND HERE, BATMAN!
BUT, *CROOKS* NONETHELESS, ROBIN. AND THEY WILL BE *DEALT WITH!*

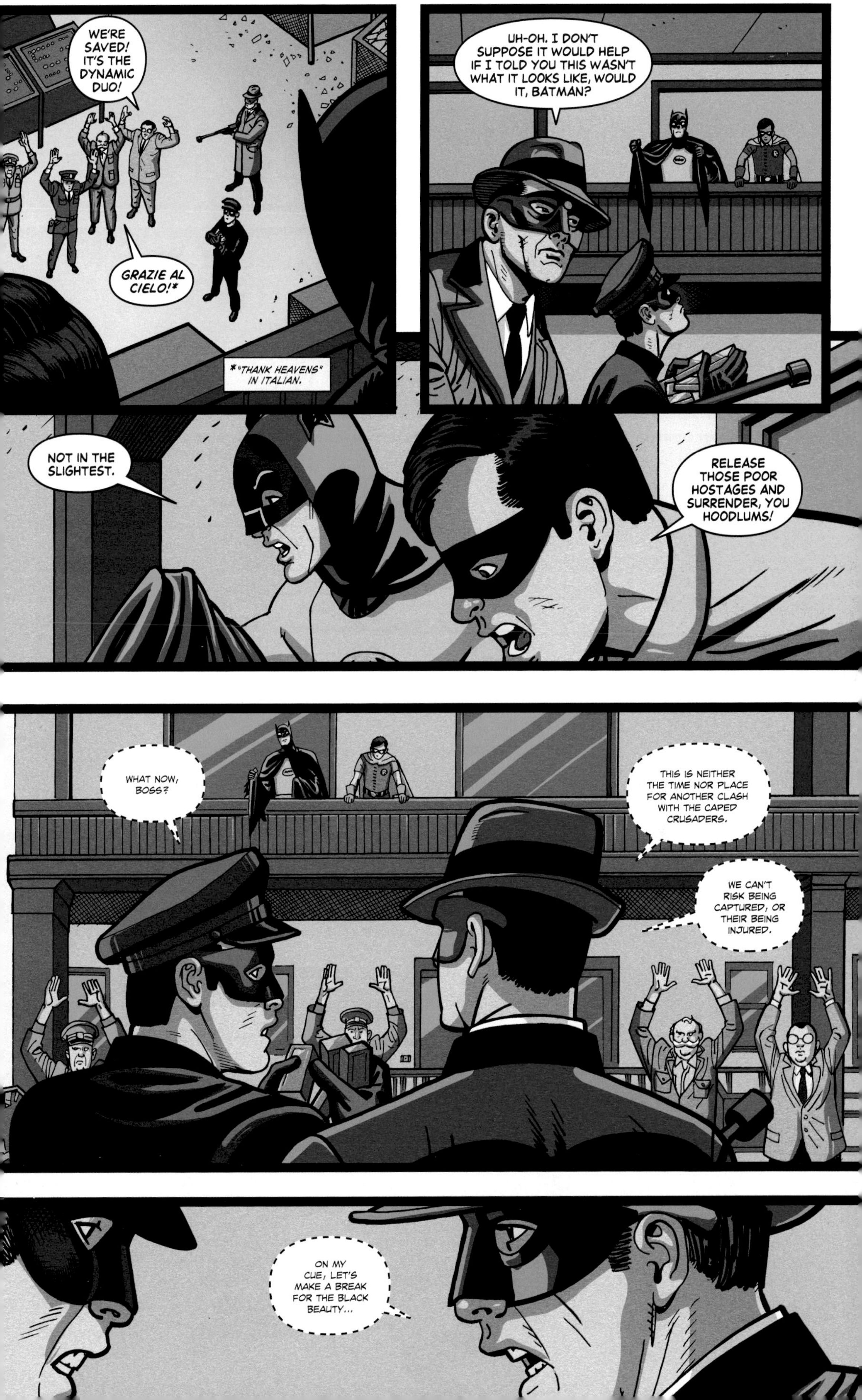
WE'RE SAVED! IT'S THE DYNAMIC DUO!
GRAZIE AL CIELO!*
*"THANK HEAVENS" IN ITALIAN.
UH-OH. I DON'T SUPPOSE IT WOULD HELP IF I TOLD YOU THIS WASN'T WHAT IT LOOKS LIKE, WOULD IT, BATMAN?
NOT IN THE SLIGHTEST.
RELEASE THOSE POOR HOSTAGES AND SURRENDER, YOU HOODLUMS!
WHAT NOW, BOSS?
THIS IS NEITHER THE TIME NOR PLACE FOR ANOTHER CLASH WITH THE CAPED CRUSADERS.
WE CAN'T RISK BEING CAPTURED, OR THEIR BEING INJURED.
ON MY CUE, LET'S MAKE A BREAK FOR THE BLACK BEAUTY...

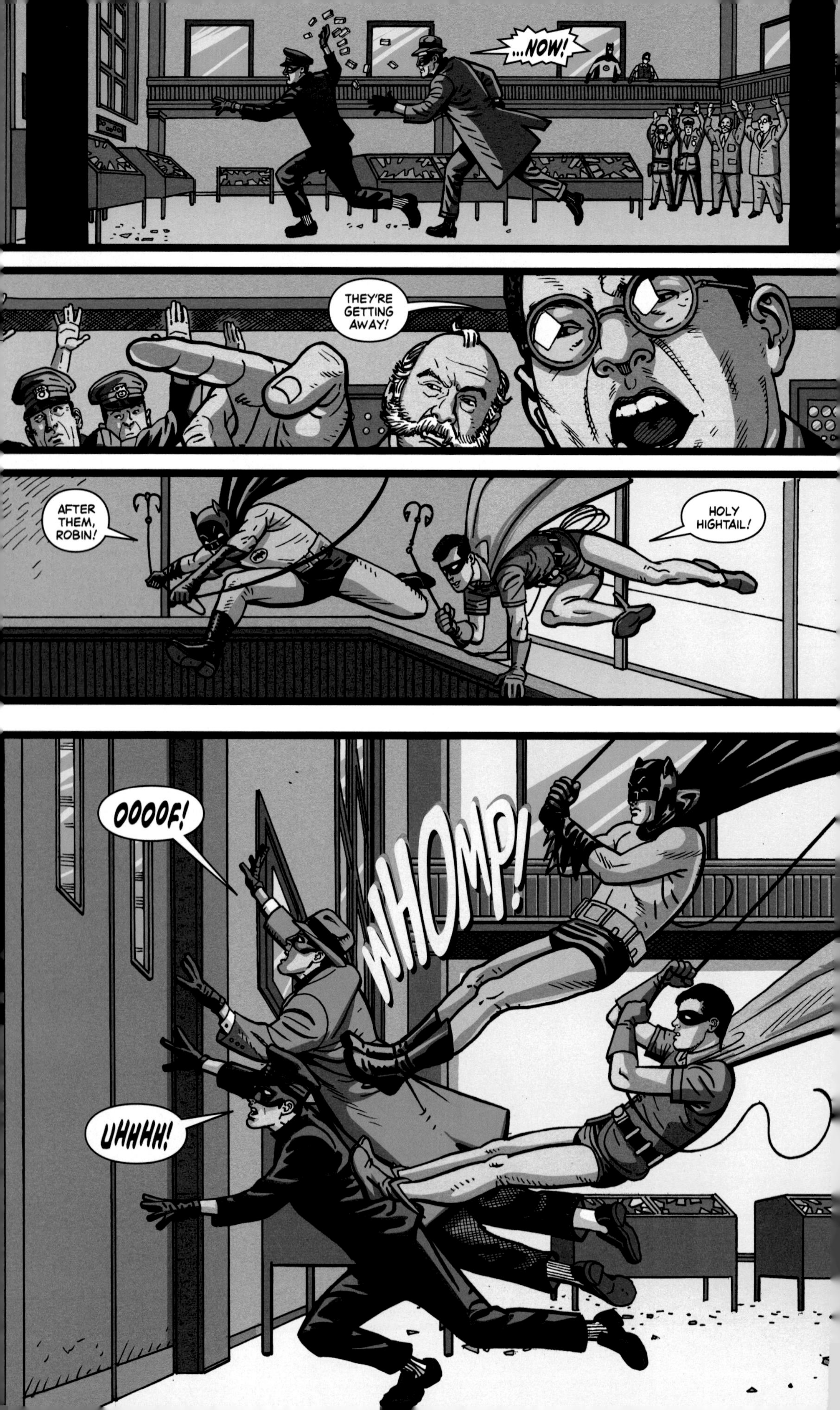
...NOW!
THEY'RE GETTING AWAY!
AFTER THEM, ROBIN!
HOLY HIGHTAIL!
OOOOF!
WHOMP!
UHHHH!

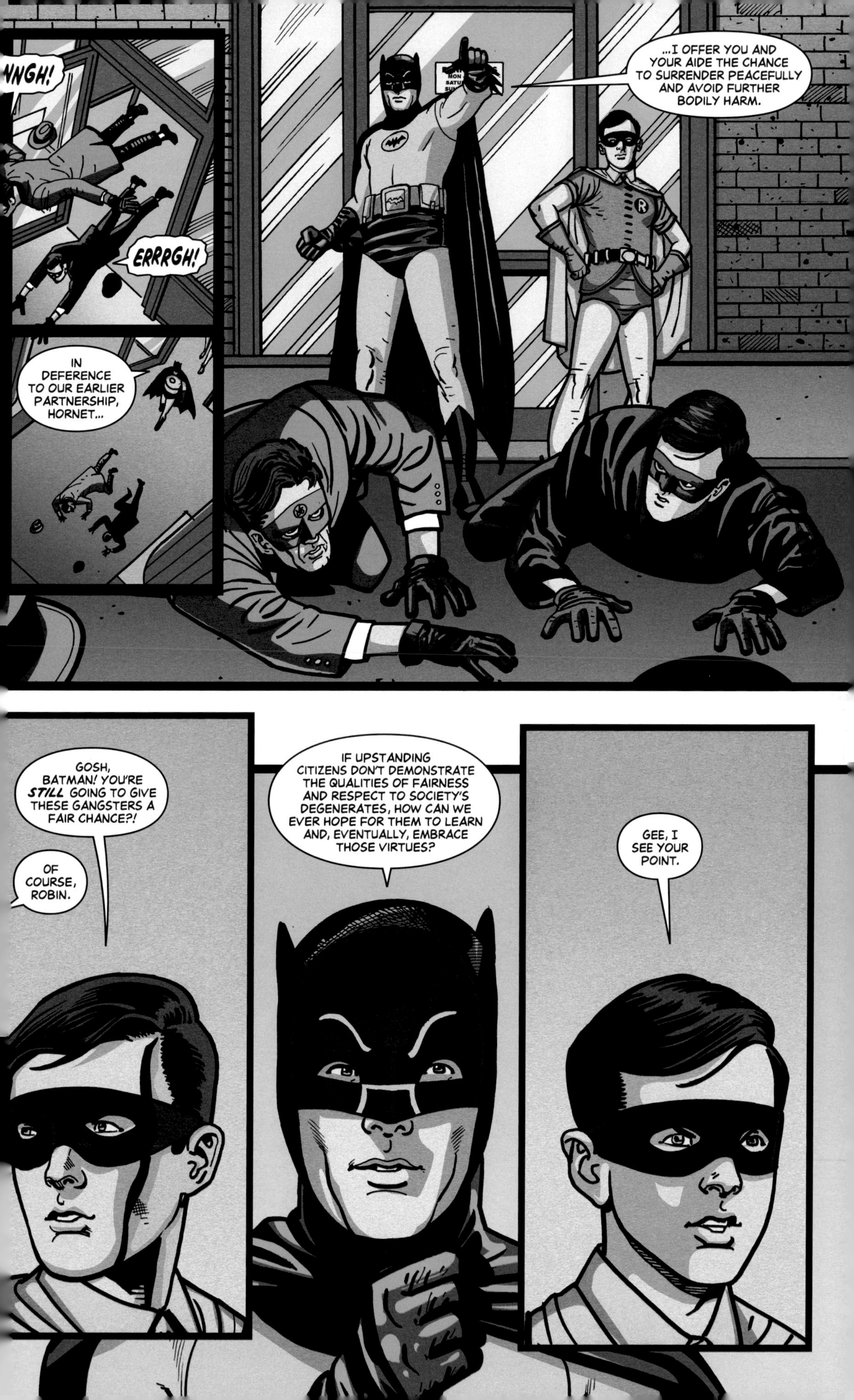
NNGH!
ERRRGH!
IN DEFERENCE TO OUR EARLIER PARTNERSHIP, HORNET...
...I OFFER YOU AND YOUR AIDE THE CHANCE TO SURRENDER PEACEFULLY AND AVOID FURTHER BODILY HARM.
GOSH, BATMAN! YOU'RE STILL GOING TO GIVE THESE GANGSTERS A FAIR CHANCE?!
OF COURSE, ROBIN.
IF UPSTANDING CITIZENS DON'T DEMONSTRATE THE QUALITIES OF FAIRNESS AND RESPECT TO SOCIETY'S DEGENERATES, HOW CAN WE EVER HOPE FOR THEM TO LEARN AND, EVENTUALLY, EMBRACE THOSE VIRTUES?
GEE, I SEE YOUR POINT.

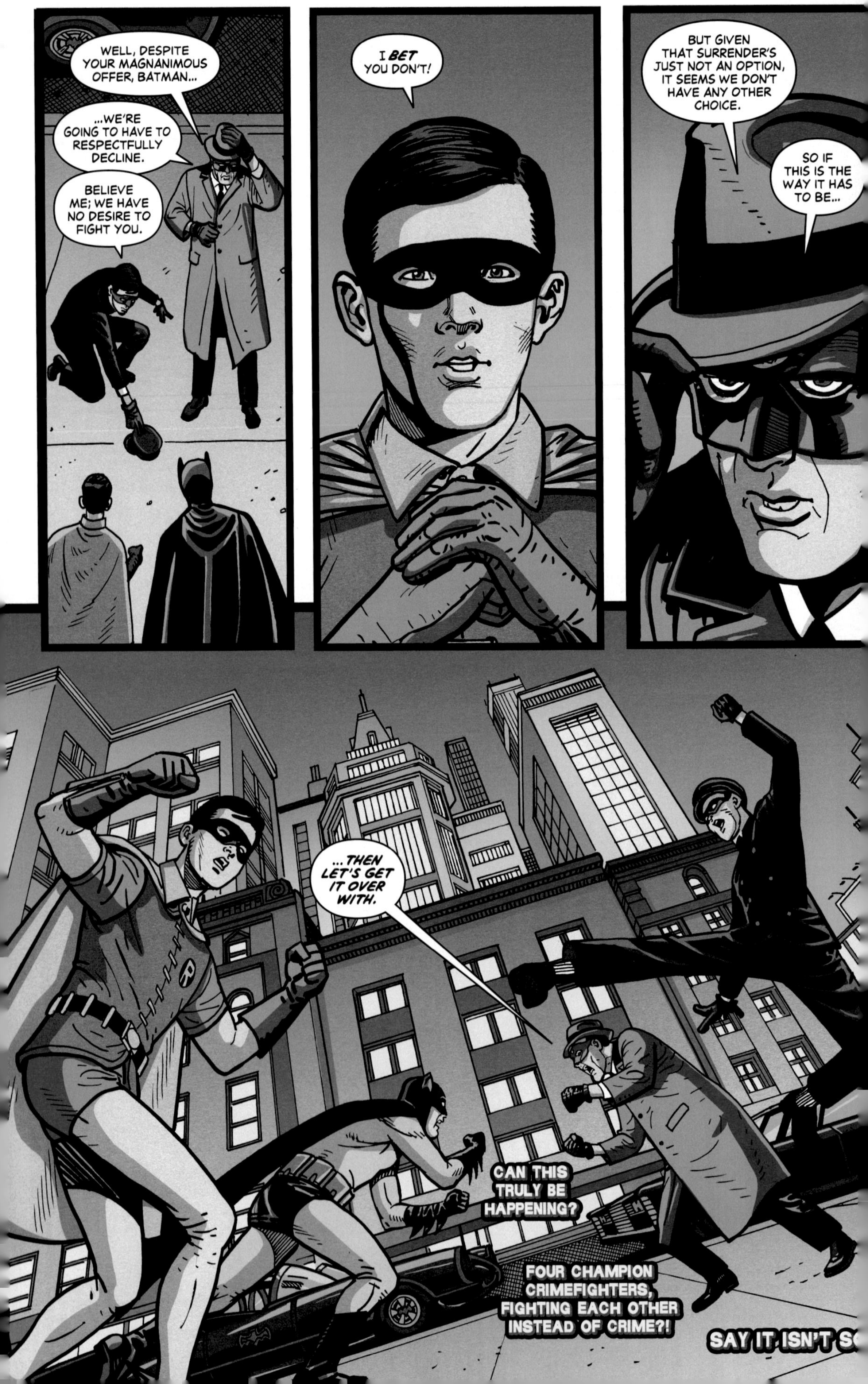
WELL, DESPITE YOUR MAGNANIMOUS OFFER, BATMAN...
...WE'RE GOING TO HAVE TO RESPECTFULLY DECLINE.
BELIEVE ME; WE HAVE NO DESIRE TO FIGHT YOU.
I BET YOU DON'T!
BUT GIVEN THAT SURRENDER'S JUST NOT AN OPTION, IT SEEMS WE DON'T HAVE ANY OTHER CHOICE.
SO IF THIS IS THE WAY IT HAS TO BE...
...THEN LET'S GET IT OVER WITH.
CAN THIS TRULY BE HAPPENING?
FOUR CHAMPION CRIMEFIGHTERS, FIGHTING EACH OTHER INSTEAD OF CRIME?!

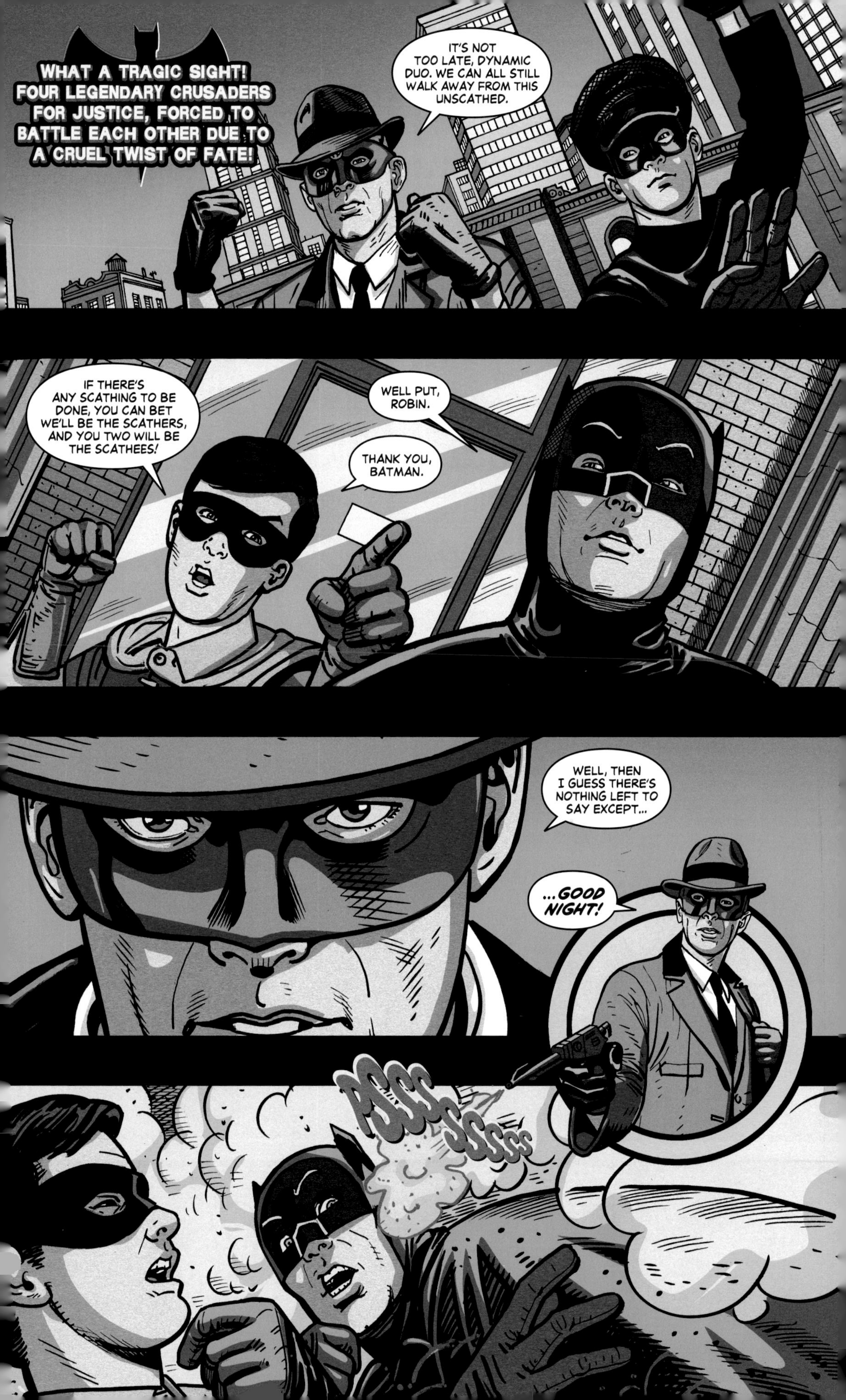
WHAT A TRAGIC SIGHT! FOUR LEGENDARY CRUSADERS FOR JUSTICE, FORCED TO BATTLE EACH OTHER DUE TO A CRUEL TWIST OF FATE!
IT'S NOT TOO LATE, DYNAMIC DUO. WE CAN ALL STILL WALK AWAY FROM THIS UNSCATHED.
IF THERE'S ANY SCATHING TO BE DONE, YOU CAN BET WE'LL BE THE SCATHERS, AND YOU TWO WILL BE THE SCATHEES!
WELL PUT, ROBIN.
THANK YOU, BATMAN.
WELL, THEN I GUESS THERE'S NOTHING LEFT TO SAY EXCEPT...
...GOOD NIGHT!
PSSSSSSSSSS

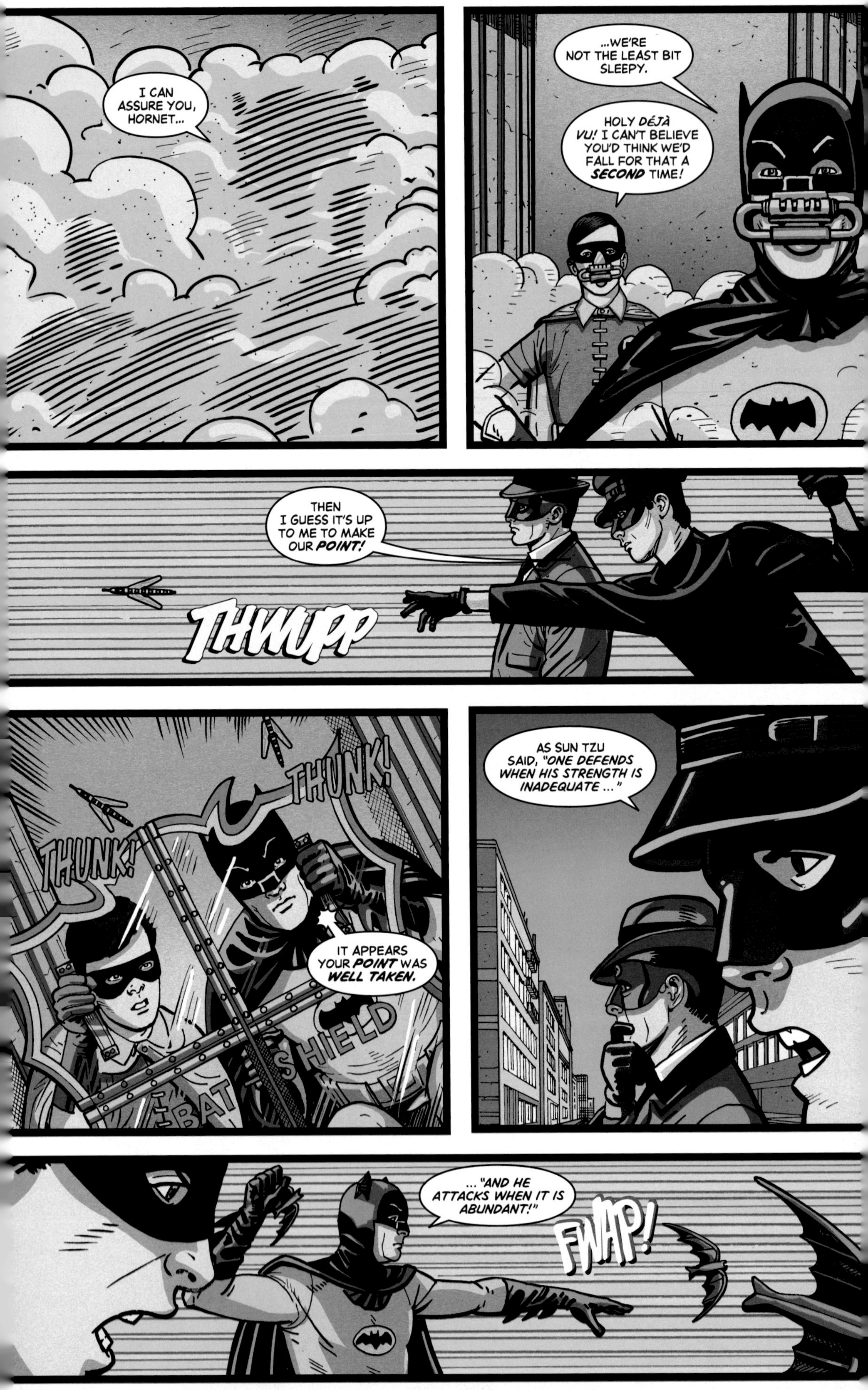
I CAN ASSURE YOU, HORNET...
...WE'RE NOT THE LEAST BIT SLEEPY.
HOLY *DÉJÀ VU!* I CAN'T BELIEVE YOU'D THINK WE'D FALL FOR THAT A ***SECOND*** TIME!
THEN I GUESS IT'S UP TO ME TO MAKE OUR ***POINT!***
THWUPP
THUNK!
THUNK!
IT APPEARS YOUR ***POINT*** WAS ***WELL TAKEN.***
BAT SHIELD
AS SUN TZU SAID, *"ONE DEFENDS WHEN HIS STRENGTH IS INADEQUATE ..."*
... *"AND HE ATTACKS WHEN IT IS ABUNDANT!"*
FWAP!

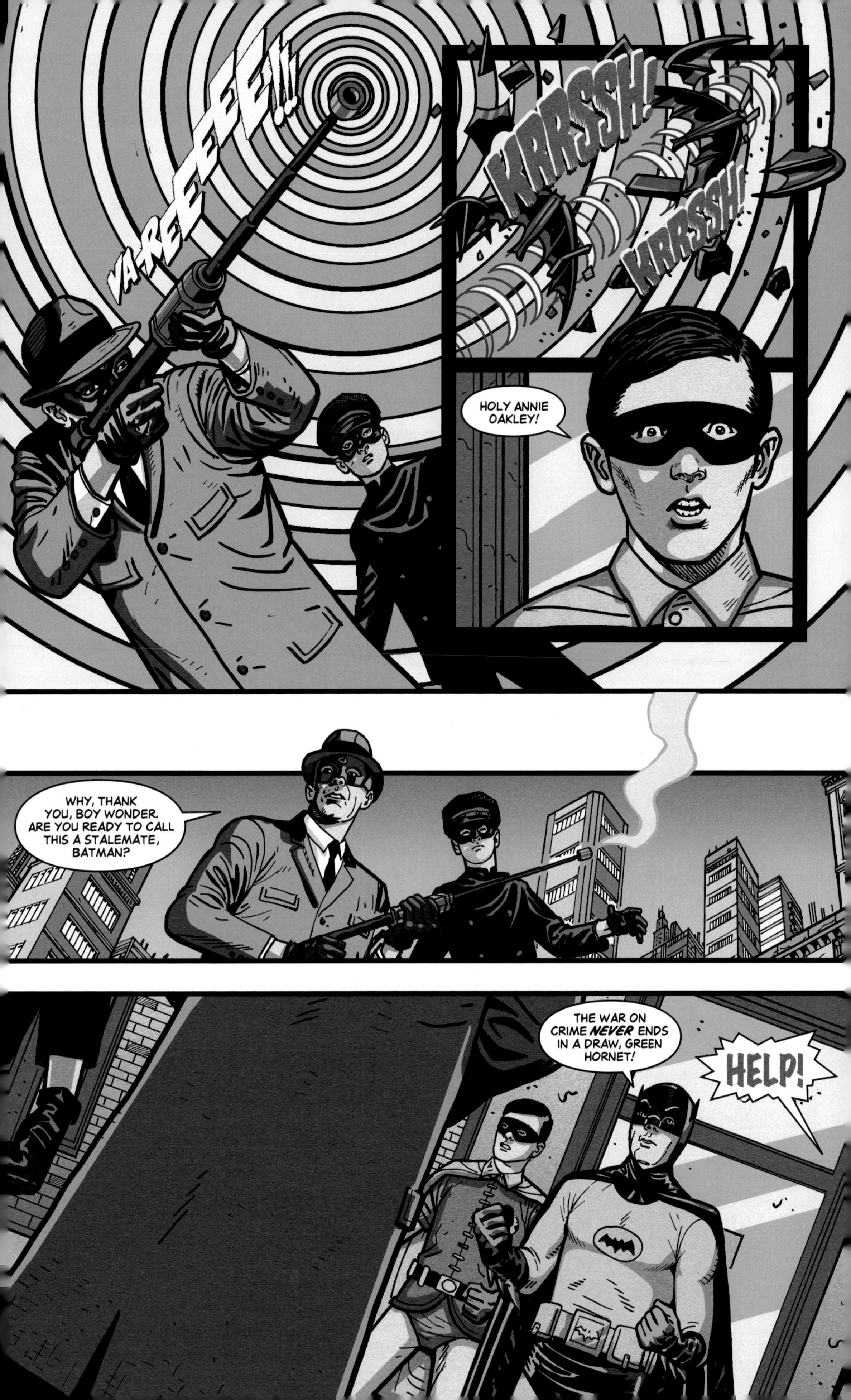
VA-REEEEE!!!
KRRSSH!
KRRSSH!
HOLY ANNIE OAKLEY!
WHY, THANK YOU, BOY WONDER. ARE YOU READY TO CALL THIS A STALEMATE, BATMAN?
THE WAR ON CRIME NEVER ENDS IN A DRAW, GREEN HORNET!
HELP!

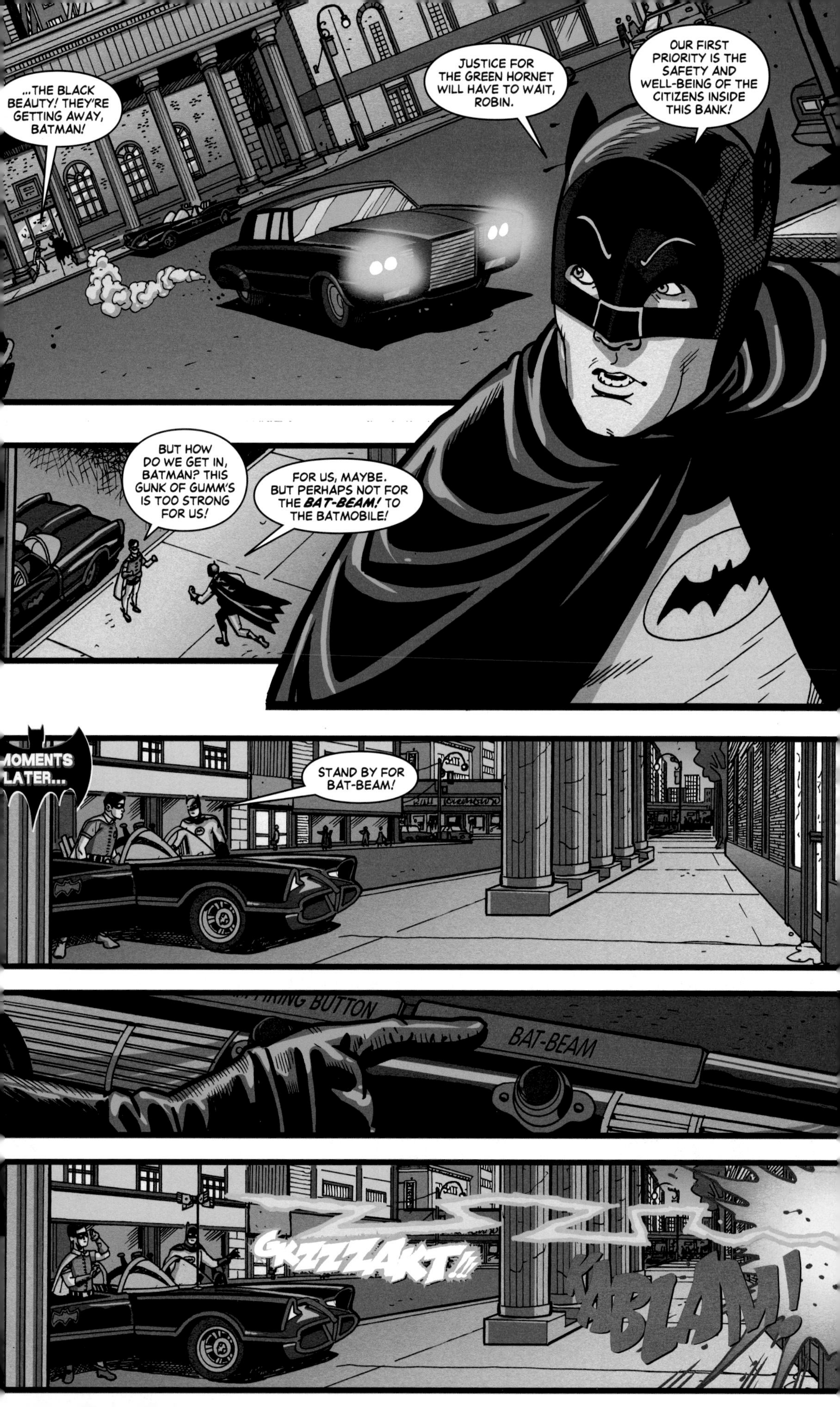

...THE BLACK BEAUTY! THEY'RE GETTING AWAY, BATMAN!
JUSTICE FOR THE GREEN HORNET WILL HAVE TO WAIT, ROBIN.
OUR FIRST PRIORITY IS THE SAFETY AND WELL-BEING OF THE CITIZENS INSIDE THIS BANK!
BUT HOW DO WE GET IN, BATMAN? THIS GUNK OF GUMM'S IS TOO STRONG FOR US!
FOR US, MAYBE. BUT PERHAPS NOT FOR THE BAT-BEAM! TO THE BATMOBILE!
MOMENTS LATER...
STAND BY FOR BAT-BEAM!
FIRING BUTTON
BAT-BEAM
GKZZZZAKT!!!
KABLAM!

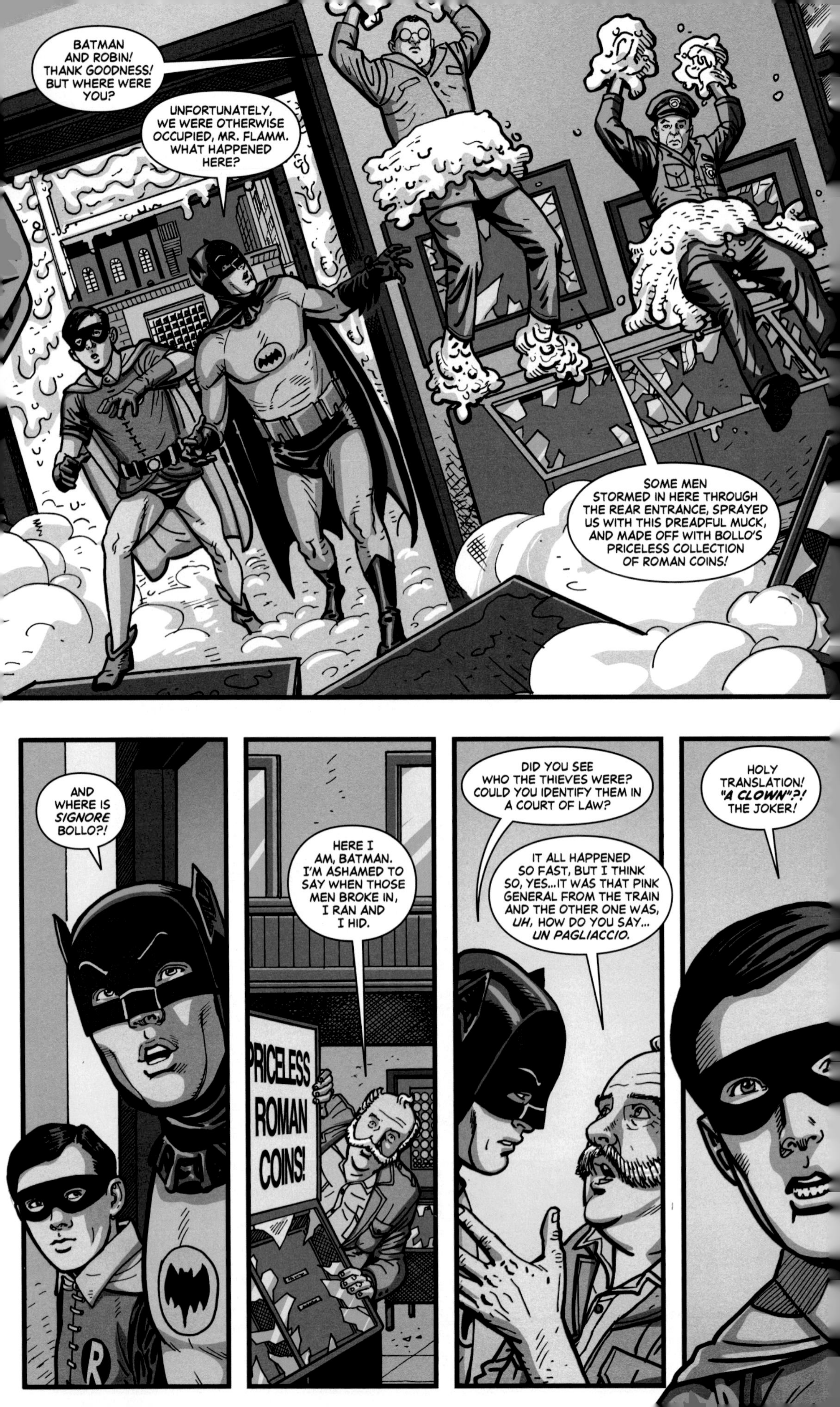

BATMAN AND ROBIN! THANK GOODNESS! BUT WHERE WERE YOU?
UNFORTUNATELY, WE WERE OTHERWISE OCCUPIED, MR. FLAMM. WHAT HAPPENED HERE?
SOME MEN STORMED IN HERE THROUGH THE REAR ENTRANCE, SPRAYED US WITH THIS DREADFUL MUCK, AND MADE OFF WITH BOLLO'S PRICELESS COLLECTION OF ROMAN COINS!
AND WHERE IS *SIGNORE* BOLLO?!
HERE I AM, BATMAN. I'M ASHAMED TO SAY WHEN THOSE MEN BROKE IN, I RAN AND I HID.
PRICELESS ROMAN COINS!
DID YOU SEE WHO THE THIEVES WERE? COULD YOU IDENTIFY THEM IN A COURT OF LAW?
IT ALL HAPPENED SO FAST, BUT I THINK SO, YES...IT WAS THAT PINK GENERAL FROM THE TRAIN AND THE OTHER ONE WAS, *UH,* HOW DO YOU SAY... *UN PAGLIACCIO.*
HOLY TRANSLATION! *"A CLOWN"?!* THE JOKER!

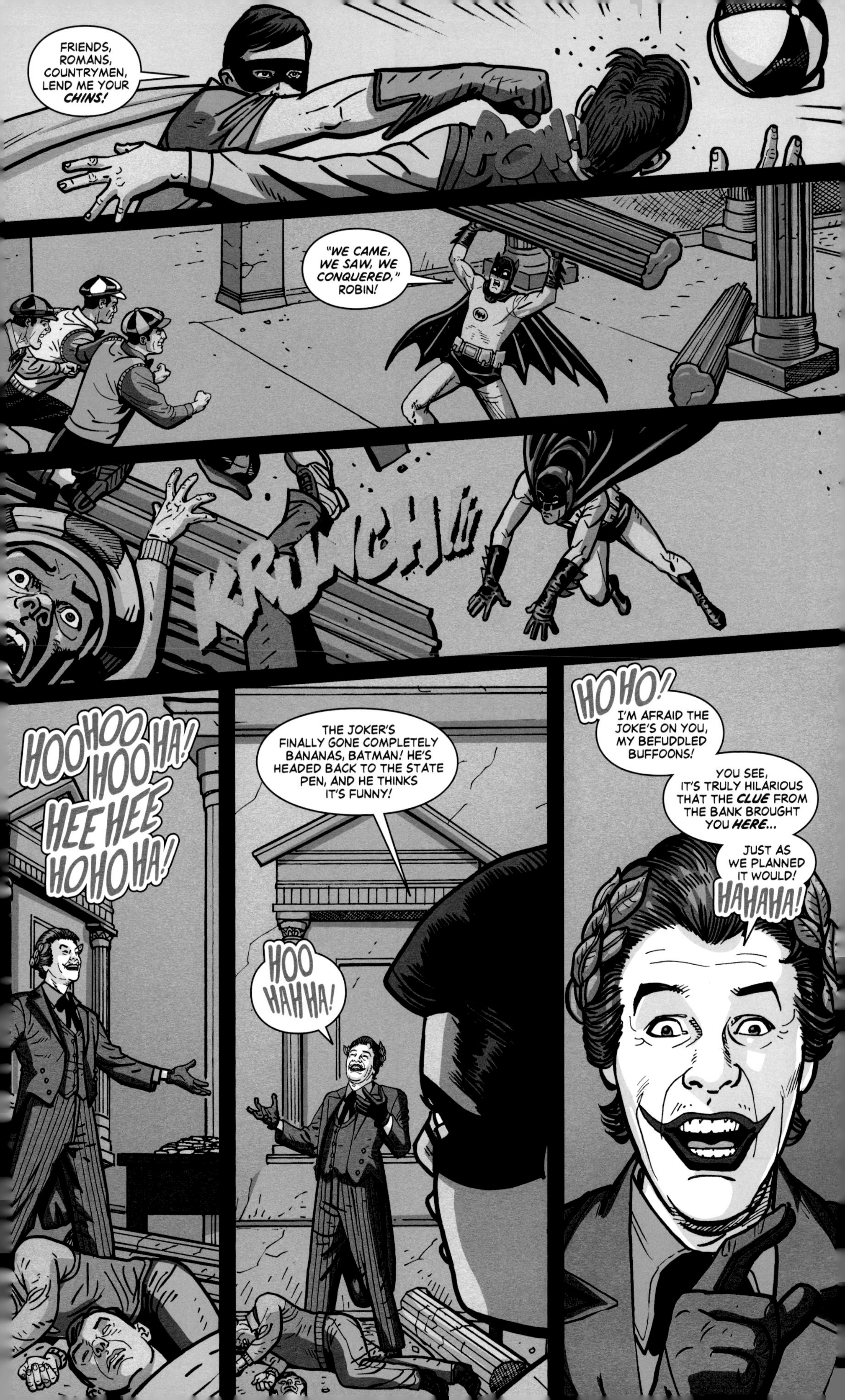
FRIENDS, ROMANS, COUNTRYMEN, LEND ME YOUR CHINS!
POW!
"WE CAME, WE SAW, WE CONQUERED," ROBIN!
KRUNCH!!!
HOOHOO HOOHA! HEE HEE HOHOHA!
THE JOKER'S FINALLY GONE COMPLETELY BANANAS, BATMAN! HE'S HEADED BACK TO THE STATE PEN, AND HE THINKS IT'S FUNNY!
HOO HAHHA!
HOHO! I'M AFRAID THE JOKE'S ON YOU, MY BEFUDDLED BUFFOONS!
YOU SEE, IT'S TRULY HILARIOUS THAT THE CLUE FROM THE BANK BROUGHT YOU HERE...
JUST AS WE PLANNED IT WOULD! HAHAHA!

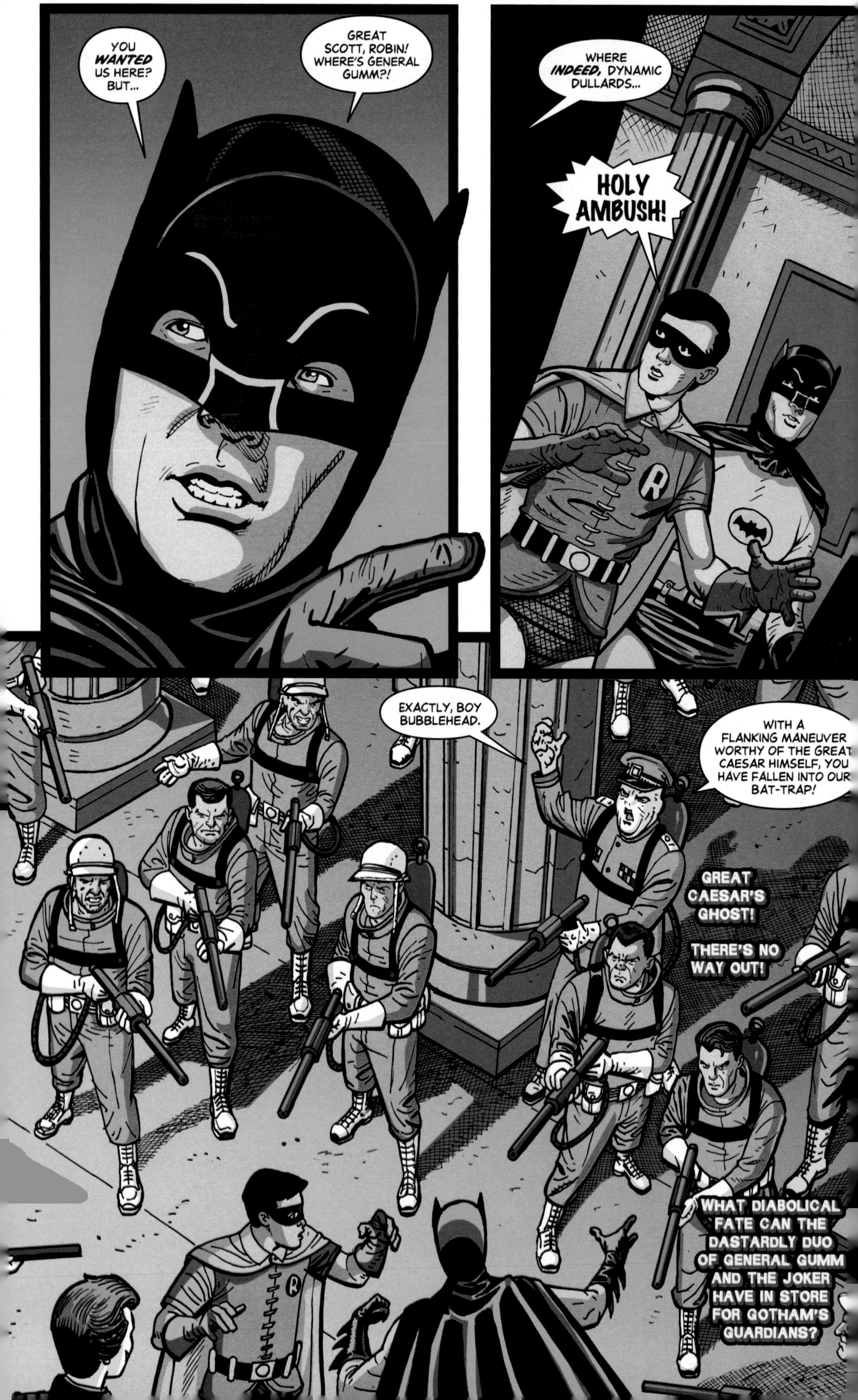
YOU *WANTED* US HERE? BUT...
GREAT SCOTT, ROBIN! WHERE'S GENERAL GUMM?!
WHERE *INDEED,* DYNAMIC DULLARDS...
HOLY AMBUSH!
EXACTLY, BOY BUBBLEHEAD.
WITH A FLANKING MANEUVER WORTHY OF THE GREAT CAESAR HIMSELF, YOU HAVE FALLEN INTO OUR BAT-TRAP!
GREAT CAESAR'S GHOST!
THERE'S NO WAY OUT!
WHAT DIABOLICAL FATE CAN THE DASTARDLY DUO OF GENERAL GUMM AND THE JOKER HAVE IN STORE FOR GOTHAM'S GUARDIANS?

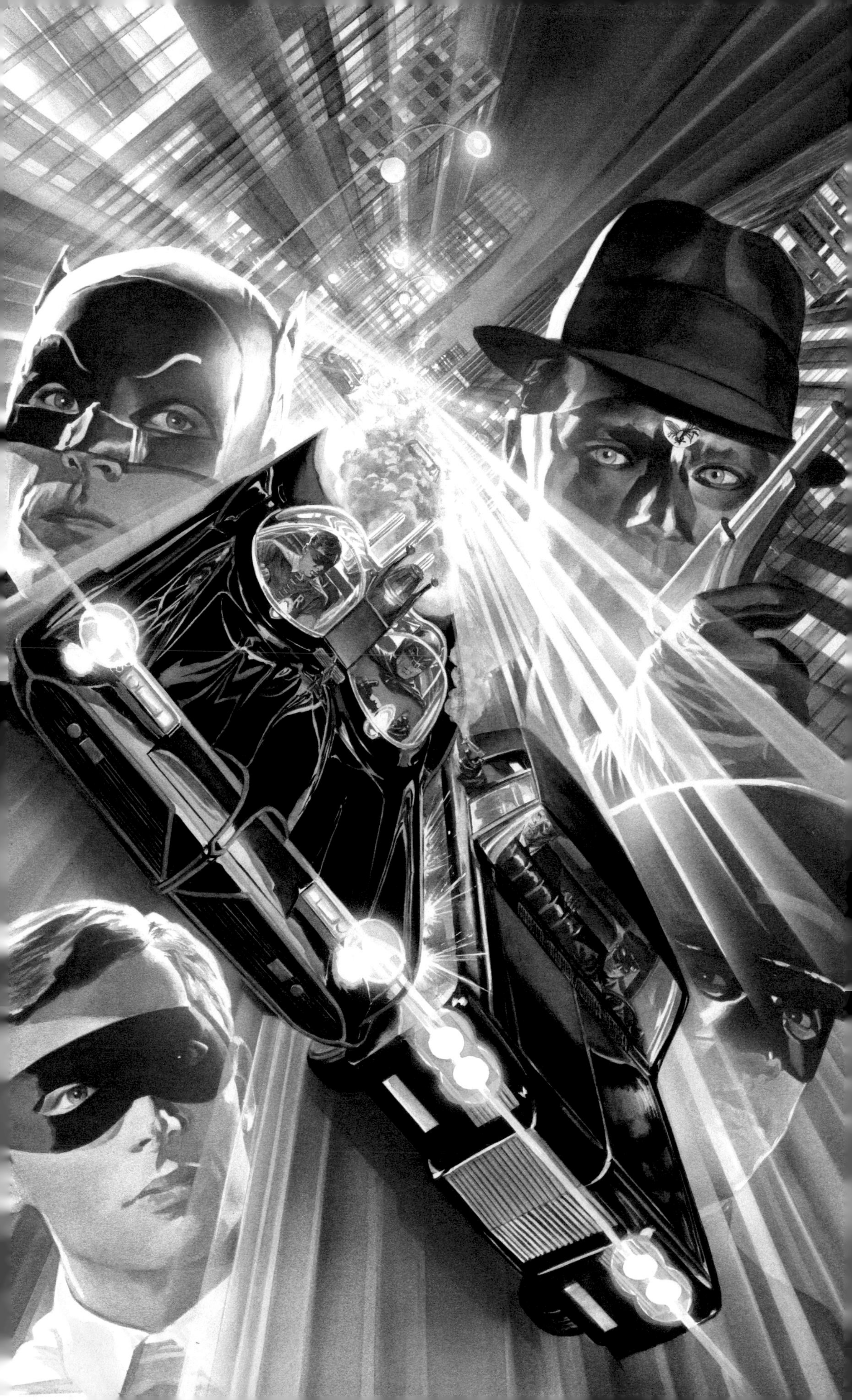

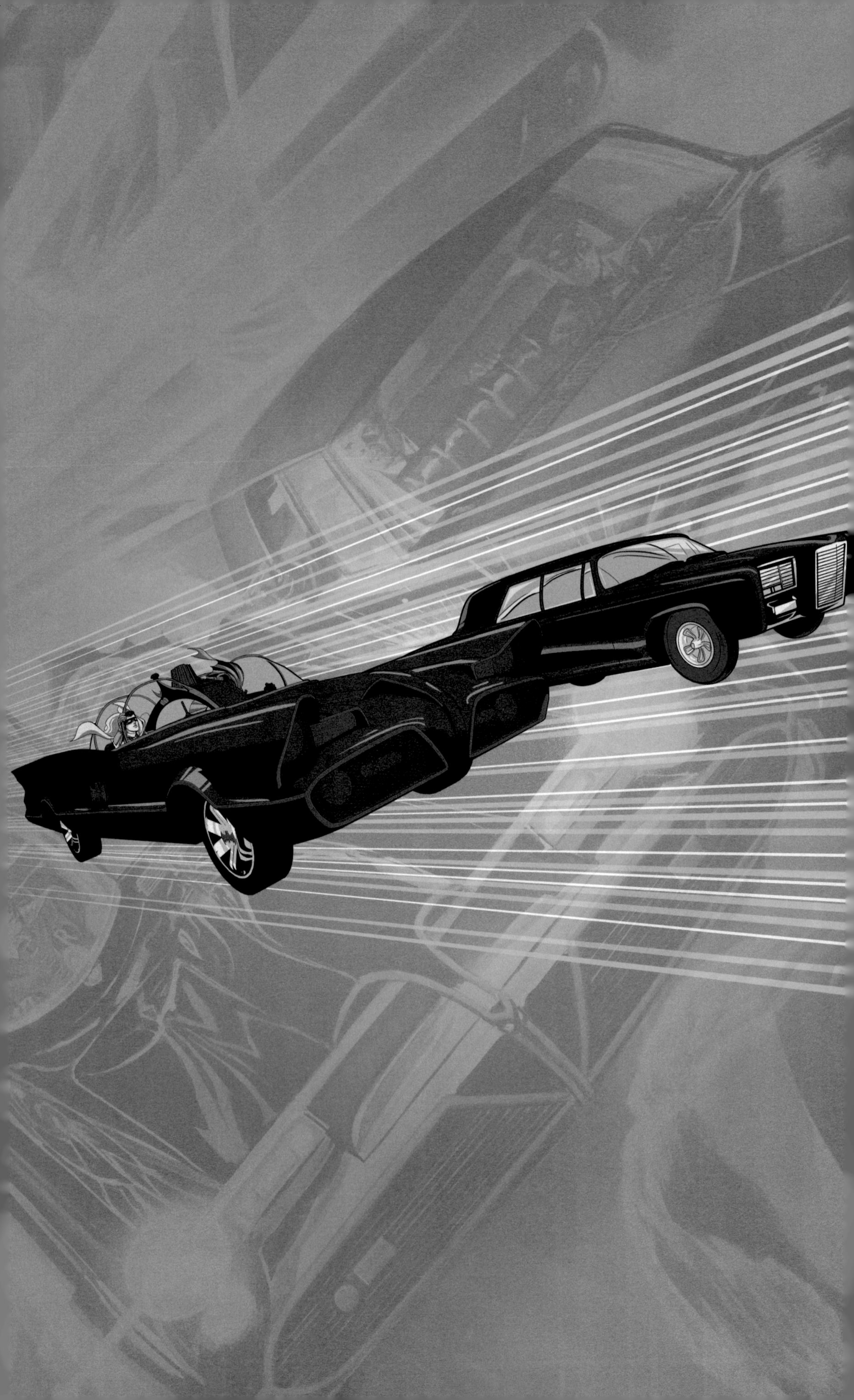

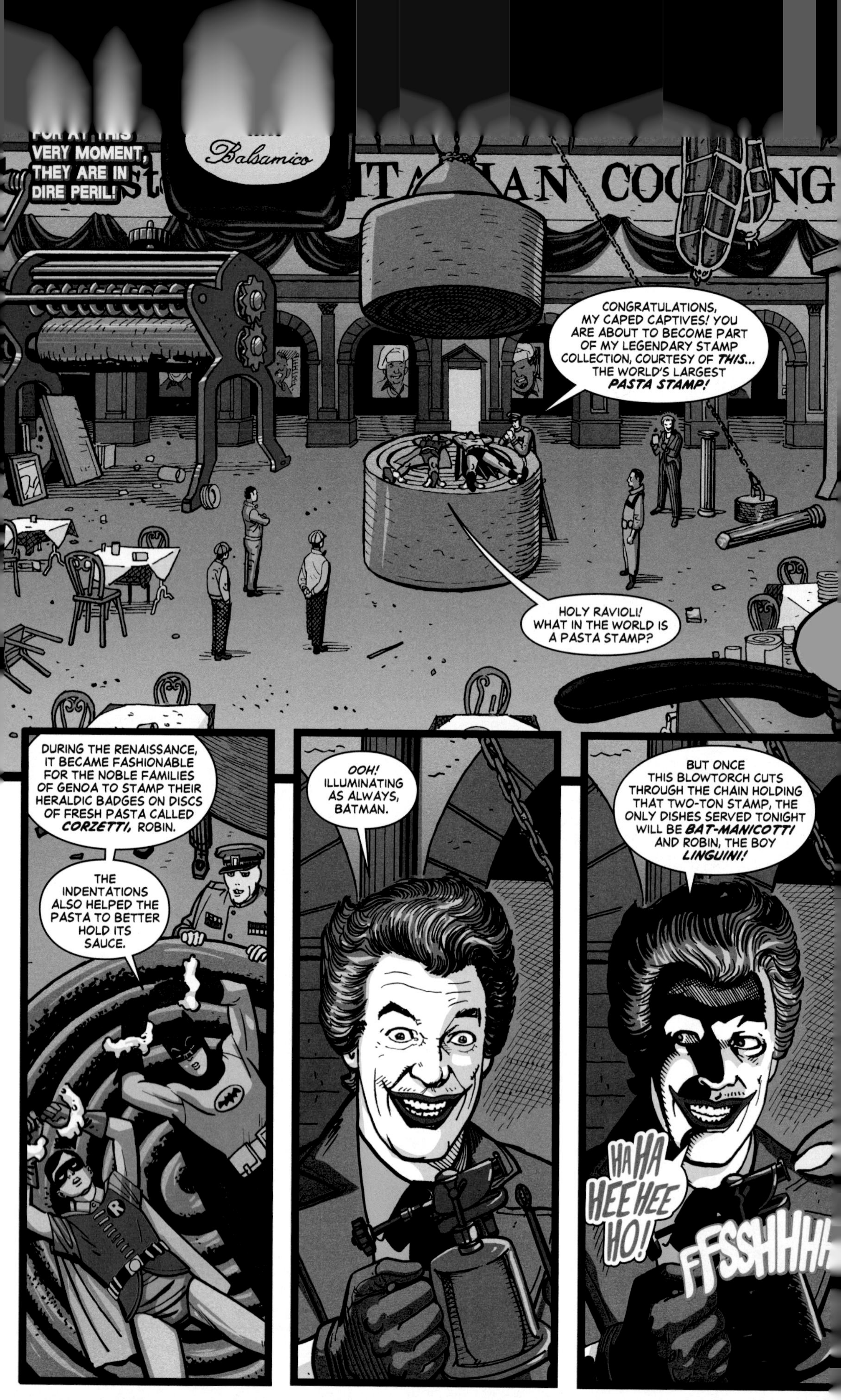
FOR AT THIS VERY MOMENT, THEY ARE IN DIRE PERIL!
Balsamico
ITALIAN COOKING
CONGRATULATIONS, MY CAPED CAPTIVES! YOU ARE ABOUT TO BECOME PART OF MY LEGENDARY STAMP COLLECTION, COURTESY OF *THIS*... THE WORLD'S LARGEST ***PASTA STAMP!***
HOLY RAVIOLI! WHAT IN THE WORLD IS A PASTA STAMP?
DURING THE RENAISSANCE, IT BECAME FASHIONABLE FOR THE NOBLE FAMILIES OF GENOA TO STAMP THEIR HERALDIC BADGES ON DISCS OF FRESH PASTA CALLED ***CORZETTI,*** ROBIN.
THE INDENTATIONS ALSO HELPED THE PASTA TO BETTER HOLD ITS SAUCE.
OOH! ILLUMINATING AS ALWAYS, BATMAN.
BUT ONCE THIS BLOWTORCH CUTS THROUGH THE CHAIN HOLDING THAT TWO-TON STAMP, THE ONLY DISHES SERVED TONIGHT WILL BE ***BAT-MANICOTTI*** AND ROBIN, THE BOY ***LINGUINI!***
HAHA HEEHEE HO!
FFSSHHHH

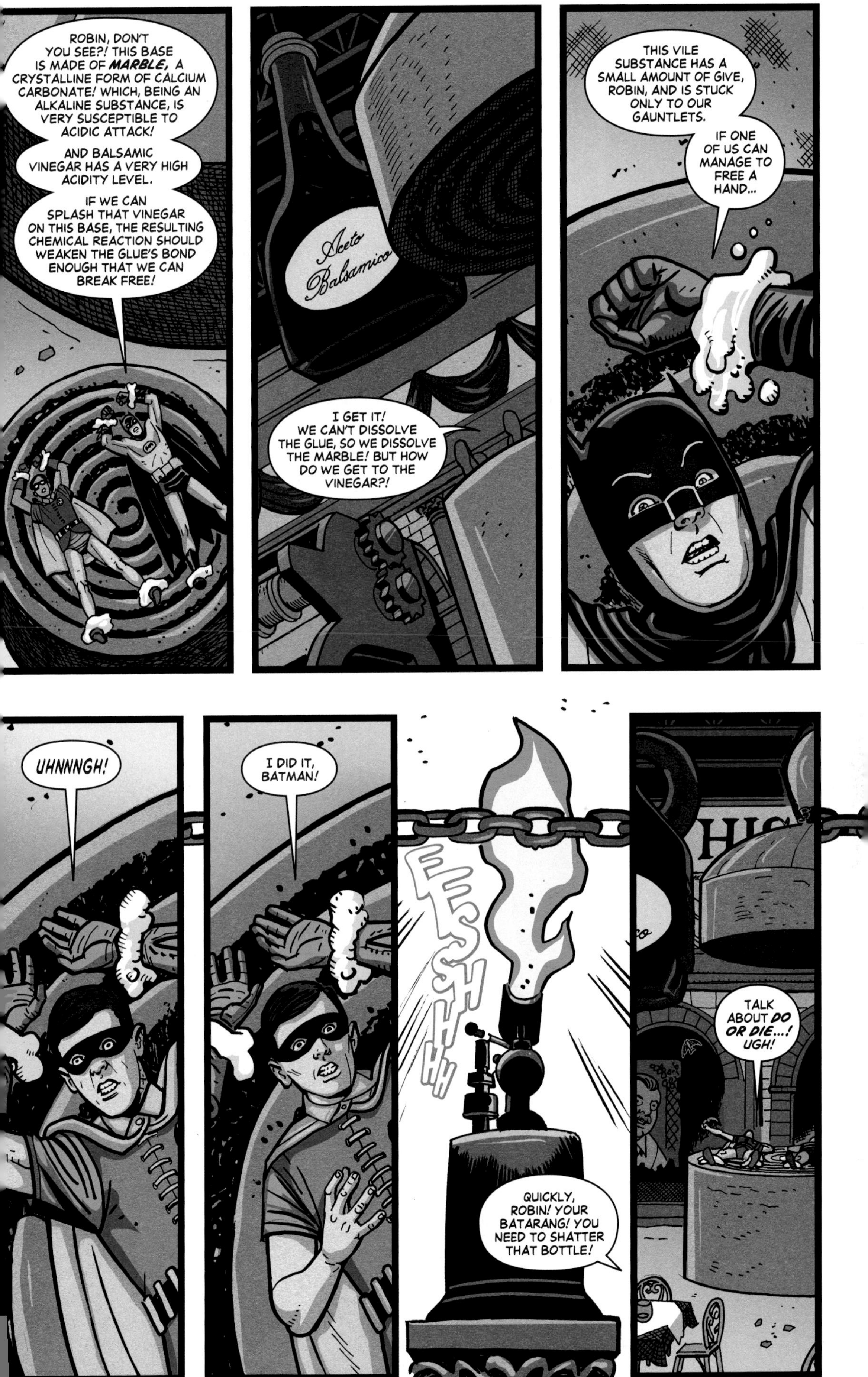
ROBIN, DON'T YOU SEE?! THIS BASE IS MADE OF MARBLE, A CRYSTALLINE FORM OF CALCIUM CARBONATE! WHICH, BEING AN ALKALINE SUBSTANCE, IS VERY SUSCEPTIBLE TO ACIDIC ATTACK!
AND BALSAMIC VINEGAR HAS A VERY HIGH ACIDITY LEVEL.
IF WE CAN SPLASH THAT VINEGAR ON THIS BASE, THE RESULTING CHEMICAL REACTION SHOULD WEAKEN THE GLUE'S BOND ENOUGH THAT WE CAN BREAK FREE!
Aceto Balsamico
I GET IT! WE CAN'T DISSOLVE THE GLUE, SO WE DISSOLVE THE MARBLE! BUT HOW DO WE GET TO THE VINEGAR?!
THIS VILE SUBSTANCE HAS A SMALL AMOUNT OF GIVE, ROBIN, AND IS STUCK ONLY TO OUR GAUNTLETS.
IF ONE OF US CAN MANAGE TO FREE A HAND...
UHNNNGH!
I DID IT, BATMAN!
FFSHHHH
QUICKLY, ROBIN! YOUR BATARANG! YOU NEED TO SHATTER THAT BOTTLE!
TALK ABOUT DO OR DIE...! UGH!

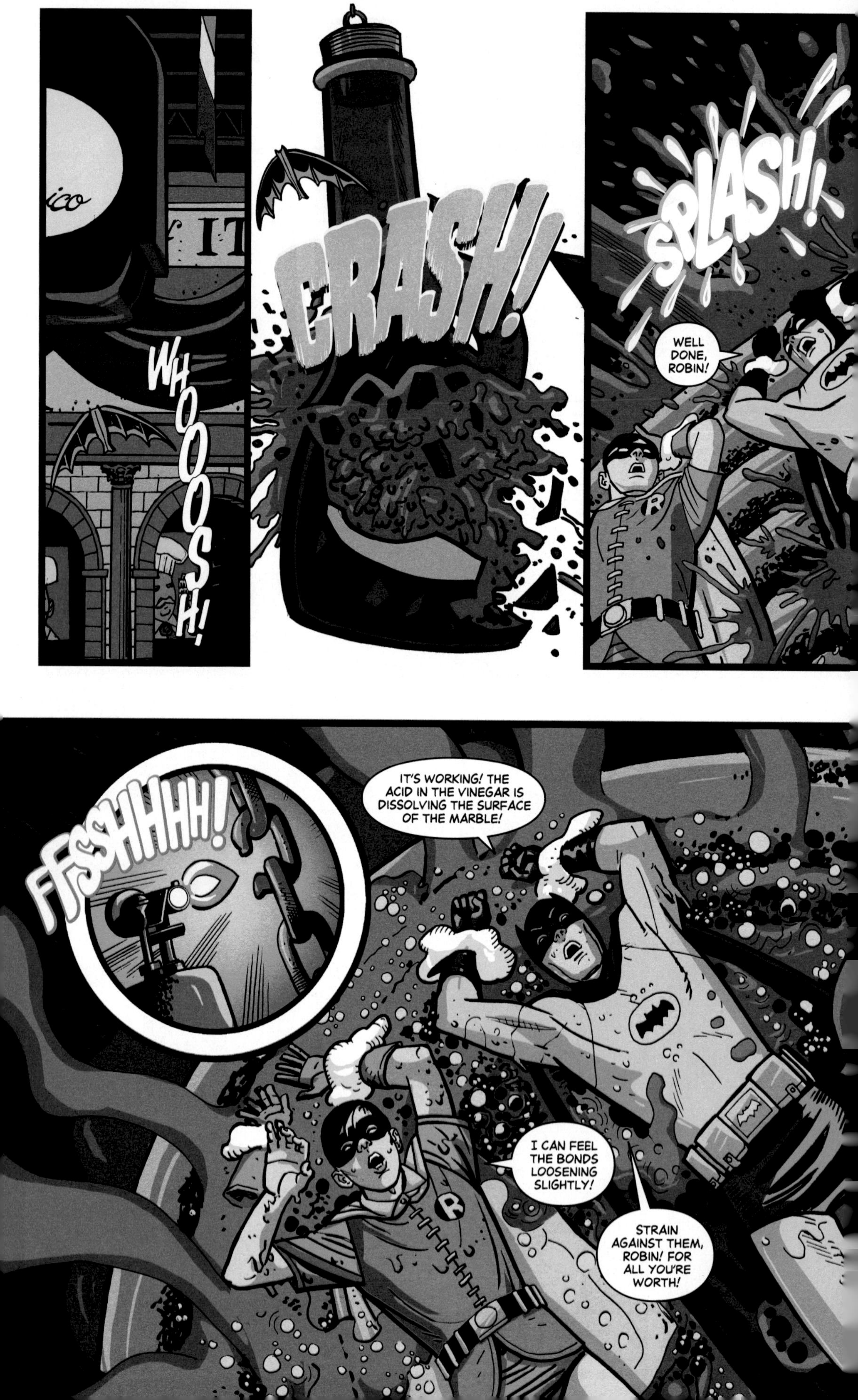
WHOOOOSH!
CRASH!
SPLASH!
WELL DONE, ROBIN!
FFSSHHHHH!
IT'S WORKING! THE ACID IN THE VINEGAR IS DISSOLVING THE SURFACE OF THE MARBLE!
I CAN FEEL THE BONDS LOOSENING SLIGHTLY!
STRAIN AGAINST THEM, ROBIN! FOR ALL YOU'RE WORTH!

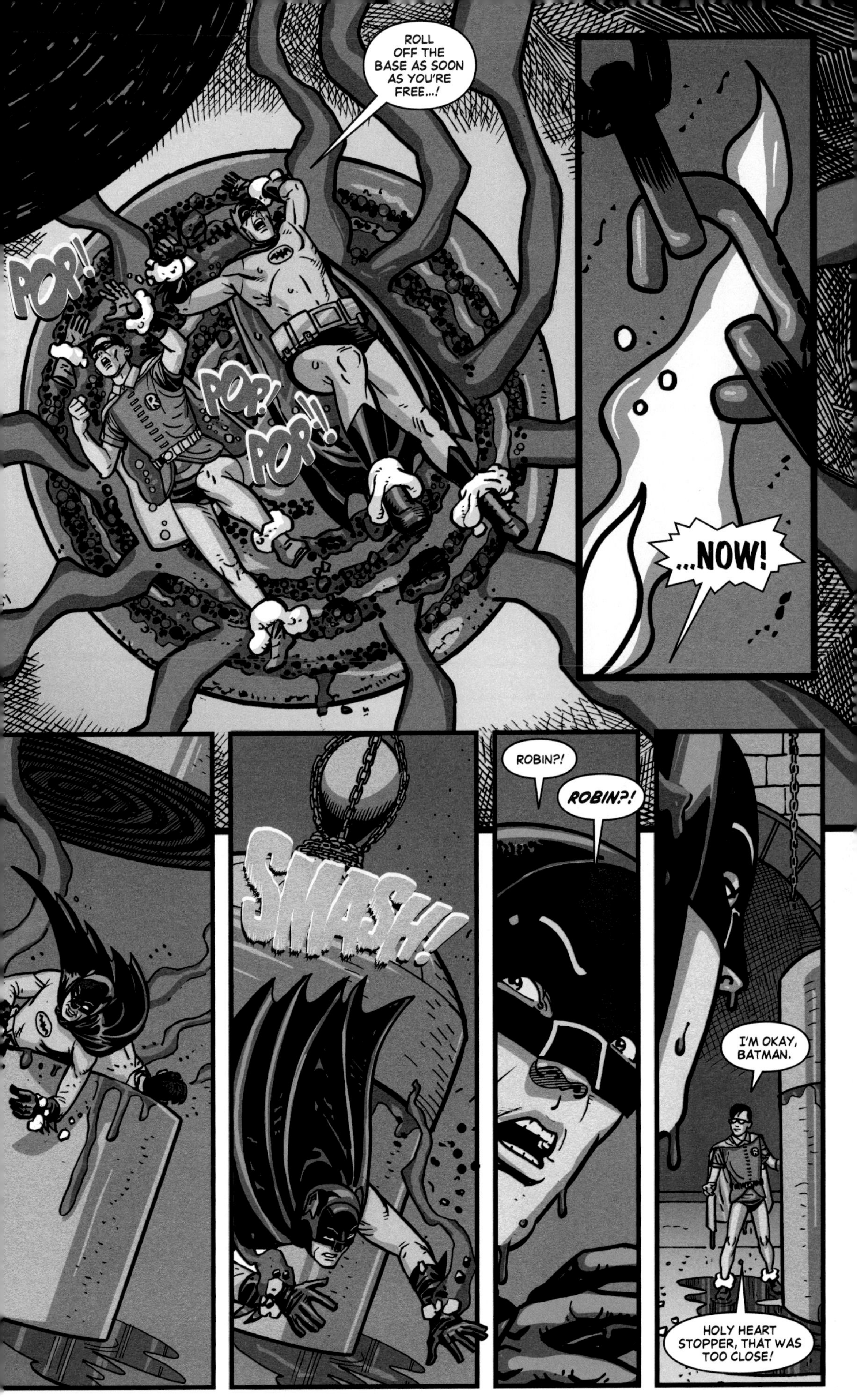
ROLL OFF THE BASE AS SOON AS YOU'RE FREE...!
POP!
POP!
POP!!
...NOW!
SMASH!
ROBIN?!
ROBIN?!
I'M OKAY, BATMAN.
HOLY HEART STOPPER, THAT WAS TOO CLOSE!

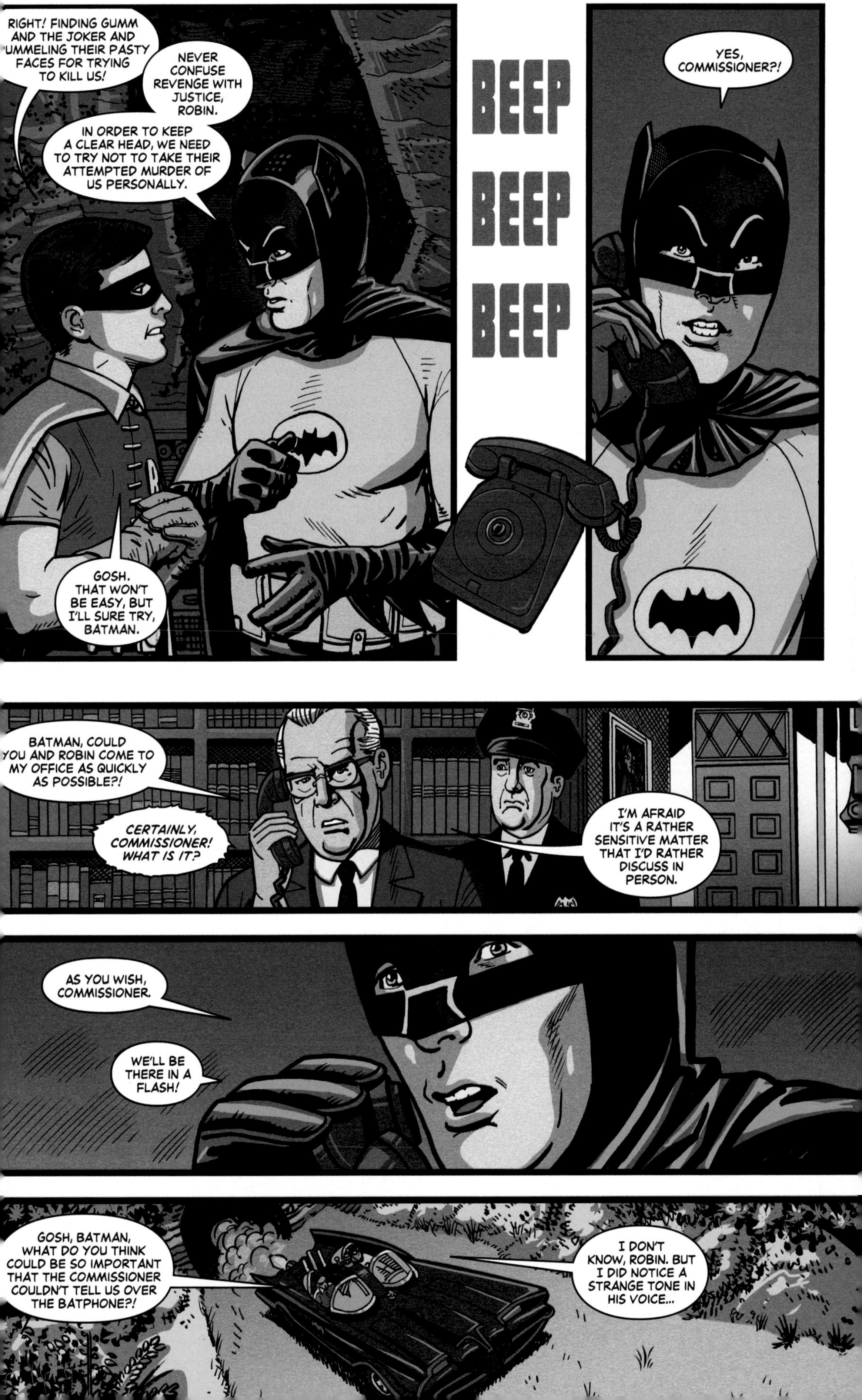

RIGHT! FINDING GUMM AND THE JOKER AND PUMMELING THEIR PASTY FACES FOR TRYING TO KILL US!
NEVER CONFUSE REVENGE WITH JUSTICE, ROBIN.
IN ORDER TO KEEP A CLEAR HEAD, WE NEED TO TRY NOT TO TAKE THEIR ATTEMPTED MURDER OF US PERSONALLY.
GOSH. THAT WON'T BE EASY, BUT I'LL SURE TRY, BATMAN.
BEEP
BEEP
BEEP
YES, COMMISSIONER?!
BATMAN, COULD YOU AND ROBIN COME TO MY OFFICE AS QUICKLY AS POSSIBLE?!
CERTAINLY, COMMISSIONER! WHAT IS IT?
I'M AFRAID IT'S A RATHER SENSITIVE MATTER THAT I'D RATHER DISCUSS IN PERSON.
AS YOU WISH, COMMISSIONER.
WE'LL BE THERE IN A FLASH!
GOSH, BATMAN, WHAT DO YOU THINK COULD BE SO IMPORTANT THAT THE COMMISSIONER COULDN'T TELL US OVER THE BATPHONE?!
I DON'T KNOW, ROBIN. BUT I DID NOTICE A STRANGE TONE IN HIS VOICE...

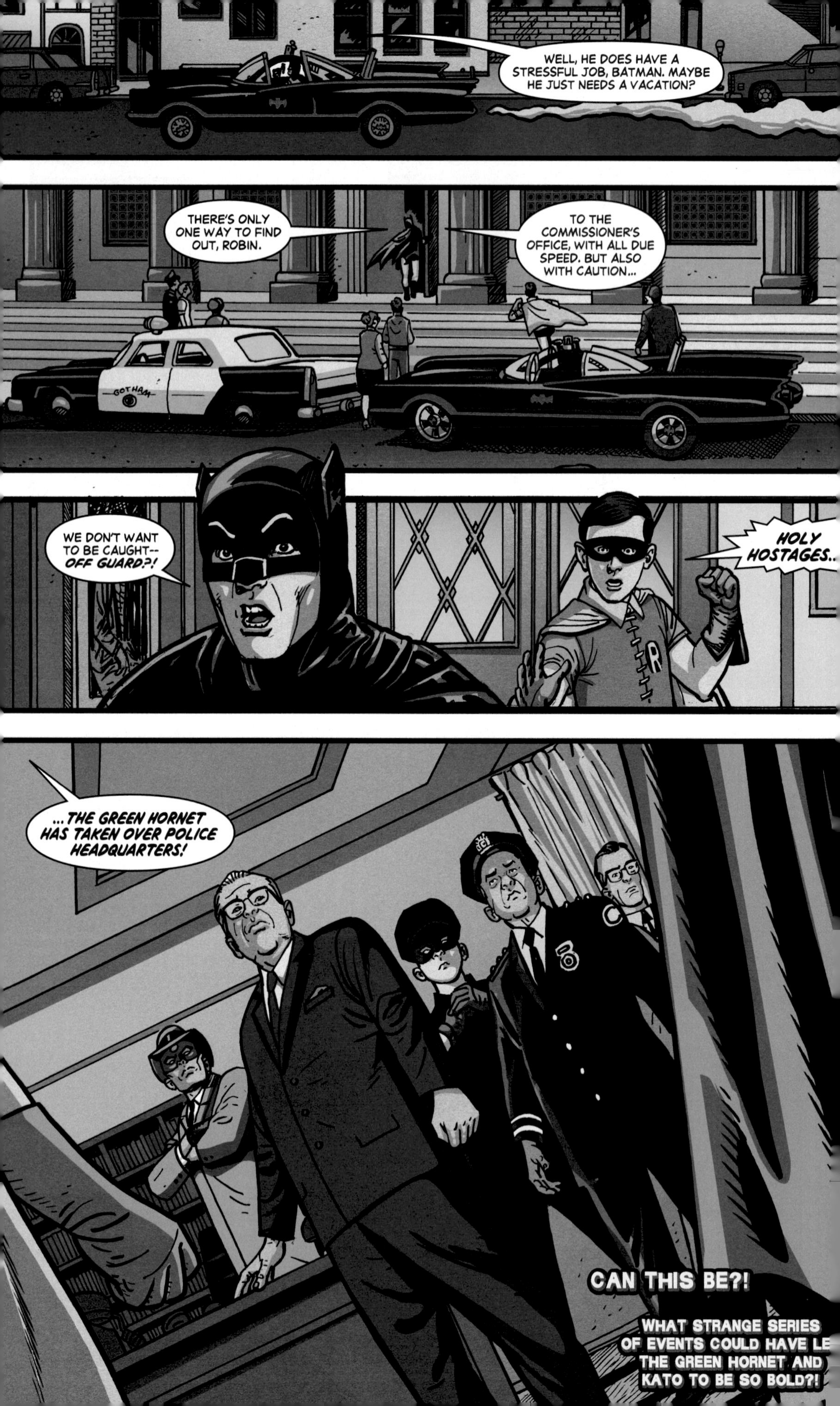
WELL, HE DOES HAVE A STRESSFUL JOB, BATMAN. MAYBE HE JUST NEEDS A VACATION?
THERE'S ONLY ONE WAY TO FIND OUT, ROBIN.
TO THE COMMISSIONER'S OFFICE, WITH ALL DUE SPEED. BUT ALSO WITH CAUTION...
GOTHAM
WE DON'T WANT TO BE CAUGHT-- OFF GUARD?!
HOLY HOSTAGES...
...THE GREEN HORNET HAS TAKEN OVER POLICE HEADQUARTERS!
CAN THIS BE?!
WHAT STRANGE SERIES OF EVENTS COULD HAVE LE THE GREEN HORNET AND KATO TO BE SO BOLD?!

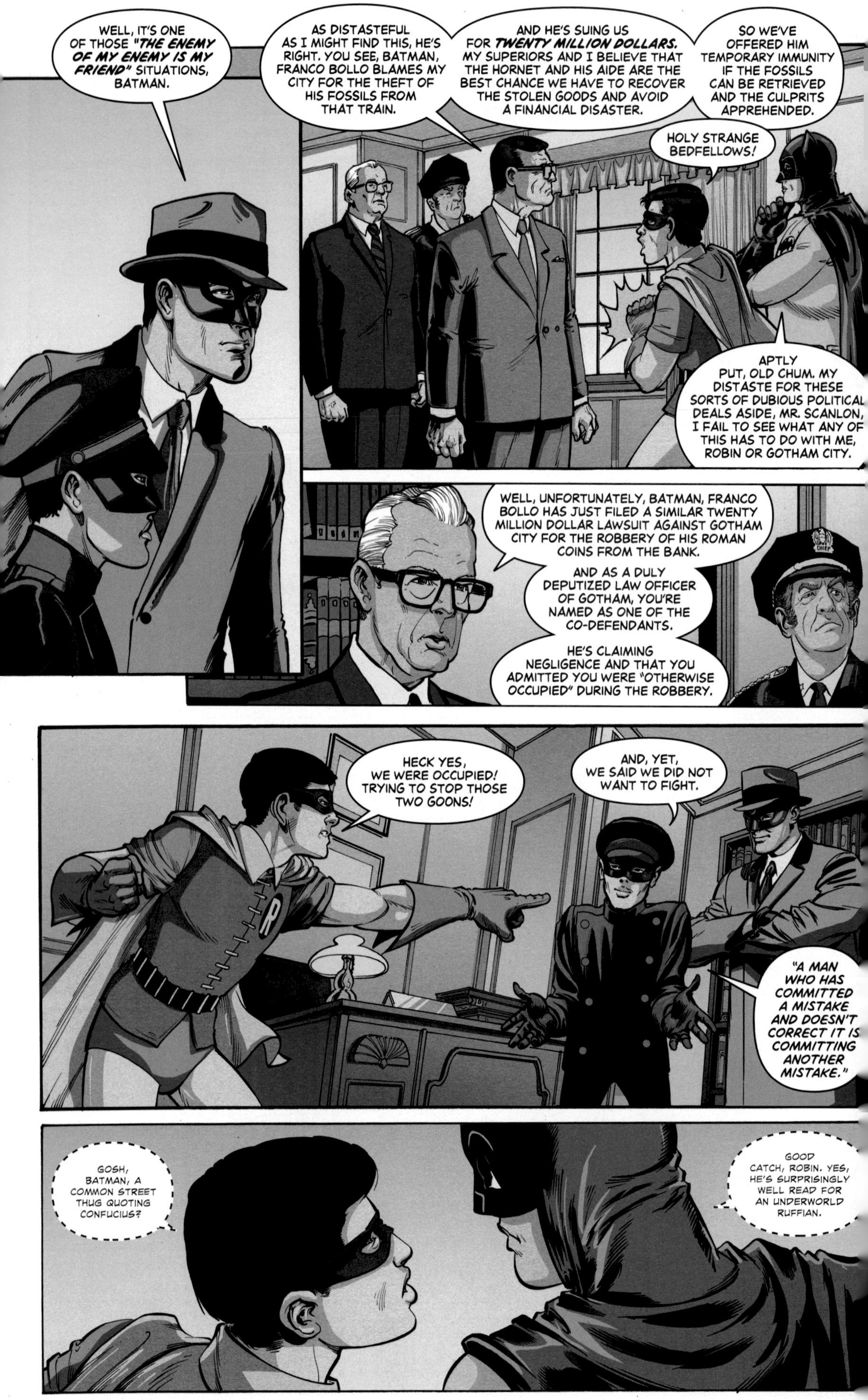
WELL, IT'S ONE OF THOSE "THE ENEMY OF MY ENEMY IS MY FRIEND" SITUATIONS, BATMAN.
AS DISTASTEFUL AS I MIGHT FIND THIS, HE'S RIGHT. YOU SEE, BATMAN, FRANCO BOLLO BLAMES MY CITY FOR THE THEFT OF HIS FOSSILS FROM THAT TRAIN.
AND HE'S SUING US FOR TWENTY MILLION DOLLARS. MY SUPERIORS AND I BELIEVE THAT THE HORNET AND HIS AIDE ARE THE BEST CHANCE WE HAVE TO RECOVER THE STOLEN GOODS AND AVOID A FINANCIAL DISASTER.
SO WE'VE OFFERED HIM TEMPORARY IMMUNITY IF THE FOSSILS CAN BE RETRIEVED AND THE CULPRITS APPREHENDED.
HOLY STRANGE BEDFELLOWS!
APTLY PUT, OLD CHUM. MY DISTASTE FOR THESE SORTS OF DUBIOUS POLITICAL DEALS ASIDE, MR. SCANLON, I FAIL TO SEE WHAT ANY OF THIS HAS TO DO WITH ME, ROBIN OR GOTHAM CITY.
WELL, UNFORTUNATELY, BATMAN, FRANCO BOLLO HAS JUST FILED A SIMILAR TWENTY MILLION DOLLAR LAWSUIT AGAINST GOTHAM CITY FOR THE ROBBERY OF HIS ROMAN COINS FROM THE BANK.
AND AS A DULY DEPUTIZED LAW OFFICER OF GOTHAM, YOU'RE NAMED AS ONE OF THE CO-DEFENDANTS.
HE'S CLAIMING NEGLIGENCE AND THAT YOU ADMITTED YOU WERE "OTHERWISE OCCUPIED" DURING THE ROBBERY.
CHIEF
HECK YES, WE WERE OCCUPIED! TRYING TO STOP THOSE TWO GOONS!
AND, YET, WE SAID WE DID NOT WANT TO FIGHT.
"A MAN WHO HAS COMMITTED A MISTAKE AND DOESN'T CORRECT IT IS COMMITTING ANOTHER MISTAKE."
GOSH, BATMAN, A COMMON STREET THUG QUOTING CONFUCIUS?
GOOD CATCH, ROBIN. YES, HE'S SURPRISINGLY WELL READ FOR AN UNDERWORLD RUFFIAN.

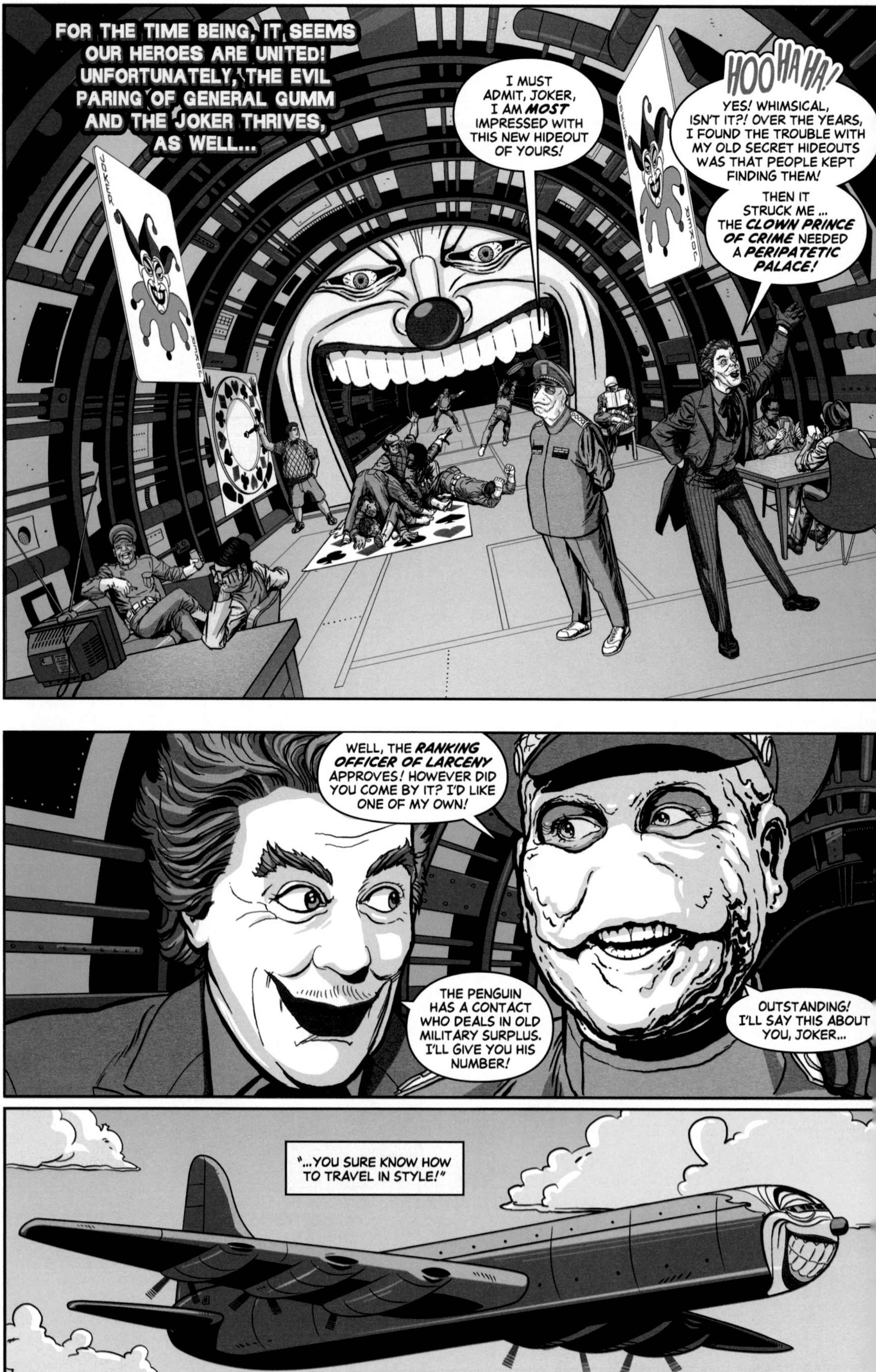

FOR THE TIME BEING, IT SEEMS OUR HEROES ARE UNITED! UNFORTUNATELY, THE EVIL PARING OF GENERAL GUMM AND THE JOKER THRIVES, AS WELL...
I MUST ADMIT, JOKER, I AM MOST IMPRESSED WITH THIS NEW HIDEOUT OF YOURS!
HOOHAHA!
YES! WHIMSICAL, ISN'T IT?! OVER THE YEARS, I FOUND THE TROUBLE WITH MY OLD SECRET HIDEOUTS WAS THAT PEOPLE KEPT FINDING THEM!
THEN IT STRUCK ME ... THE CLOWN PRINCE OF CRIME NEEDED A PERIPATETIC PALACE!
JOKER
WELL, THE RANKING OFFICER OF LARCENY APPROVES! HOWEVER DID YOU COME BY IT? I'D LIKE ONE OF MY OWN!
THE PENGUIN HAS A CONTACT WHO DEALS IN OLD MILITARY SURPLUS. I'LL GIVE YOU HIS NUMBER!
OUTSTANDING! I'LL SAY THIS ABOUT YOU, JOKER...
"...YOU SURE KNOW HOW TO TRAVEL IN STYLE!"

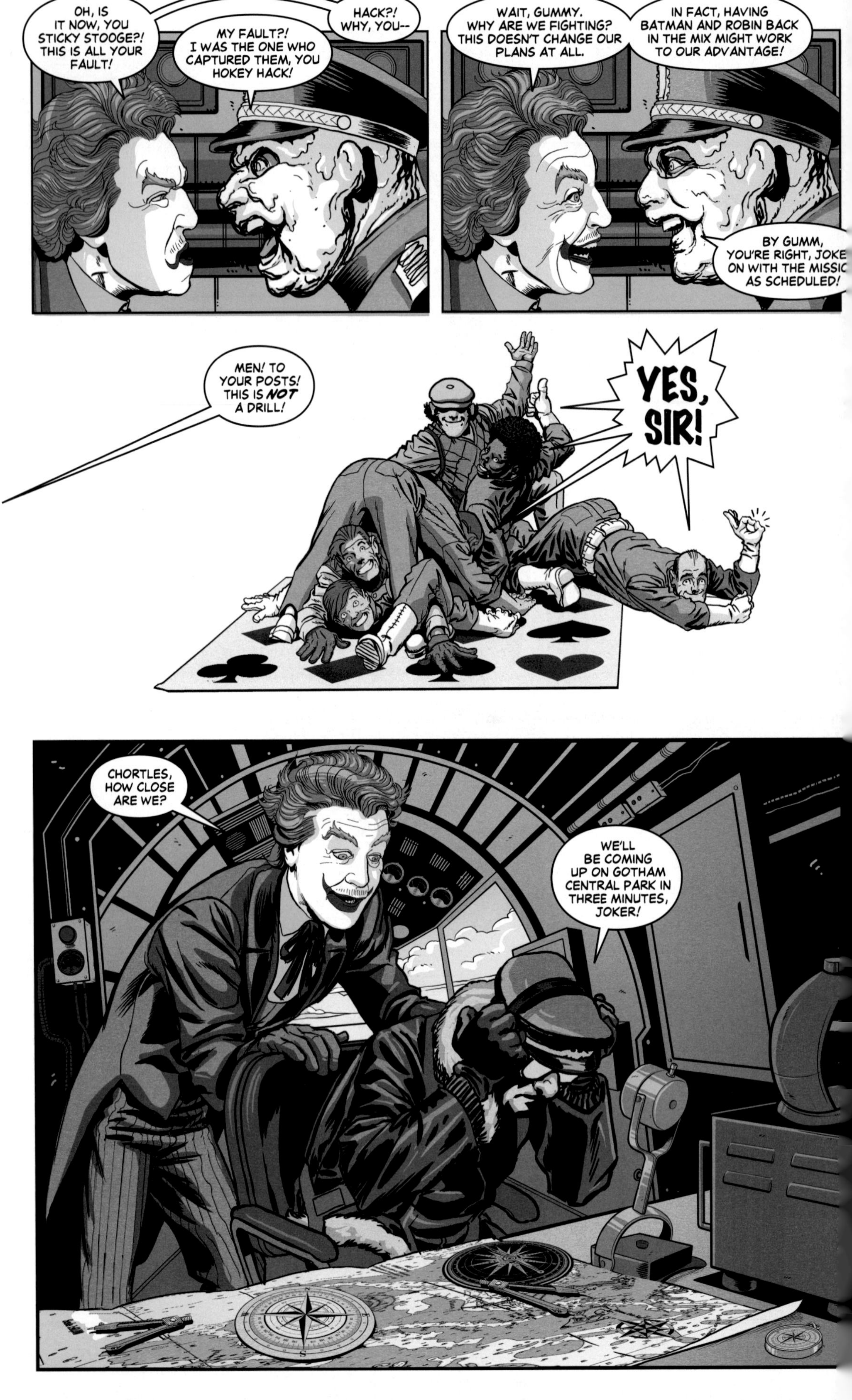
OH, IS IT NOW, YOU STICKY STOOGE?! THIS IS ALL YOUR FAULT!
MY FAULT?! I WAS THE ONE WHO CAPTURED THEM, YOU HOKEY HACK!
HACK?! WHY, YOU--
WAIT, GUMMY. WHY ARE WE FIGHTING? THIS DOESN'T CHANGE OUR PLANS AT ALL.
IN FACT, HAVING BATMAN AND ROBIN BACK IN THE MIX MIGHT WORK TO OUR ADVANTAGE!
BY GUMM, YOU'RE RIGHT, JOKE ON WITH THE MISSIC AS SCHEDULED!
MEN! TO YOUR POSTS! THIS IS NOT A DRILL!
YES, SIR!
CHORTLES, HOW CLOSE ARE WE?
WE'LL BE COMING UP ON GOTHAM CENTRAL PARK IN THREE MINUTES, JOKER!

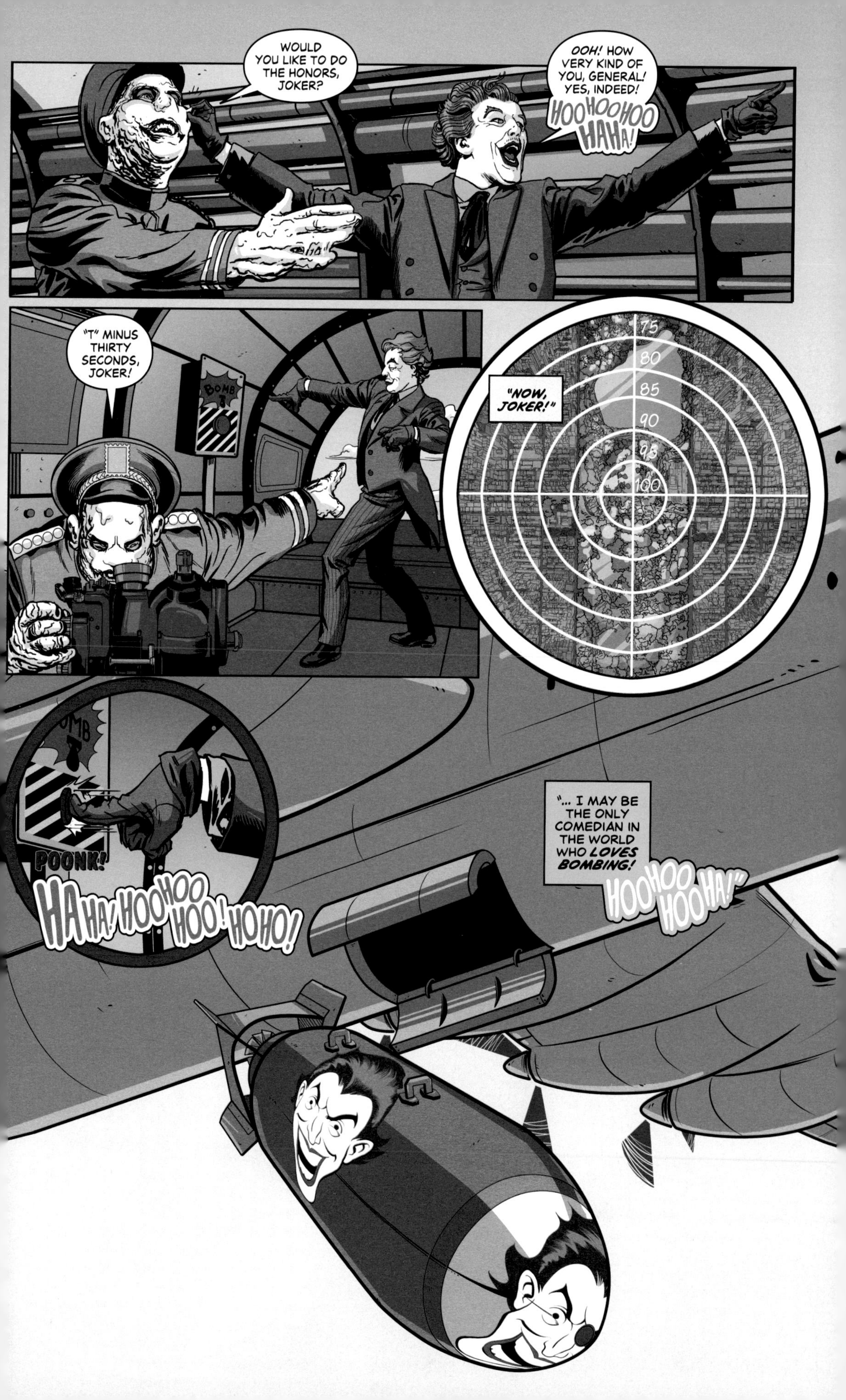
WOULD YOU LIKE TO DO THE HONORS, JOKER?
OOH! HOW VERY KIND OF YOU, GENERAL! YES, INDEED!
HOOHOOHOO HAHA!
"T" MINUS THIRTY SECONDS, JOKER!
BOMB
"NOW, JOKER!"
75
80
85
90
95
100
BOMB
POONK!
HAHA! HOOHOO HOO! HOHO!
"... I MAY BE THE ONLY COMEDIAN IN THE WORLD WHO LOVES BOMBING!
HOOHOO HOOHA!"

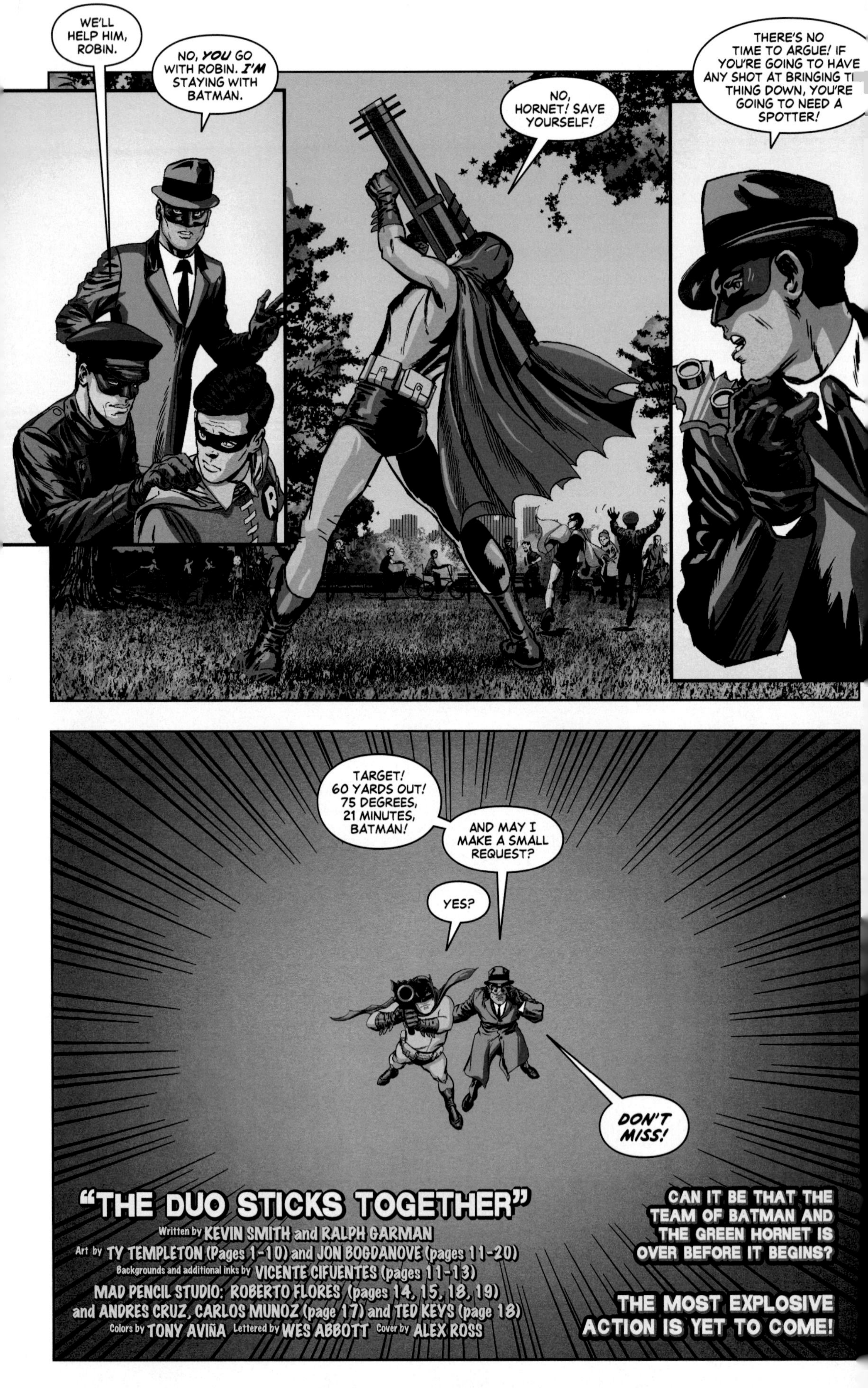
WE'LL HELP HIM, ROBIN.
NO, YOU GO WITH ROBIN. I'M STAYING WITH BATMAN.
NO, HORNET! SAVE YOURSELF!
THERE'S NO TIME TO ARGUE! IF YOU'RE GOING TO HAVE ANY SHOT AT BRINGING T THING DOWN, YOU'RE GOING TO NEED A SPOTTER!
TARGET! 60 YARDS OUT! 75 DEGREES, 21 MINUTES, BATMAN!
AND MAY I MAKE A SMALL REQUEST?
YES?
DON'T MISS!
"THE DUO STICKS TOGETHER"
Written by KEVIN SMITH and RALPH GARMAN
Art by TY TEMPLETON (Pages 1-10) and JON BOGDANOVE (pages 11-20)
Backgrounds and additional inks by VICENTE CIFUENTES (pages 11-13)
MAD PENCIL STUDIO: ROBERTO FLORES (pages 14, 15, 18, 19)
and ANDRES CRUZ, CARLOS MUNOZ (page 17) and TED KEYS (page 18)
Colors by TONY AVIÑA Lettered by WES ABBOTT Cover by ALEX ROSS
CAN IT BE THAT THE TEAM OF BATMAN AND THE GREEN HORNET IS OVER BEFORE IT BEGINS?
THE MOST EXPLOSIVE ACTION IS YET TO COME!

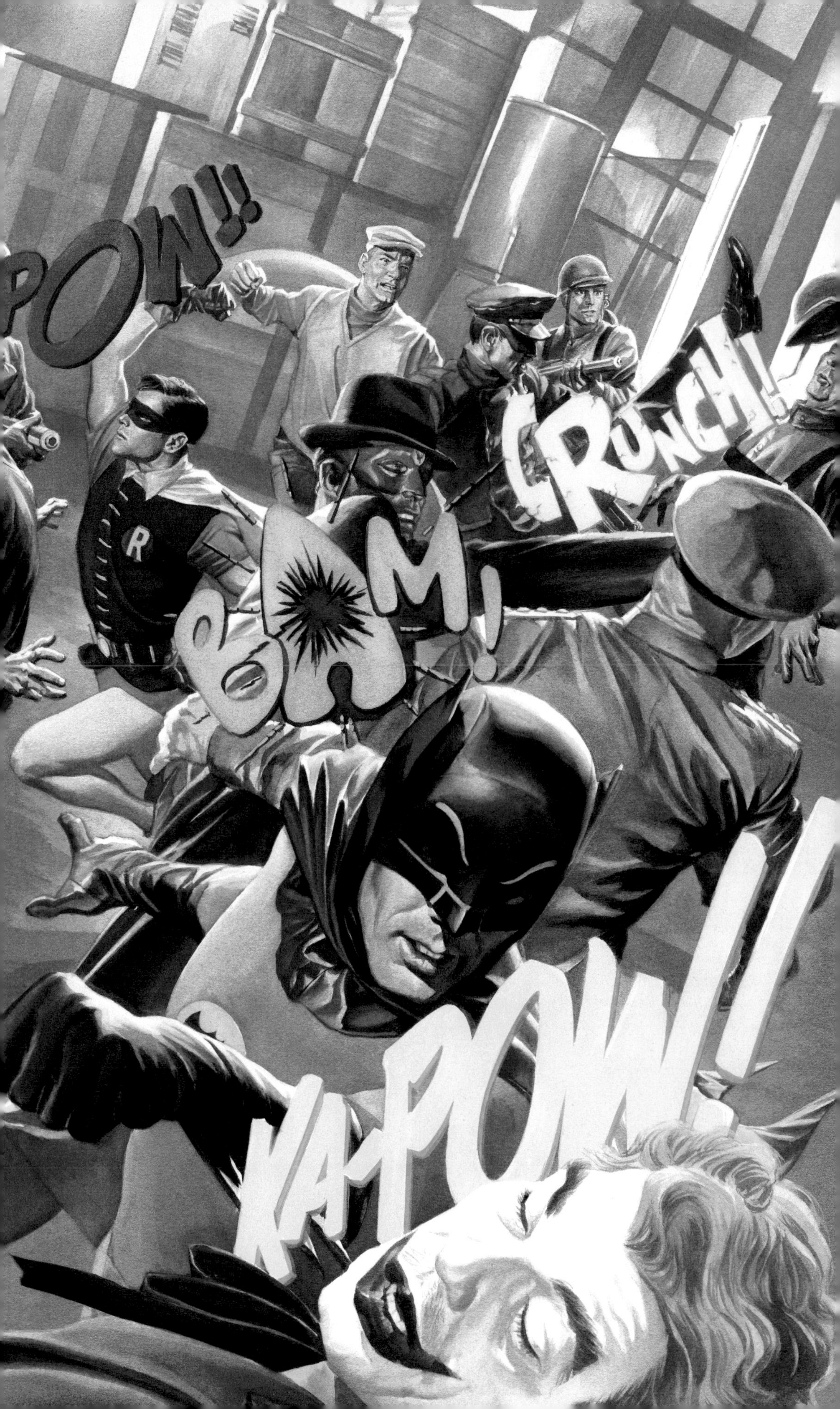
POW!!
BAM!
CRUNCH!
KA-POW!!

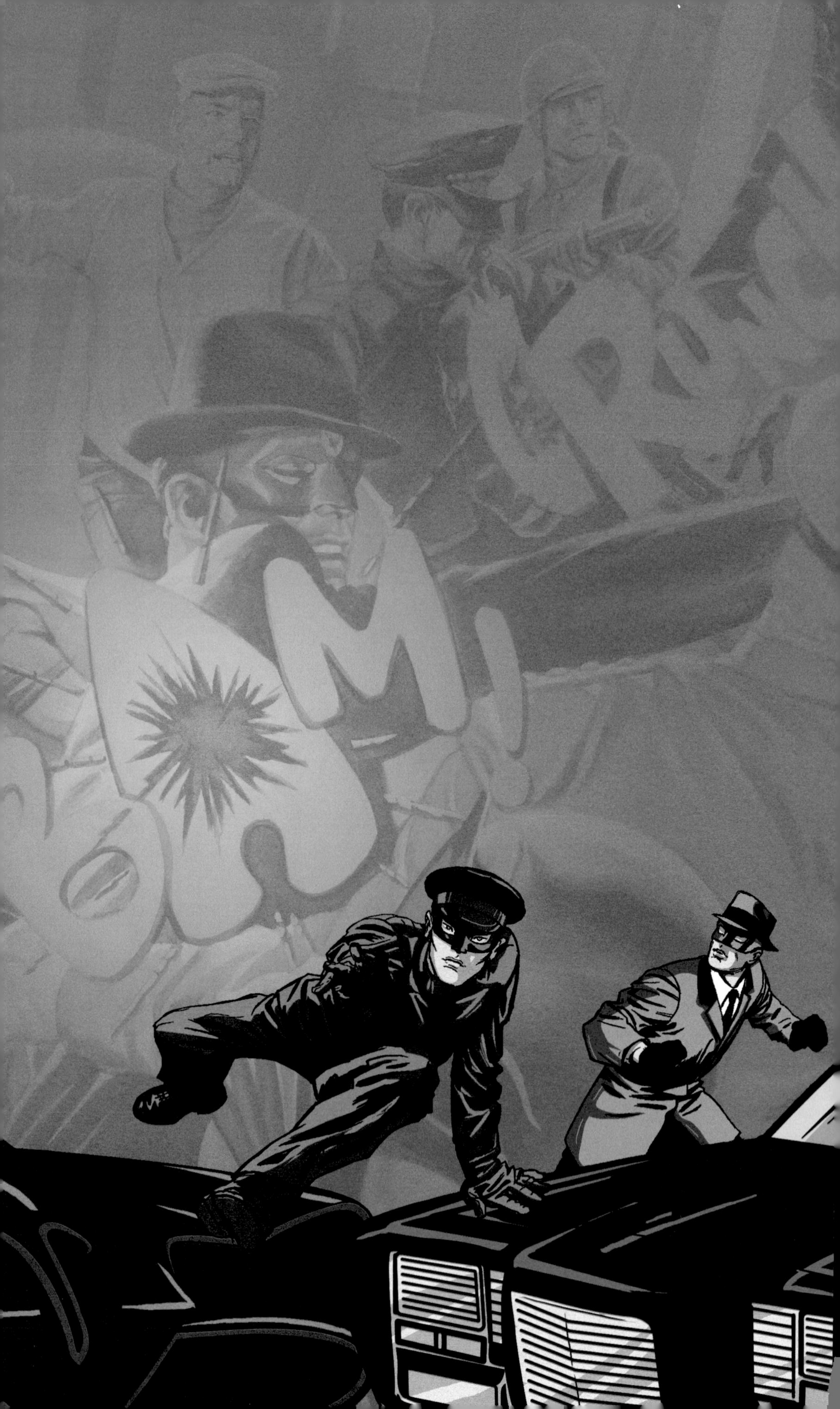

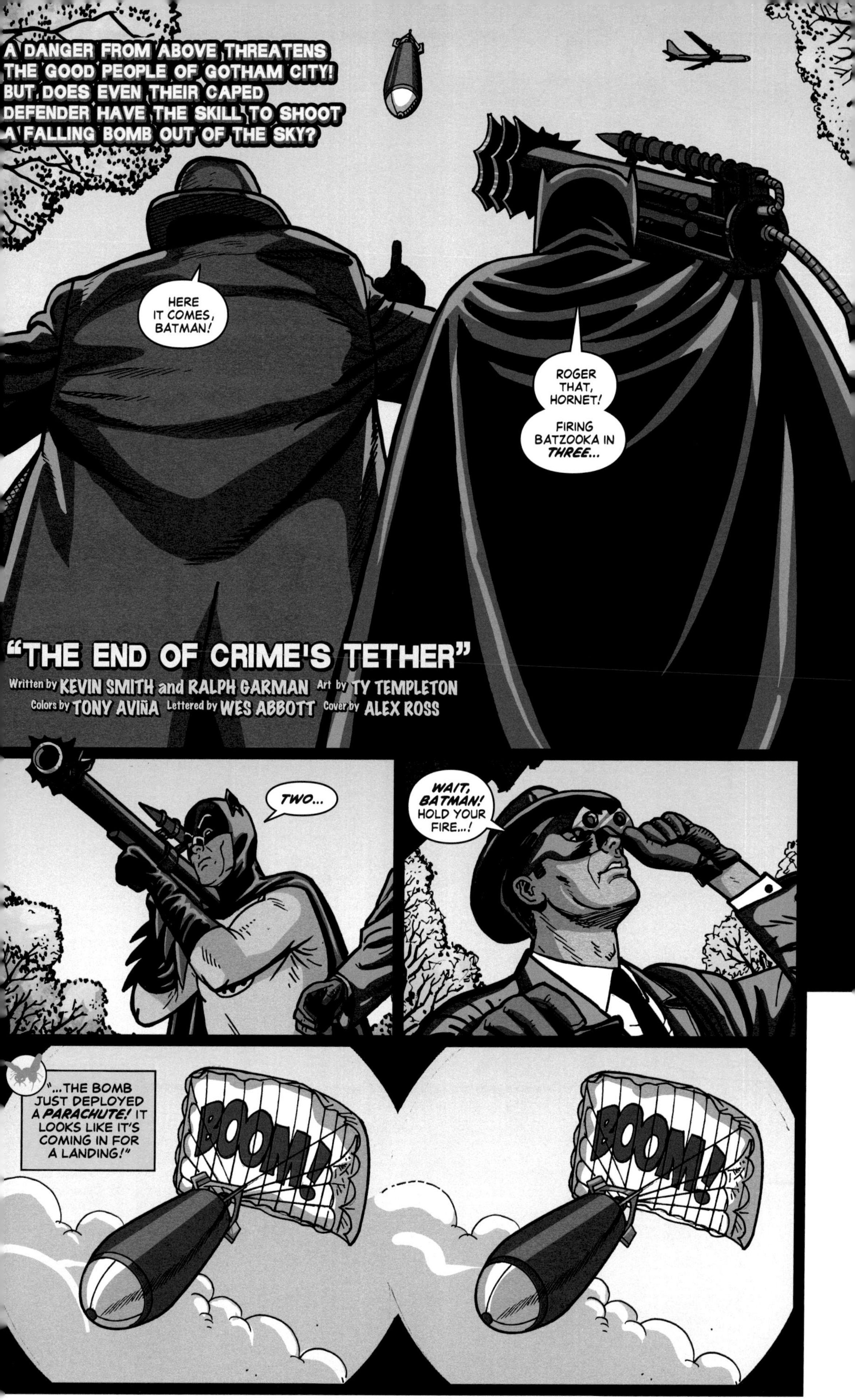
A DANGER FROM ABOVE THREATENS THE GOOD PEOPLE OF GOTHAM CITY! BUT DOES EVEN THEIR CAPED DEFENDER HAVE THE SKILL TO SHOOT A FALLING BOMB OUT OF THE SKY?
HERE IT COMES, BATMAN!
ROGER THAT, HORNET!
FIRING BATZOOKA IN THREE...
"THE END OF CRIME'S TETHER"
Written by KEVIN SMITH and RALPH GARMAN Art by TY TEMPLETON
Colors by TONY AVIÑA Lettered by WES ABBOTT Cover by ALEX ROSS
TWO...
WAIT, BATMAN! HOLD YOUR FIRE...!
"...THE BOMB JUST DEPLOYED A PARACHUTE! IT LOOKS LIKE IT'S COMING IN FOR A LANDING!"
BOOM!
BOOM!

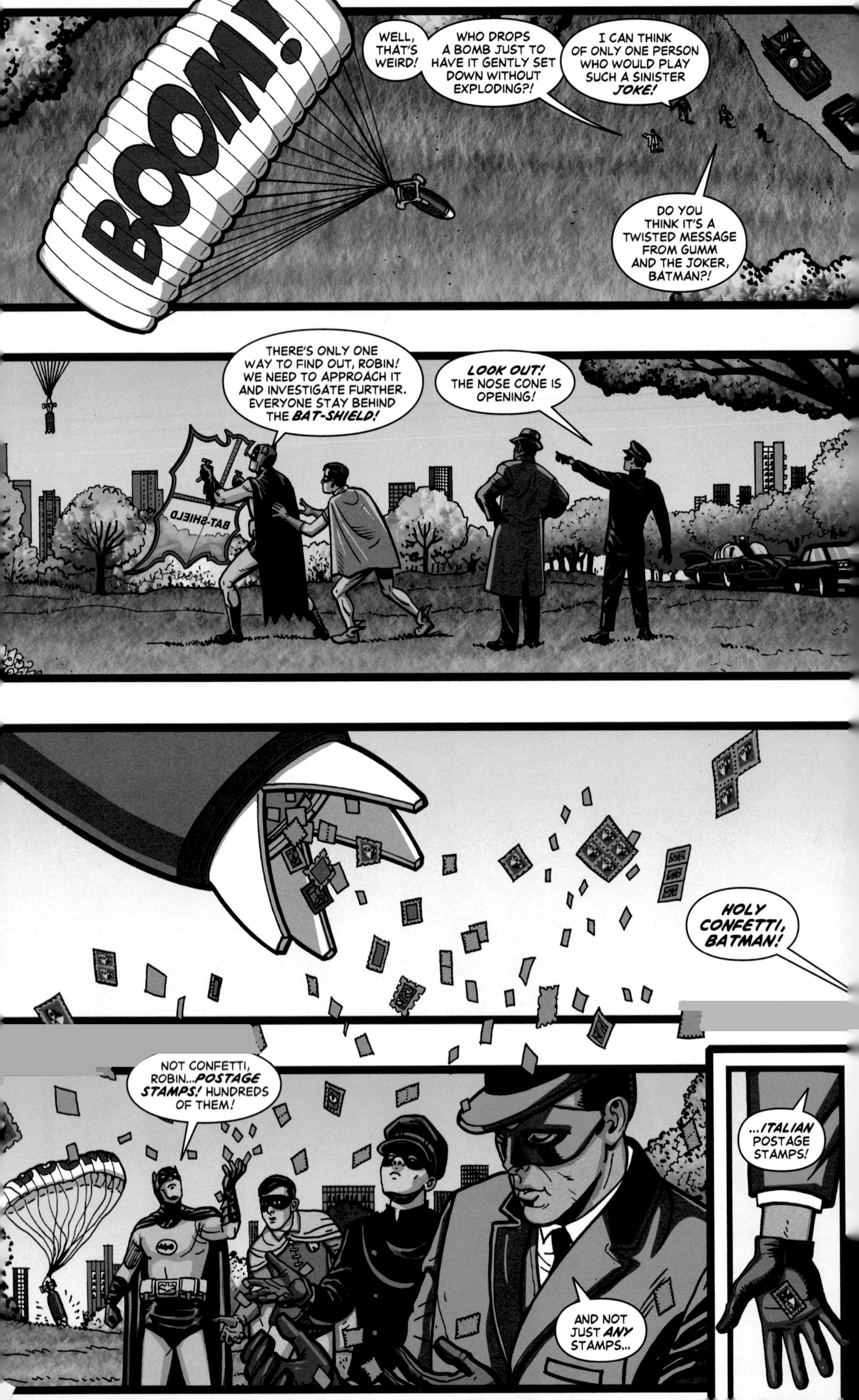
BOOM!
WELL, THAT'S WEIRD!
WHO DROPS A BOMB JUST TO HAVE IT GENTLY SET DOWN WITHOUT EXPLODING?!
I CAN THINK OF ONLY ONE PERSON WHO WOULD PLAY SUCH A SINISTER *JOKE!*
DO YOU THINK IT'S A TWISTED MESSAGE FROM GUMM AND THE JOKER, BATMAN?!
THERE'S ONLY ONE WAY TO FIND OUT, ROBIN! WE NEED TO APPROACH IT AND INVESTIGATE FURTHER. EVERYONE STAY BEHIND THE *BAT-SHIELD!*
LOOK OUT! THE NOSE CONE IS OPENING!
BAT-SHIELD
HOLY CONFETTI, BATMAN!
NOT CONFETTI, ROBIN...*POSTAGE STAMPS!* HUNDREDS OF THEM!
AND NOT JUST *ANY* STAMPS...
...*ITALIAN* POSTAGE STAMPS!

NOTHING REMARKABLE ABOUT THESE AT FIRST GLANCE.

OF COURSE, WE'LL KNOW MORE WHEN WE FURTHER EXAMINE A SAMPLE IN THE BATCAVE!

THE BATCAVE?!

YEAH. JUST WAIT UNTIL YOU SEE THIS PLACE.

OF COURSE, THEY DO HAVE TO KNOCK US OUT TO TAKE US THERE.

OF COURSE. WELL THEN, I GUESS I'LL SEE YOU WHEN WE WAKE UP.

A SHORT TIME LATER, IN THE SECRET BATCAVE, A REVIVED GREEN HORNET AND KATO JOIN THE CAPED CRUSADERS AS THEY PUT THEIR NEW CLUES THROUGH EVERY IMAGINABLE SCIENTIFIC TEST!

WELL, THAT'S IT. EVEN THE BAT-SPECTROGRAPHIC ANALYZER SHOWS THESE STAMPS ARE NOTHING MORE THAN INK, PAPER AND ORDINARY ADHESIVE.

GOSH, BATMAN, MAYBE THE CLUE ISN'T IN THE STAMPS THEMSELVES.

MAYBE THEY SYMBOLIZE SOMETHING ELSE?

THAT'S GOOD THINKING, ROBIN. LET'S CONSIDER THE RECURRING THEMES OF THIS CAPER SO FAR.

FOR EXAMPLE, THERE'S GUMM'S SUPER GLUE...

WELL, THERE'S THE *STAMPS,* OF COURSE. STAMPED FOSSILS, STAMPED COINS, PASTA STAMPS...

AND ITALY. ROMAN GODS, THE ITALIAN PAVILION...

...AND *ONE* ITALIAN IN PARTICULAR, *FRANCO BOLLO!*

BAT-SPECTROGRAPHIC ANALYZE

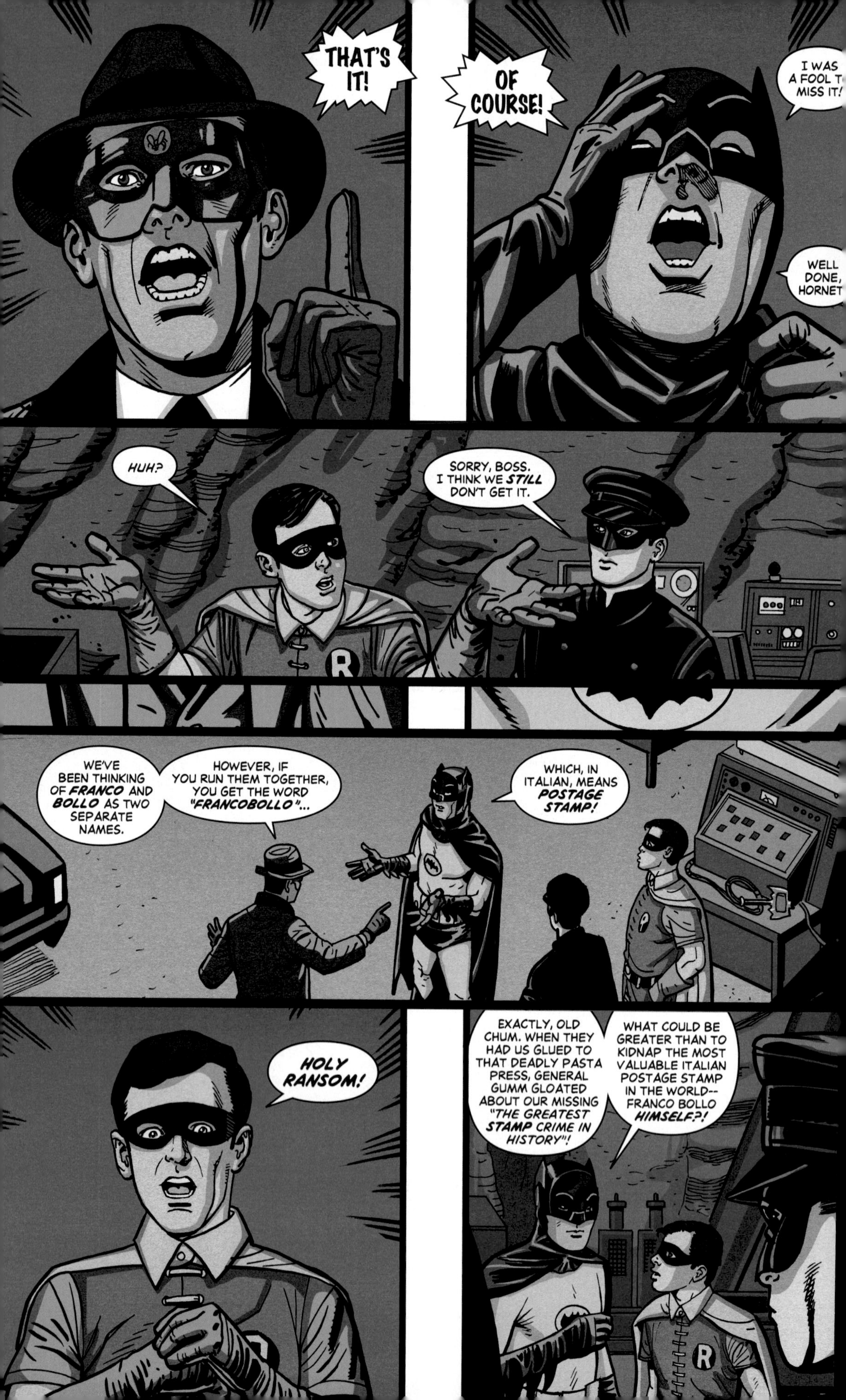

THAT'S IT!
OF COURSE!
I WAS A FOOL TO MISS IT!
WELL DONE, HORNET
HUH?
SORRY, BOSS. I THINK WE STILL DON'T GET IT.
WE'VE BEEN THINKING OF FRANCO AND BOLLO AS TWO SEPARATE NAMES.
HOWEVER, IF YOU RUN THEM TOGETHER, YOU GET THE WORD "FRANCOBOLLO"...
WHICH, IN ITALIAN, MEANS POSTAGE STAMP!
HOLY RANSOM!
EXACTLY, OLD CHUM. WHEN THEY HAD US GLUED TO THAT DEADLY PASTA PRESS, GENERAL GUMM GLOATED ABOUT OUR MISSING "THE GREATEST STAMP CRIME IN HISTORY"!
WHAT COULD BE GREATER THAN TO KIDNAP THE MOST VALUABLE ITALIAN POSTAGE STAMP IN THE WORLD-- FRANCO BOLLO HIMSELF?!

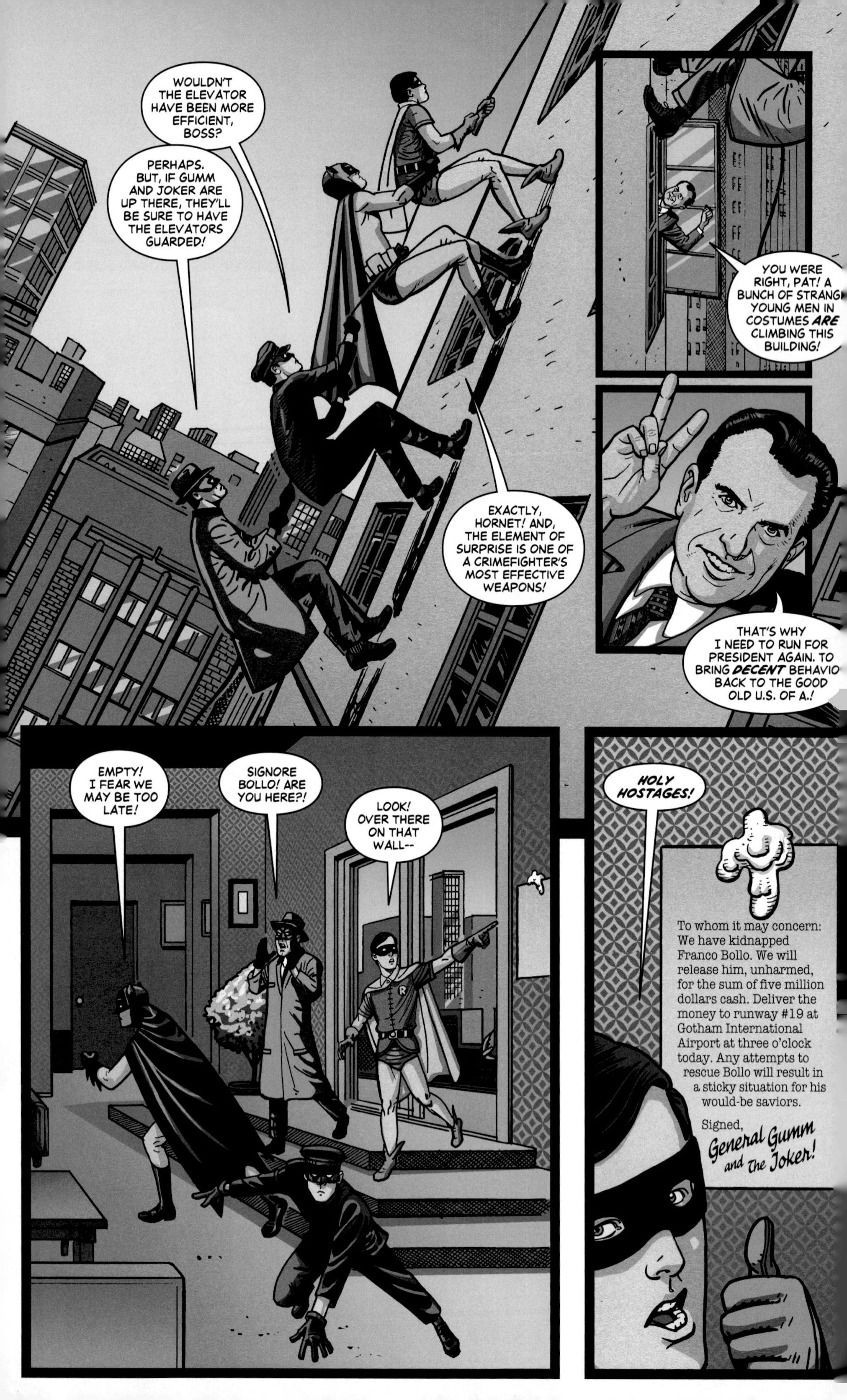

WOULDN'T THE ELEVATOR HAVE BEEN MORE EFFICIENT, BOSS?
PERHAPS. BUT, IF GUMM AND JOKER ARE UP THERE, THEY'LL BE SURE TO HAVE THE ELEVATORS GUARDED!
EXACTLY, HORNET! AND, THE ELEMENT OF SURPRISE IS ONE OF A CRIMEFIGHTER'S MOST EFFECTIVE WEAPONS!
YOU WERE RIGHT, PAT! A BUNCH OF STRANG YOUNG MEN IN COSTUMES *ARE* CLIMBING THIS BUILDING!
THAT'S WHY I NEED TO RUN FOR PRESIDENT AGAIN. TO BRING *DECENT* BEHAVIO BACK TO THE GOOD OLD U.S. OF A.!
EMPTY! I FEAR WE MAY BE TOO LATE!
SIGNORE BOLLO! ARE YOU HERE?!
LOOK! OVER THERE ON THAT WALL--
HOLY HOSTAGES!
To whom it may concern: We have kidnapped Franco Bollo. We will release him, unharmed, for the sum of five million dollars cash. Deliver the money to runway #19 at Gotham International Airport at three o'clock today. Any attempts to rescue Bollo will result in a sticky situation for his would-be saviors.
Signed,
General Gumm and The Joker!

RRRRRRRRGHHHHHHHHHWRRRRRRRRGGG

OOH, I JUST WISH I COULD GET ME MITTS ON THEM!

AND I WISH THE CAPED CRUSADERS WERE HERE!

WHEN WE SPOKE ON THE BAT-PHONE, ROBIN SEEMED TO THINK BATMAN HAD A WAY TO CIRCUMVENT THIS SYRUPY SNARE.

NE DO NOT CROS

AND IT LOOKS LIKE HE DOES BEGORRAH!

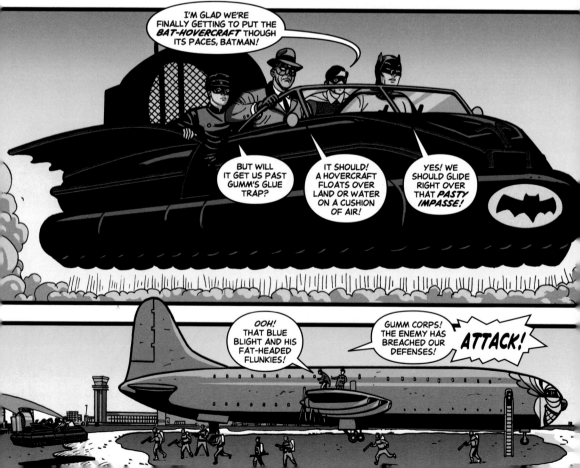

I'M GLAD WE'RE FINALLY GETTING TO PUT THE *BAT-HOVERCRAFT* THOUGH ITS PACES, BATMAN!

BUT WILL IT GET US PAST GUMM'S GLUE TRAP?

IT SHOULD! A HOVERCRAFT FLOATS OVER LAND OR WATER ON A CUSHION OF AIR!

YES! WE SHOULD GLIDE RIGHT OVER THAT *PASTY IMPASSE!*

OOH! THAT BLUE BLIGHT AND HIS FAT-HEADED FLUNKIES!

GUMM CORPS! THE ENEMY HAS BREACHED OUR DEFENSES!

ATTACK!

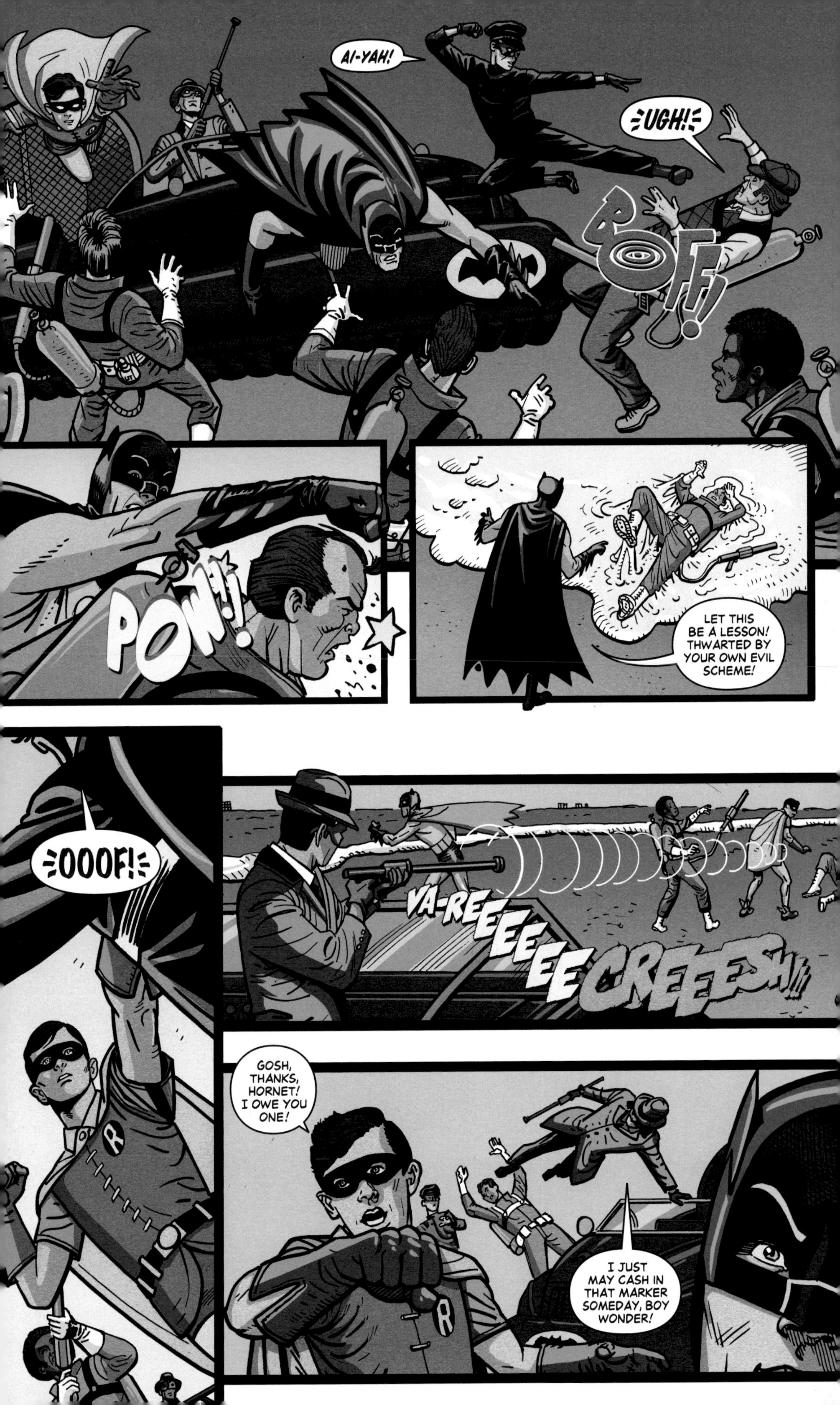
AI-YAH!
UGH!
BOFF!
POW!!
LET THIS BE A LESSON! THWARTED BY YOUR OWN EVIL SCHEME!
OOOF!
VA-REEEEEEE CREEESH!!
GOSH, THANKS, HORNET! I OWE YOU ONE!
I JUST MAY CASH IN THAT MARKER SOMEDAY, BOY WONDER!

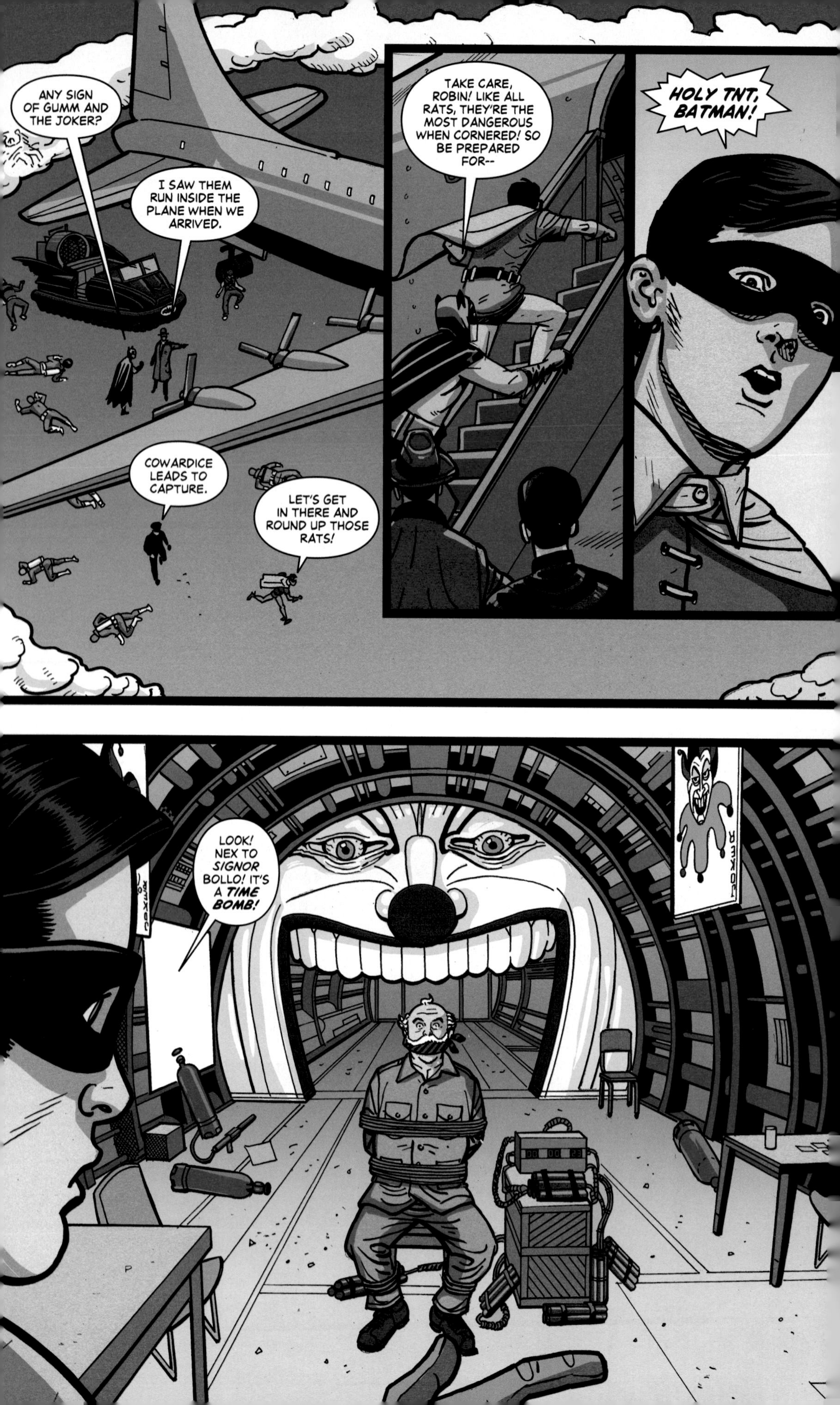
ANY SIGN OF GUMM AND THE JOKER?
I SAW THEM RUN INSIDE THE PLANE WHEN WE ARRIVED.
COWARDICE LEADS TO CAPTURE.
LET'S GET IN THERE AND ROUND UP THOSE RATS!
TAKE CARE, ROBIN! LIKE ALL RATS, THEY'RE THE MOST DANGEROUS WHEN CORNERED! SO BE PREPARED FOR--
HOLY TNT, BATMAN!
LOOK! NEX TO *SIGNOR* BOLLO! IT'S A ***TIME BOMB!***

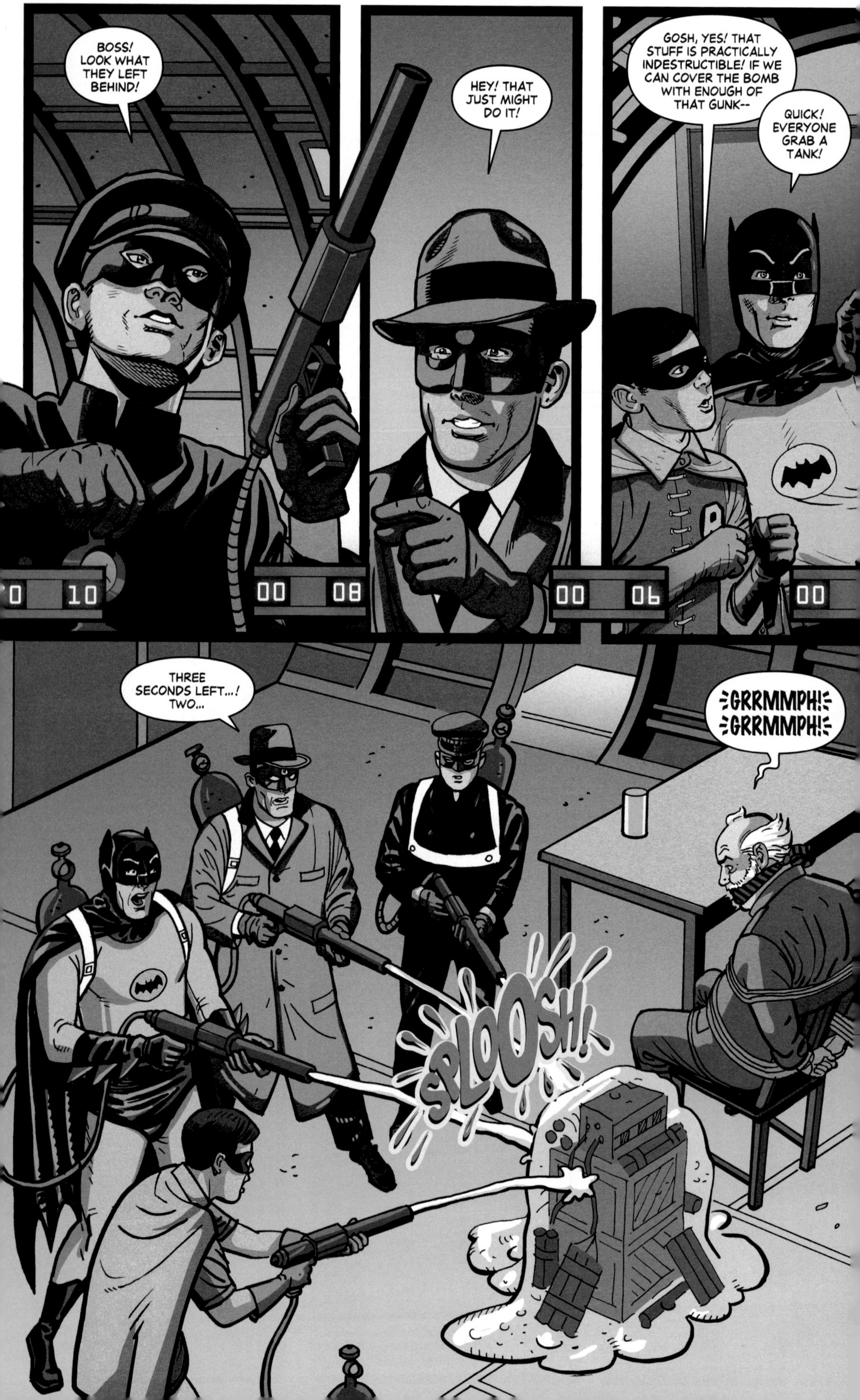
BOSS! LOOK WHAT THEY LEFT BEHIND!
0 10
HEY! THAT JUST MIGHT DO IT!
00 08
GOSH, YES! THAT STUFF IS PRACTICALLY INDESTRUCTIBLE! IF WE CAN COVER THE BOMB WITH ENOUGH OF THAT GUNK--
QUICK! EVERYONE GRAB A TANK!
00 06
00
THREE SECONDS LEFT...! TWO...
GRRMMPH! GRRMMPH!
SPLOOSH!

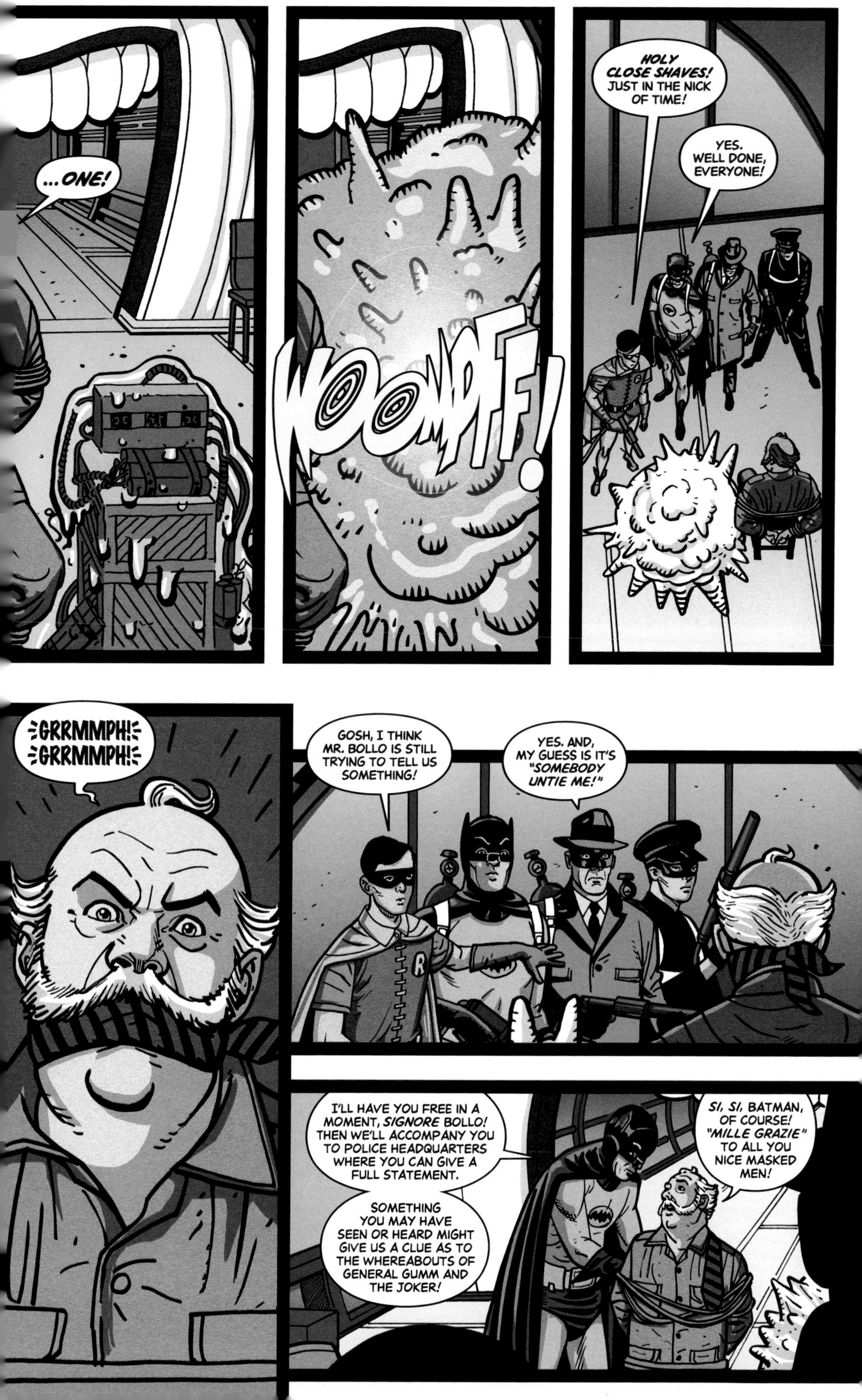

...ONE!
WOOMPFF!
HOLY CLOSE SHAVES! JUST IN THE NICK OF TIME!
YES. WELL DONE, EVERYONE!
GRRMMPH! GRRMMPH!
GOSH, I THINK MR. BOLLO IS STILL TRYING TO TELL US SOMETHING!
YES. AND, MY GUESS IS IT'S "SOMEBODY UNTIE ME!"
I'LL HAVE YOU FREE IN A MOMENT, SIGNORE BOLLO! THEN WE'LL ACCOMPANY YOU TO POLICE HEADQUARTERS WHERE YOU CAN GIVE A FULL STATEMENT.
SOMETHING YOU MAY HAVE SEEN OR HEARD MIGHT GIVE US A CLUE AS TO THE WHEREABOUTS OF GENERAL GUMM AND THE JOKER!
SI, SI, BATMAN, OF COURSE! "MILLE GRAZIE" TO ALL YOU NICE MASKED MEN!

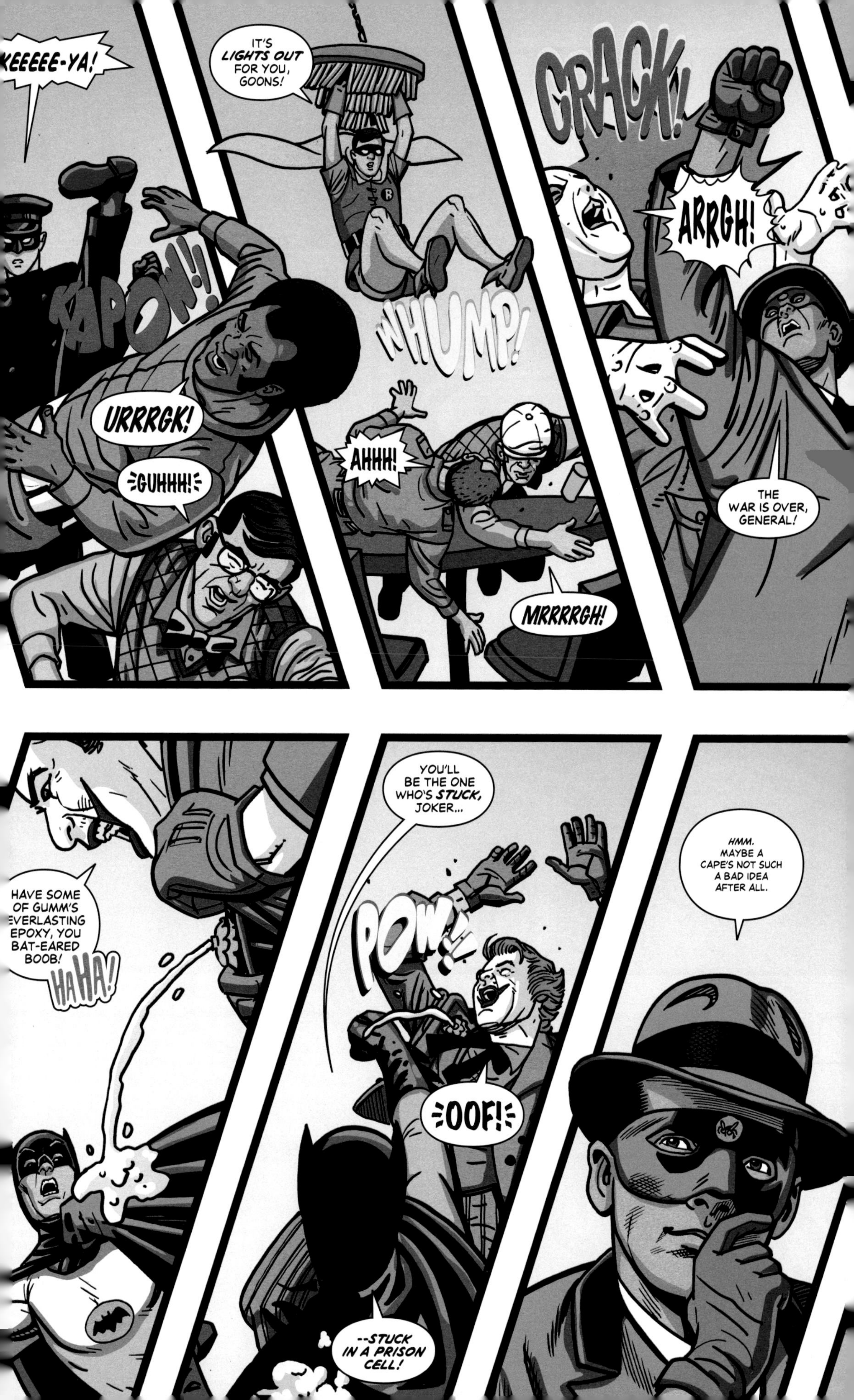
KEEEEE-YA!
KAPOW!!
URRRGK!
GUHHH!
IT'S LIGHTS OUT FOR YOU, GOONS!
WHUMP!
AHHH!
MRRRRGH!
CRACK!
ARRGH!
THE WAR IS OVER, GENERAL!
HAVE SOME OF GUMM'S EVERLASTING EPOXY, YOU BAT-EARED BOOB!
HAHA!
YOU'LL BE THE ONE WHO'S STUCK, JOKER...
POW!
OOF!
--STUCK IN A PRISON CELL!
HMM. MAYBE A CAPE'S NOT SUCH A BAD IDEA AFTER ALL.

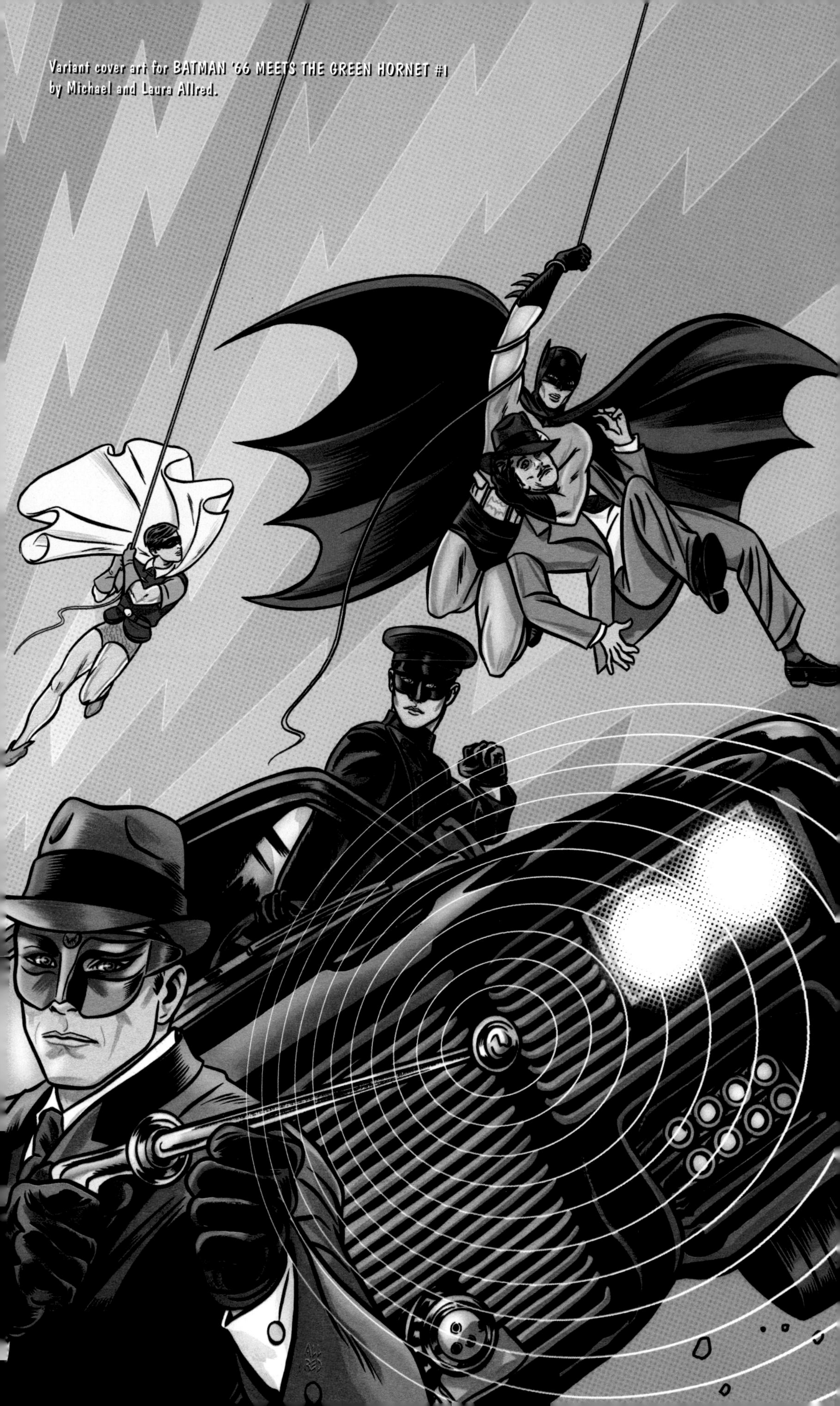

Variant cover art for BATMAN '66 MEETS THE GREEN HORNET #1 by Michael and Laura Allred.

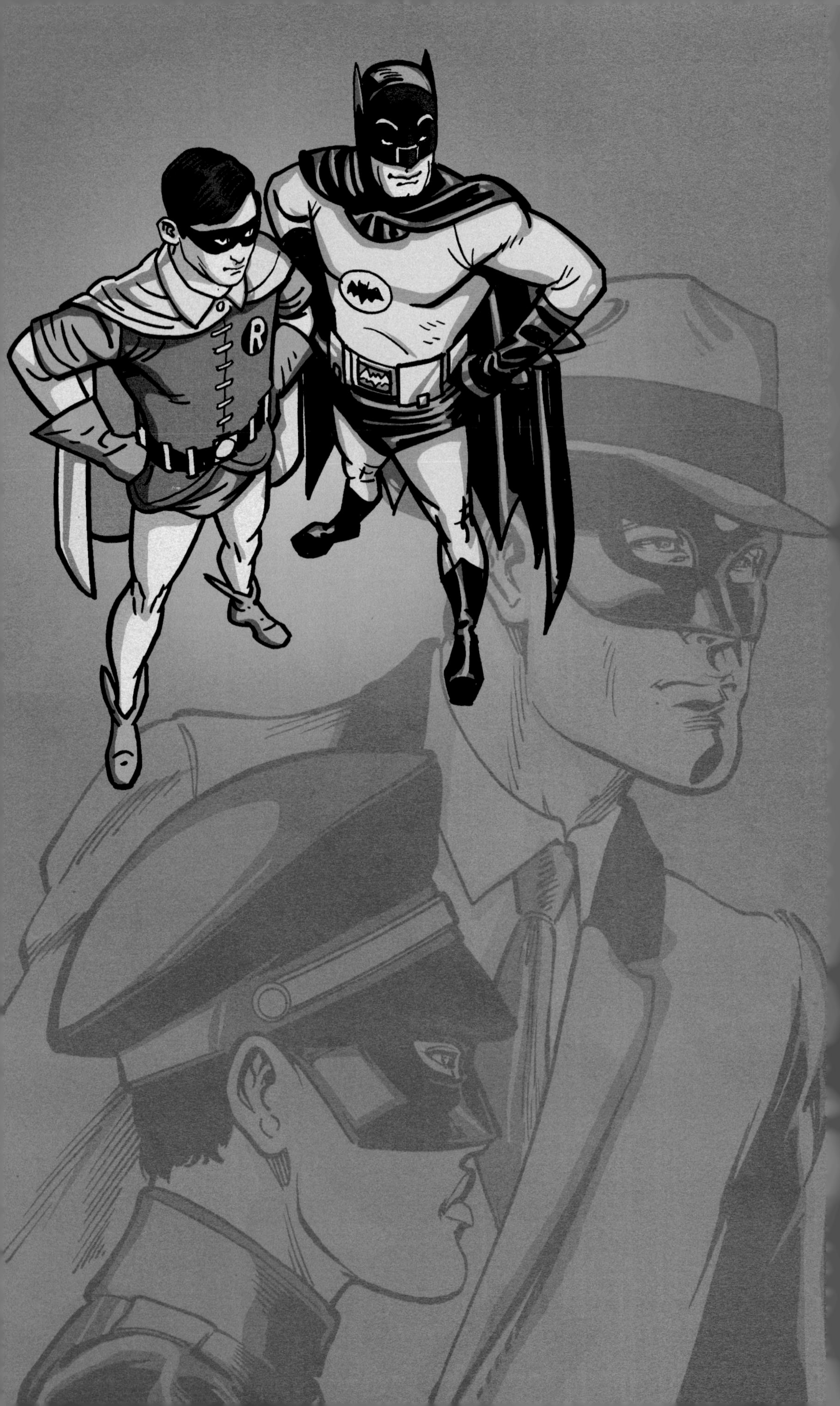

DC COMICS™

"Groundbreaking."
—USA TODAY

"It's film noir in cartoon panels."
—VANITY FAIR

"Frank Miller absolutely revolutionized the Dark Knight and his influence can be felt throughout comics, even 20 years later...true masterpiece of storytelling."
—IGN

FROM THE CREATOR OF *300* and *SIN CITY*

FRANK MILLER

with KLAUS JANSON

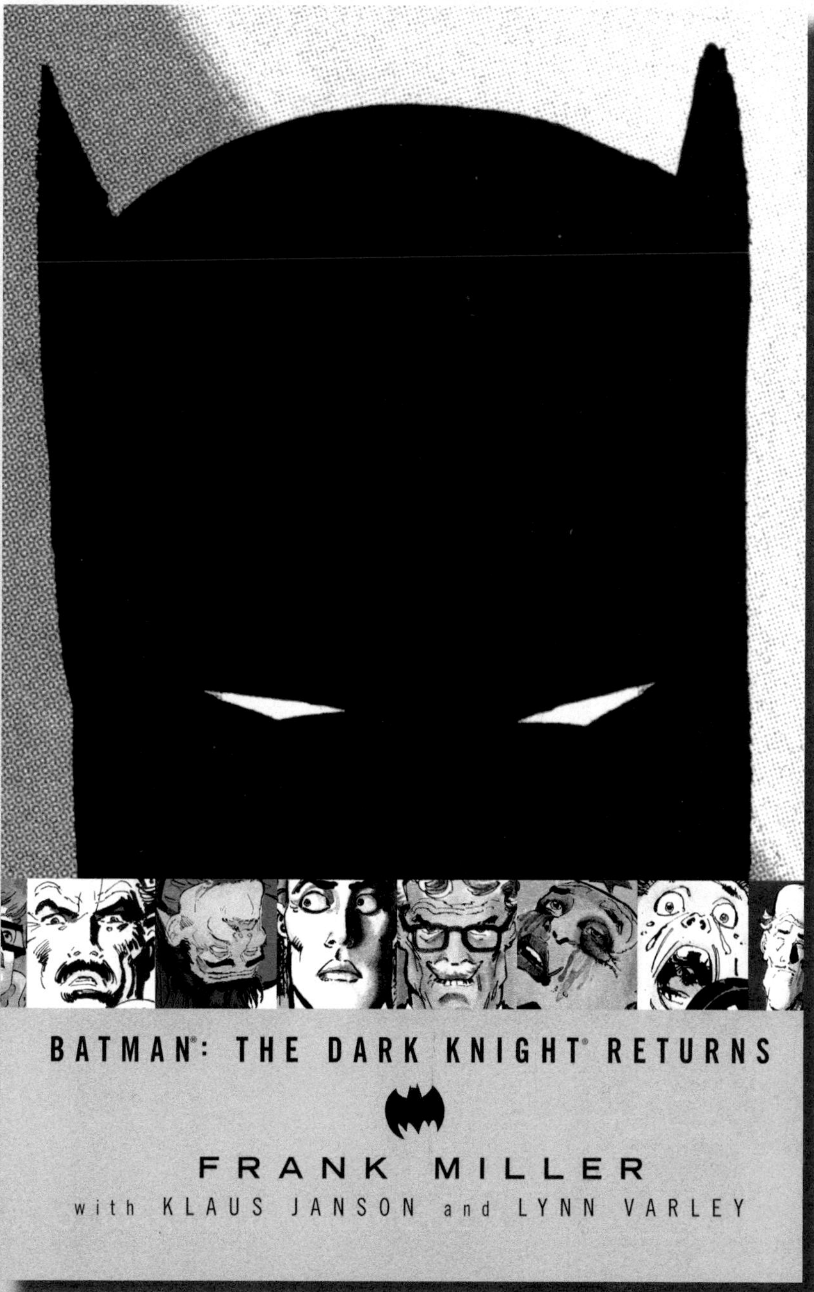

BATMAN®: THE DARK KNIGHT® RETURNS
FRANK MILLER
with KLAUS JANSON and LYNN VARLEY

BATMAN: THE DARK KNIGHT STRIKES AGAIN

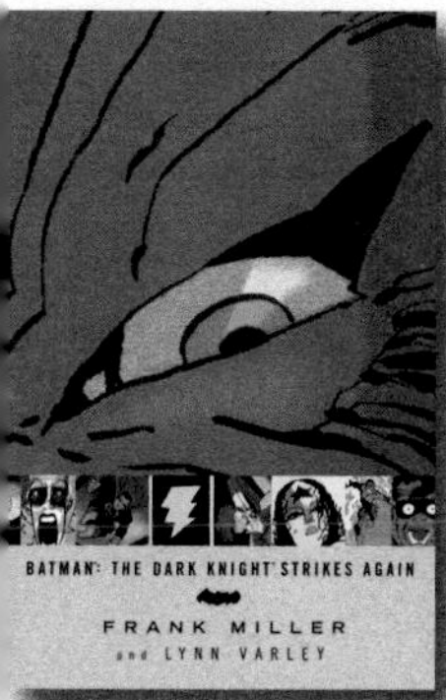

BATMAN: THE DARK KNIGHT STRIKES AGAIN
FRANK MILLER
and LYNN VARLEY

BATMAN: YEAR ONE DELUXE EDITION

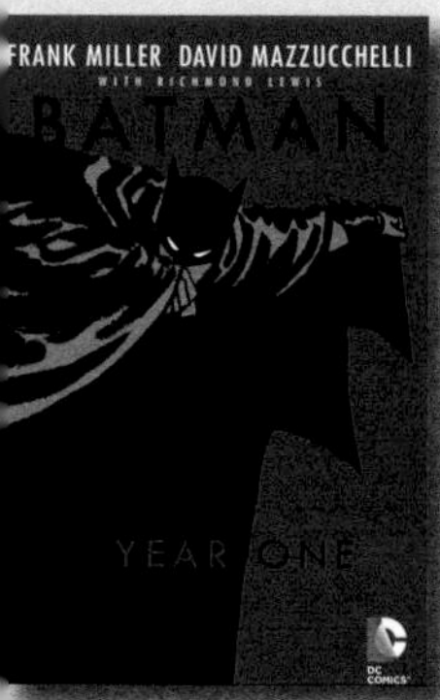

FRANK MILLER DAVID MAZZUCCHELLI
BATMAN
YEAR ONE

with DAVID MAZZUCCHELLI

ALL-STAR BATMAN & ROBIN, THE BOY WONDER VOL. 1

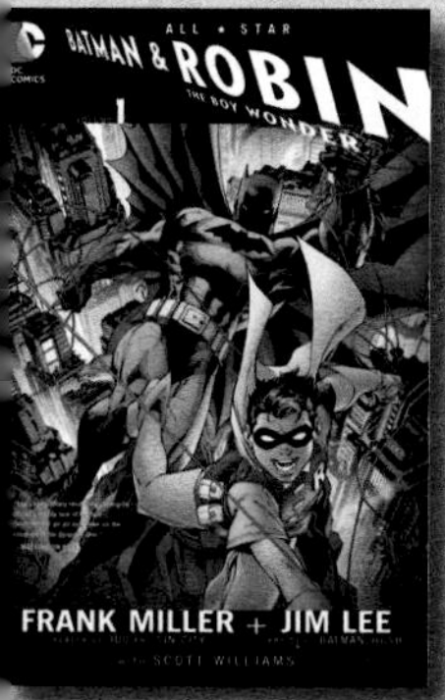

ALL ★ STAR
BATMAN & ROBIN
THE BOY WONDER
FRANK MILLER + JIM LEE

with JIM LEE

"[Writer Scott Snyder] pulls from the oldest aspects of the Batman myth, combines it with sinister-comi elements from the series' best period, and gives the whole thing terrific forward-spin."—ENTERTAINMENT WEEKLY

START AT THE BEGINNING!

BATMAN VOLUME 1: THE COURT OF OWLS

BATMAN VOL. 2: THE CITY OF OWLS

with SCOTT SNYDER and GREG CAPULLO

BATMAN VOL. 3: DEATH OF THE FAMILY

with SCOTT SNYDER and GREG CAPULLO

BATMAN: NIGHT OF THE OWLS

with SCOTT SNYDER and GREG CAPULLO

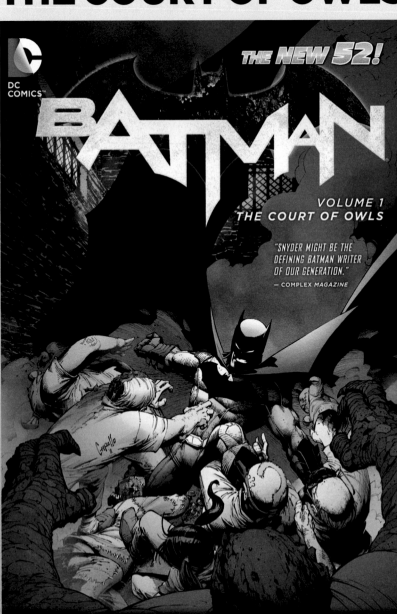

THE NEW 52!

DC COMICS™

BATMAN

VOLUME 1
THE COURT OF OWLS

"SNYDER MIGHT BE THE DEFINING BATMAN WRITER OF OUR GENERATION."
— COMPLEX MAGAZINE

SCOTT **SNYDER**   GREG **CAPULLO**   JONATHAN **GLAPION**

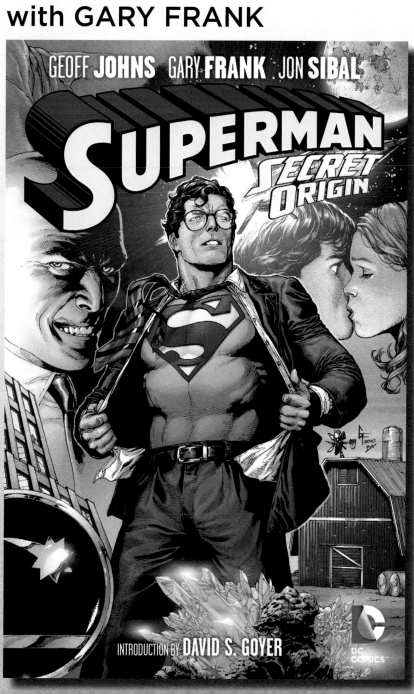

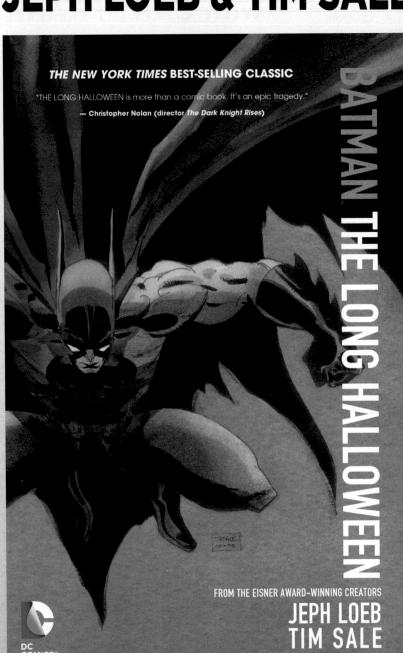